The Jonah Complex

THE
JONAH
COMPLEX

André Lacocque
and
Pierre-Emmanuel
Lacocque

foreword by Mircea Eliade

John Knox Press
ATLANTA

Library of Congress Cataloging in Publication Data

Lacocque, André.
  The Jonah complex.

  Includes the authors' translation of the Book of Jonah.
  Bibliography: p.
  Includes indexes.
  1. Bible. O.T. Jonah—Criticism, interpretation,
etc. I. Lacocque, Pierre-Emmanuel, 1952-
II. Bible. O.T. Jonah. English. Lacocque. 1981.
III. Title.
BS1605.2.L33   224'.9206   80-84649
ISBN 0-8042-0091-2   AACR2
ISBN 0-8042-0092-0 (pbk.)

10 9 8 7 6 5 4 3 2 1

Printed in the United States of America
John Knox Press
Atlanta, Georgia 30365

To David and Rebecca

And if we obey God, we must disobey ourselves, and it is in this disobeying ourselves, wherein the hardness of obeying God consists.

Sermon of Father Mapple in Herman Melville's
Moby Dick

Table of Contents

Foreword

What is striking in the history of religions is not the almost universal presence of some important rituals, myths and symbols, but the fact that their significance is never *exactly* the same. Of course, this considerable variety of meanings is not immediately evident to the nonspecialist. Thus, many followers of the three "religions of the Book" are sometimes embarrassed to discover that a belief, symbol, or rite considered to belong exclusively to *their* faith is in fact profusely distributed throughout the world. On the other hand, agnostics, atheists or religiously indifferent scholars emphasize triumphantly the almost universal presence of some central symbols and ideas which characterize the biblical and Christian traditions. Thus, when solar mythology was in vogue, scholars and dilettantes discovered solar elements in the Old and the New Testaments and, as a matter of fact, everywhere else in the world. After the publication of *The Golden Bough,* corn-mothers, fertility-demons and dying-gods were identified in numberless religions and folklores and, of course, in the Jewish, Christian and Muslim myths, rituals and beliefs.

It is useless to multiply examples. Suffice it to say that, leaving aside the grotesque exaggerations of many partisans of solar mythology and of Frazerian or "Myth-and-Ritual" schools, these researchers were correct in pointing out the analogies and the similarities of a great number of mythological themes, symbolisms and religious structures. In fact, it is difficult to imagine the situation otherwise. As far as we know, from the very beginning prehistoric man was *homo religiosus, homo faber* and *homo ludens.* That is to say, the "sacred" is an element in the structure of consciousness and not a stage in the history of consciousness. Furthermore, the experience of the "sacred" is expressed in a limited number of acts, images, ideas and narratives. In the case of the three "religions of the Book," their "pagan" analogies are explained by the fact that they developed historically in the context of ancient Near Eastern, Mediterranean and Hellenistic syncretistic cultures. As a matter of fact, we cannot understand them outside of their historical context.

But as I said, for a historian of religions, even more important than the similarities between *religious expressions* belonging to different cultures and periods is the inexaustible variety of their *significance.* To cite an example: in all the higher cultures of Asia, as well as among archaic societies, the images of cosmos, house and human body were equivalent; moreover, all of them present, or are susceptible to receive, an "opening" which allows passage into another world. To the "hole" in the sky through which the *axis mundi* passes corresponds the smoke-hole of the house or the "eye" of the dome and, in Indian speculations, the "opening" at the top of the head (*brāhmarandhra*), through which the soul escapes at the moment of death.

But Gautama Buddha gave a new and more profound meaning to this traditional anthropo-cosmic imagery. To express the passage from a conditioned existence to an unconditioned mode of being (*nirvāna, samādhi,* etc.) the Buddhist texts utilize a double image, that of breaking through the roof and flying through the air. Arhats shatter the roofs of their "houses" (i.e., the skull) and fly up into the sky. This means that the transcending of the human condition is figuratively expressed by the imagery of the destruction of the "house," that is to say, of the personal cosmos which has been chosen for a home. Every "stable dwelling" wherein one is "installed" is equivalent, in Indian thought, to an existential situation which one assumes. But the Buddhist interpretation of "breaking through the roof" proclaims that the Arhat has now *abolished* every "situation" and has chosen *not* installation in the world but the absolute freedom which implies the annihilation of every conditioned world.

We may also recall the Christian revalorization of two archaic and universally distributed cosmological symbolisms: the Waters (and the immersion in water) and the World-Tree. In a great many religious contexts, waters are creative, purifying and regenerative. The Fathers did not fail to explore some of the pre-Christian and universal values of aquatic symbolisms, but they enriched them with new meaning. For Tertullian (*De baptismo,* III-IV), water was the "first seat of divine Spirit," and it was water which "first produced that which has life." Through the descent of Holy Spirit, waters were sanctified and "in their turn impregnated with sanctifying virtue . . . and procures salvation in eternity." According to John Chrysostom (*Homil. in Joh.,* XXV, 2), baptism represents "death and entombment, life and resurrection . . . When we plunge our head into water, as into a sepulchre, the old man is immersed, altogether buried; when we come out of the water the new man simultaneously appears." But the valorization of baptism as a descent into the Waters of Death was made possible, for the Christian, by Christ's descent into the Jordan, that is to say, by an episode in "sacred history." Moreover, the baptism of Christ in the Jordan was compared by the Fathers with Noah, rising victorious from the Waters to become the head of a new race, and with Adam (baptismal nakedness being the abandonment of the old vesture of corruption and sin in which Adam had been clothed since the Fall).

Likewise, Christianity has utilized, amplified and revalorized the symbol-

ism of the Cosmic Tree. A Homily of pseudo-Chrysostom speaks of the
Cross as a tree which "rises from the earth to the heaven. A plant immortal,
it stands at the centre of heaven and earth; strong pillar of the universe, bond
of all things, support of all the inhabited earth," etc. The Byzantine liturgy
sings even now, in the day of the exaltation of the Holy Cross, of the "tree of
life planted in Calvary . . ., which springing from the depths of the earth, has
risen to the center of the earth and sanctifies the Universe unto its limits."
Many texts compare the Cross to a ladder, a column or a mountain—and
these are universally attested images of the "Center of the World," the *axis
mundi*. It is as a symbol of the "Center of the World" that the Cross has been
likened to the Cosmic Tree. But, of course, for Christians the Cross was
sanctified through the agony and death of Jesus: it became the instrument of
salvation. [We may add, however, that the idea of salvation prolongs and
completes the notion of perpetual renovation and cosmic regeneration, of
universal fecundity and sanctity, of absolute reality and, in the final reckon-
ing, of immortality—all of which coexist in the symbolism of the World-
Tree (see my *Images and Symbols,* pp. 44 ff., 161 ff.).]

* * * * * * * *

The book of Jonah—considered by some theologians to be the most important text of the Old Testament—brilliantly illustrates the revalorization
(one is tempted to say re-creation) of some archaic and universally distributed symbols and mythico-ritual scenarios. Apropos of Jonah's flight to Tarshish, one may compare the resistance of the future shaman against his
"call," his election by supernatural beings. One need not insist on the rich
symbolism of the Sea and the Tempest. In regard to the swallowing of Jonah
by a marine monster, the historian of religions can evoke not only parallel
stories (Herakles, the Finnish shaman-sage Väinämoinen, a number of Poly-
nesian heroes, etc.) but also many initiation rites in which the novice is symbolically placed in the body of a giant snake or a marine monster. The
significance of such rites is obvious: the novice "dies" to the "natural" life in
order to be reborn as a new "spiritual" (i.e., initiated) man.

From a certain point of view, the swallowing of Jonah, and the three days
and nights in the whale's belly, can be compared to a *descensus ad infernos,*
thus to an initiation rite. But the comparison with the well-known pattern of
initiatory death and resurrection (= rebirth) stops here, for Jonah is not *exis-
tentially changed* when the whale, on God's order, vomits him on the shore.

André and Pierre-Emmanuel Lacocque do not elaborate a comparative
analysis of such universal themes as resistance to God's call, the Sea and
Tempest, or the symbolism of being swallowed and regurgitated by a marine
monster. On the contrary, their hermeneutical endeavor concentrates on

the new, more complex and deeper meanings susceptible to decipherment in the book of Jonah. The great merit of their work resides in the minute, delicate and multilateral analysis of this enigmatic narrative. They critically examine the different interpretations elaborated by Jewish and Christian exegetes from antiquity to our days; they further discuss a number of contemporary evaluations of Jonah's narrative structure, psychological implications and religious message. It is this interdisciplinary approach—from textual criticism and theology to contemporary psychologies and historical events—which confers a unique value on the work of André and Pierre-Emmanuel Lacocque.

One may wonder why the authors invited a historian of religions to write a Preface to a book manifestly involved in the problems of, and the crises provoked by, the confrontation of the Judeo-Christian message with the contemporary Western World. Perhaps they are aware of the growing risks of "provincialization" of the Judeo-Christian, as well as the entire Mediterranean and Near Eastern, heritage. Although they honestly acknowledge their fidelity to Christianity, perhaps they too ask themselves the question which today obsesses every responsible Western individual: What significance may Jewish-Christian theologies have (in our case, Jonah's *saga* and its religious and ethical implications) for a Hindu, a Buddhist or a member of the Third World? We do not know the answer because a genuine and free dialogue between the religions of the world has hardly begun. But in order to pursue a meaningful dialogue with the representatives of non-Western religions, it is indispensable to know at least some of the "universal" symbols, myths and religious ideas. Certainly, as I said, there is a discontinuity between the shaman's resistance to his "call" and the flight of Jonah to Tarshish as well as between the archaic myths and rites of initiation and Jonah's being swallowed by the whale. But this means that, in a very remote past, *there was a continuity,* interrupted by what the Israelites and the Christians consider as their "sacred history." Nevertheless, if, one day, Jonah's adventure should interest *religiously* a Hindu or a "primitive," it will be thanks to their "old myths" of the Ocean and the marine monsters, of their initiation rituals and of the sacred stories of shamans and saints who vainly tried to resist the "call" of a divine Being.

Mircea Eliade
University of Chicago

Preface

We speak of God in a "non-religious" way.

—Dietrich Bonhoeffer, *Letters and Papers
from Prison* (New York: Macmillan,
1953), p. 362.

Writing a book is always an adventure. It is also an enormously expensive proposition—in time, effort, research, and especially expectation. The personal investment is immeasurable; this is even more true for the authors of this book, for they are father and son. What they have here produced had in their eyes inestimable value even *before* anything was put in writing, for a miracle was occurring which we both will always remember—we were dialoguing, we were experiencing the authentic encounter.

When we started it was not clear to the biblicist that psychology was not some sort of disguised narcissism. The psychologist, on the other hand, was not sure that theology was not a sophisticated way to kid oneself with empty concepts having no real bearing on humanity and the world. Indeed the dialogue started in part because of that mutual curiosity about the choice of the other. For the rest, we started to speak to one another because of a deep mutual respect.

Conversation is never more real than when a terrain is found where each of the two partners has to cover one third of the distance—one third for the one, one third for the other, and one third for the terrain itself which, the two partners should acknowledge in advance, will always transcend their reflections and formulations. It is indeed the last third, lying in the center, where the two authentically encounter each other and, perhaps, God himself.

The terrain was, we knew, all important. We decided on Jonah, a biblical book that we thought could be "interesting" for a psychologist and a theologian. We did not know at that time (some two years ago) how profoundly moved and enthusiastic (literally, filled with the numinous) we would be through a regular commerce with that unassuming, tongue-in-cheek, understating narrative. From the outset Jonah had features that claimed our attention. A short story told with disarming simplicity by the "singer of tales," its purpose is far from obvious, though its language is familiar to the Bible student. It speaks of the God of Israel, of a Jewish prophet, of well-known places, of an oracle, of attributes of God celebrated in biblical liturgies, of movements of repentance in people and even in God—themes appearing frequently elsewhere in the Scriptures.

The psychologist also felt attuned to Jonah as a popular narrative, a folktale, a parable in a skillfully symbolic form, and he readily recognized this literary piece as a mirror of the soul. Jonah as a character is very human, overwhelmed like an epic hero by extraordinary events and phenomena (not even the dragon is absent), but he is more an antihero than a model of courage and virtue. Such a picaresque personage—some twenty centuries before that literary genre was invented in Europe—was all the more fascinating, since he is the antipode of the Greek "oversized" hero— the hero usually selected by psychological scientists to exemplify the complexes, syndromes, neuroses and psychoses of John Does confronted in reality neither by father-assassins nor mother-whores, neither by powerful soothsayers nor cryptic sphynxes, but more generally (and it may appear, trivially) by the call (the urge, the drive, the inner necessity) to become what they actually are.

So, is Jonah a "theological" pamphlet or a "psychological" symbolic tale? The literary critic looking at the Bible as literature may consider the religious overtones of the story as culture-bound "externalia." The "Alttestamentler" on the contrary may have the tendency to play down the literary genre and stress the theological "kerygma." But form and content are one, and they must be received together. The story of Jonah is a *story* that happens to belong to a canonical literature, to Israel's Bible. Jonah can be understood only if those two components (biblical narrative) are equally appreciated. In other words, the exegete, in order to read Jonah must be more than a biblical theologian, and the literary critic or the psychologist also must reach beyond the usual boundaries of those disciplines.

André and Pierre had thus to start with the *given:* Jonah is a biblical narrative. What it means for a text to be in the Bible had to be assessed in Chapter I, and what it means for a text to be a story had to be appraised in Chapter II. Further, the historical "setting in life" (*Sitz im Leben*) of the parable (always world-subverting, says John D. Crossan) had to be carefully pondered, since there are texts whose meaning depends entirely upon their setting in life. For example, Jonathan Swift's Gulliver stories can bear different interpretations depending on whether they are read as pure imaginative fancy or as critiques of eighteenth-century England.

Similarly, Jonah is no "world citizen"; he is a Jew. The city to which he is called is not just any metropolis; it is the archenemy of his people, Nineveh. The message he is commissioned to proclaim is not just any curse; it describes the fate of Sodom and Gomorrah. The *dénouement* is unimaginable outside of the Israelite parameters within which the story is told, and the absence of a normal ending tells something about the creative milieu of such tales.

From this perspective, Jonah cannot be equated by means of cheap theological anti-Semitism with a petty stiff-necked Jew, nor by means of facile psychologcal typology, *à la* Molière, with "the coward," or "the irredentic untrustful missionary," or again "the reluctant missionary." The singer of the Jonah tale had much more on his mind than a caricature of his own race, and indeed he had a greater respect for his audience, for us, than to waste our time with shallow polemical satire, so general in its sway as to be addressed finally to no one. The historical circumstances of fifth-century Jerusalem were not conducive to the light-headed vanities that prevailed at the court of Louis XIV. Jonah was written on the morrow of the return from Exile, when prophetic promises were not realized. The subsequent frustration in Jerusalem caused some to turn to religious isolationism and to proclaim the advent of theocracy in Zion, while others wrote prophecies like Joel or Zechariah and stories like Ruth or Jonah, protesting against the complacency and the lack of theological vision of the conservative party. The Hasidic author of Jonah could easily have been so provincial in his interests and so narrow in his scope as to render his story unusable for other times and other peoples. But he was a genius. He molded his specific message to specific opponents in such universal categories (like the Psalms) that the tableau he painted revealed a profound human character—a character present in fifth-century B.C.E. Israel as well as in twentieth-century C.E. America—the "Jonah complex."

Others before us have written about the so-called "Jonah-syndrome." They intuited in Jonah the presence of profoundly human feelings, but they were content with the stereotyped interpretation of the biblical book in vogue in the Christian church. Jonah thus was *type*, a caricature, a foil for human virtues. From that perspective, the Jonah-syndrome designated a distorted human behavior prompted by cowardice before life, refusal to make a commitment, fear of success, narcissism, parochialism, greed, envy. The authors of the present book felt it necessary to reassess the humanity and indeed the universality of the Jonah character, which had been so badly disfigured by preconceived notions. What resulted is expressed especially in our final two chapters, on the Outer Voice and the Jonah Complex Revisited.

Our ambition went farther. After discussing the four chapters of Jonah and blending—harmoniously we hope—our respective disciplines, we had to draw more far-reaching conclusions concerning the integration of biblical insights into modern nonreligious language. This is one of the aims of our book: the demonstration that existential psychology in cross-cultural rapport with bibilical disciplines is able to provide a language that can be understood by our contemporaries.

Such language conveys a message respectful of its audience. The author of Jonah did not become tactless in his polemics against the conservative party in power in Jerusalem. The least that modern expositors can do is to learn that lesson from Jonah and not to indulge in a cheap reduction of its hero to the dimension of a contemptible dwarf. No indeed, Jonah has nothing to do with a petty insubstantial Jew conceived by the deranged mind of an anti-Semite. Jonah is Everyman, and like Everyman he is under the commandment to respond to his human vocation. Jonah must not become Moses; he must become Jonah, which recalls a profound Hasidic story. If he is unwilling to yield to the call, it is not because he is a subhuman, the by-product of an obstinate race, but simply because he is a human being. What he imagines about himself has become more important, more attractive, than what the commandment (vocation, call) tells him he actually is. It even happens that the Being-Object, which has no voice other than his own, is to him dearer than the Being-Subject, who speaks—and says things he finds repulsive (see Jon. 4:2).

Unless—and that has been our puzzlement throughout this book—the existential issues of Jonah transcend all psychology, philosophy, and theology, it may be that the resistance of Jonah to the "voice from without" is not just a manifestation of a universal complex but—as in the story of Job—the daring ultimate act of a man opposing his justice to the justice of God in the name of the countless Jewish victims—at the hands of Ninevites, at the hands of Nazis—of a merciful God.

Acknowledgments

We wish to extend our appreciation to the following persons, whose help and support throughout our work has been most gratifying: Claire Lacocque and Vickie Quero, whose enthusiasm and everlasting encouragement have contributed greatly to the final form of this work; the Chicago Theological Seminary for allowing us to co-teach a course on Jonah.

Also, we cannot adequately acknowledge our privilege in having Mircea Eliade contribute the Foreword to this book. His input adds to an already very special relationship we have developed over the years with him and his wife Christinel.

Finally, our special thanks go to David Thurn for reading this work and making numerous helpful and cogent remarks on it.

A. L.
P. E. L.

The Book of Jonah: Translation

Chapter 1

1. Once upon a time, the word of the Lord came to Jonah ben
2. Amittai saying: "Arise! Go to Nineveh, the great city, with the proclamation against her that her evil has flown in my face."
3. But instead Jonah rose to flee to Tarshish from the Presence of the Lord! He went down to Joppa where he found a ship bound for Tarshish. He paid its fare and went down inside to
4. go with them to Tarshish, from the Lord's Presence. Then the Lord hurled a great wind toward the sea, and it became such a great sea storm that one thought the ship was being wrecked.
5. The sailors became frightened and they cried out to their respective gods; they hurled into the sea the ship's wares to lighten it. Meanwhile Jonah had gone down to the vessel's holds. He was lying there sound asleep.
6. The captain came near to him and asked him, "How can you sleep so soundly? Arise! Call to your god. Perhaps that god will notice us and we won't perish."
7. Then the sailors said one to another: "Come, let's cast lots to find out why this evil is upon us." So they cast lots and
8. the lot fell on Jonah. They thus said to him, "Tell us now, whose fault is it that this evil is upon us? What is your job? Where do you come from? What is the name of your country
9. and of your people?" He said to them, "I am a Hebrew, and I fear the Lord, the God of heaven, who has made sea and land
10. alike." Then the men became very frightened and they asked him; "How could you do this?" For the men knew from Jonah's own admission that he was fleeing from the Lord's
11. Presence. They said to him, "What should we do to you that
12. the sea may calm down—for the sea grows stormier." He said to them. "Pick me up and hurl me into the sea; then the sea will calm down. I know that it is on account of me that
13. this great storm is upon you." However, the men started to paddle hard towards the shore but without success, for the

14. sea grew still stormier against them. Then they called to the
     Lord Himself and they said, "Please, Lord, let us not perish
     on account of this one man. Do not place upon us the onus of
     innocent blood, for you are the Lord, and you do as you
15. please." They then picked up Jonah and hurled him into the
16. sea . . . and the sea stopped its raging. Then the men feared
     the Lord greatly; they offered a sacrifice to the Lord, and
     bound themselves by oaths.

Chapter 2*
1.   But the Lord appointed a great fish to swallow Jonah, and
     Jonah remained in the fish's bowels for three days and three
2.   nights. And Jonah prayed to the Lord, his God, from the fish's
3.   bowels and said:

     "I called in my distress to the Lord, and He answered
          me;
     From the belly of Sheol I cried for help—You heard my
          voice.
4.   You cast me into the depth, into the heart of the seas.
     A current whirled around me;
     Your breakers and waves all swept over me.
5.   Then I thought, 'I am driven away from Your sight,
     But I persist in gazing at Your holy Temple!'
6.   Waters choked me to death; the Abyss whirled around
          me;
     Weeds were tangled about my head.
7.   To the base of the mountains I descended;
     Of the earth the bars were forever locked on me.
     Yet You lifted my life from the pit, O Lord, my God.
8.   As my soul was faint within me, I remembered the Lord;
     My prayer came unto You, unto Your holy Temple.
9.   Those who adhered to futile idols abandoned their
          disgrace.
10. But as for me, with a song of gratitude I shall bring
          offerings to You; what I have vowed I will fulfill.
     Salvation is the Lord's!"

11.   Then on the Lord's order, the fish spewed Jonah out on
     the shore.

---

*In the English translation this is 1:17, and chapter 2 begins with the next verse.

Chapter 3

1. So the word of the Lord came to Jonah a second time say-
2. ing: "Arise! Go to Nineveh, the great city; let her hear the
3. proclamation I'm telling you." Jonah arose and went to Nineveh as he had been told by the Lord. Now Nineveh was a city
4. of huge dimensions; it took three days to walk across it. Jonah
   entered the city and walked for a day; then he made this proclamation: "Yet forty days and Nineveh shall be overthrown!"
5. The people of Nineveh believed God, and they proclaimed a fast and donned sackcloth, from the greatest to the
6. least of them. And when word reached the King of Nineveh
   he rose from his throne, stripped himself of his royal vest-
7. ment, and, covered only with sackcloth, he sat in ashes. Then
   he had it promulgated in Nineveh: "By order of the king and
   his court: Neither man nor beast in herd or flock shall even
8. taste anything; they shall neither graze nor drink water; they
   are to cover themselves with sackcloth, both human and beast,
   and fervently to invoke God. Everyone must repent from his
9. evil way of living, from the violence of his deed. Who knows
   but that God may repent and be forgiving, for if He turns
   away from His burning wrath, we shall not perish!"
10. God considered what they were doing, how they repented
    from their evil way of living; so God relented concerning the
    evil He had thought to do to them, and He did not do it.

Chapter 4

1. But Jonah resented this greatly and was incensed. He
2. prayed to the Lord and said, "Now, Lord, is not this what I
   thought while yet on my own turf? That's why I fled in the first
   place to Tarshish, for I knew all along that You are a gracious
   and merciful God, slow to anger, rich in kindness, and forgiv-
3. ing of evil intention. Now then, Lord, take back my life, for
4. I'd rather die than live." And the Lord said, "Is it fair for you
   to be angry?"
5. Jonah left the city and sat to the east of it. He made himself
   a booth on the spot to sit under its shade until he would see
6. what was going to happen to the city. Then the Lord God appointed a plant to grow up over Jonah to form a shade over his
   head and relieve him from his discomfort. And Jonah had an
   immense joy on account of the plant. But at dawn on the fol-
7. lowing day, God appointed a worm to attack the plant so that

8. it withered. Moreover, when the sun rose, God appointed a stifling east wind; the sun beat upon Jonah's head and he became faint. So Jonah asked for death, saying, "I'd rather die than live!"

9. And God said to Jonah; "Is it fair for you to be incensed

10. about the plant?" He answered, "Til my last breath, it is fair!" Then the Lord said, "You, you found it a pity about a plant for which you did not labor nor did you make it grow, and which

11. from one night to the next lived and then perished. And I— shall I not take pity upon Nineveh, the great city, in which there are more than 120,000 people who do not know their right hand from their left, and many beasts as well?"

The Jonah Complex

Chapter I

THE
BOOK
OF
JONAH
Genre and
Setting in Life

*In trying to decide what a great man meant by
his original formulations, it is always good to
find out what he was talking against at the
time . . .*

—Erik H. Erikson, *Young Man Luther: A Study on
Psychoanalysis and History* (New York: W.W.
Norton, 1961), p. 218.

The book of Jonah is unique in the Prime Testament. It bears the name of a prophet of Israel, but the only "oracle" it reports consists of a single sentence: "Yet forty days and Nineveh shall be overthrown." More important in the book of Jonah is the person of the prophet and his attitude toward his vocation, as he becomes the mouthpiece of his God in a far-away and ill-famed city. There are a number of elements that distinguish this book from all other prophetic books, and therefore one might conclude that Jonah is not representative of the prophets in the Bible and is perhaps even unimportant. In fact, however, in the words of Elias Bickerman:

> The Book of Jonah contains only forty-eight verses according to the reckoning of the ancient Hebrew scribes. But the name of no prophet is better known to the man in the street. Jonah is that man who was swallowed alive by a whale and was spewed up three days later, unhurt . . . Celsus . . . suggested that the Christians should worship not Jesus but Jonah or Daniel, whose miracles outdo the Resurrection.[1]

Thus, despite the fact that the episode of the "whale" occupies only a couple of verses and is by no means central to the book, it is precisely this motif that struck the imaginations of its readers. Its popular nature easily touched popular fibers in generations of the book's recipients, and it is not in the least paradoxical that so many attempts have been made to "prove" its historical character. Bickerman continues:

> In modern times exegetes have often tried to vindicate the episode by quoting sailor yarns. Two years after the publication of Darwin's *On the Origin of Species* Canon Pusey collected some such old salt's tales in his commentary on Jonah (1861). . . . Despite the discomfort the story arouses in the faithful, its literal historicity was declared as late as 1956 in a Catholic encyclopedia, and admitted albeit half heartedly, in a Protestant biblical dictionary in 1962.[2]

So the problem of "authenticity" is one of the main questions at the out-set of our study. It is directly dependent upon the literary genre of the book. Should we understand the story of Jonah as history or as fiction? James D. Smart puts forth several arguments to show that the latter possibility is the only viable one. He calls attention first to the fact that we have in the book of Jonah a complete absence of historical data. The monarch of Nineveh is not named; rather, he is called "King of Nineveh," an unusual and indeed unique expression in biblical and extrabiblical annals. The narrative is but a sequence of miracles (the sea calmed, the psalm in the fish's belly, the message of Jonah uttered in a foreign language, the conversion of the whole city, the tree which grew in one night, and its destruction by a worm, the dimension of Nineveh, etc.). Besides, asks Smart, what would be the nature of such a history whose aim lay in demeaning a prophet of Israel? Who would write this, and for what purpose?[3]

If, however, we consider the possibility that the tale of Jonah be a para-ble, we find abundant and striking parallels elsewhere in the Bible (e.g., 2 Sam. 12:1 ff.; Isa. 5; etc.). But then the object of that parable becomes a moot and complicated question. According to Smart, the aim of the parable is to express caustic opposition to the hostility toward the non-Jews in Israel after the exile. Jonah, as the main character of the narrative appears "ab-surd," or "idiotic," "ludicrous in the extreme," as a "sulky child," and the like, and the text of 4:2 would constitute the point of the whole parable, that is, Jonah's rejection of the God of the fathers because of his mercifulness.

As it is, Smart's reading is widely accepted in the Church. It has become customary to see Jonah as a petty, narrow-minded and stiff-necked repre-sentative of his stubborn people, and anti-Semites have always found in this book a fertile ground for their poisonous seeds. Even as careful an exegete as Gerhard von Rad—whom we quote here as a foil to anti-Semitism—called Jonah a "religionspsychologisches Monstrum"![4]

On the contrary, Bickerman entitled one of his chapters "Jonah as Friend of Israel." He sees in the reluctant attitude of the hero an unwillingness to betray his own people for the sake of speaking the word of God to the arch-enemies of his nation.

> And why should he be pained to death at the display of divine mercy? . . . The traditional Jewish explanation was that Jonah, being a prophet, knew in ad-vance that Nineveh would repent and be saved. But that would put to shame stiff-necked Israel. "Since the heathen are nearer to repentance, I might be causing Israel to be condemned." The prophet knew, says Jerome, that "the repentance of the Gentiles would be the downfall of the Jews."[5]

Such is the unanimous reading of the Rabbis at any rate,[6] and one will re-member that the NT puts the story in the same light: the Ninevites shall raise up an accusation against Jesus' generation, etc. (Matt. 12:41 and parallel). Compare *Midrash on Lamentations* Intr. No. 31: "I sent one prophet to Nineveh and he brought it to penitence and conversion. And these Israelites in Jerusalem—how many prophets have I sent to them!" [7]

Be that as it may for now, it is clear that the bulk of the evidence leans toward the fictitious character of the book of Jonah. There is, however, at least one element in the narrative that revives the whole problem, namely, the presentation of the hero in 1:1: "And the word of the Lord came unto Jonah the son of Amittai . . ." This name comes directly from 2 Kings 14:25 where we read "Jeroboam II restored the border of Israel from the entrance of Hamath unto the sea of Arabah, according to the word of the Lord, the God of Israel, which he spoke by the hand of his servant Jonah the son of Amittai, the prophet, who was of Gath-Hepher." This is the only reference in the Bible to an eighth-century prophet by the name of Jonah under the reign of Jeroboam II. This king, as is well known, is condemned severely by the Deuteronomistic historians, authors of the books of Kings, and it is all the more surprising that he receives a promise, by an oracle of the prophet Jonah, that his country would extend so far as to reach the dimensions of the Davidic empire. Evidently Jewish tradition could not read 2 Kings 14:25 as a mere prediction of bliss to a wicked king. The basis of the oracle was no doubt an unmentioned repentance of Jeroboam II, for there was no way to suspect the prophet Jonah ben Amittai of being a false witness. He is mentioned in the text of 2 Kings as God's "servant" and "prophet." The midrash (cf. *PRE* 10; *Mid. Jonah* 96) then imagines that Jonah had had the task of proclaiming the destruction of Jerusalem, but his prophecy did not materialize and Jonah was therefore known as "the false prophet." When sent to Nineveh to prophesy the downfall of the city, he knew in advance that the heathens would do penance and decided not to go. This Rabbinic development is all the more interesting in that modern scholars have, on the basis of 2 Chronicles 13:22; 24:27, suggested that the tale of Jonah is a midrash on the book of Kings. Hans Schmidt,[8] for example, thinks that Nineveh is a substitute for Jerusalem, a literary device used by the poet in order to render his argument more cogent by selecting a pagan city which God forgave because of the presence of just ones in its midst.[9] The book of Jonah thus must be read together with the prophecies of Jeremiah and Ezekiel, who had condemned the city before 586; Jonah's composition also is to be dated before 586 B.C.E.

Such a stance is, however, unwarranted. As Adolphe Lods[10] reminded his readers, prior to 586 the problem was not the inefficacy of repentance. On the contrary, the prophets made their oracles conditional, but the illusion of the nation was precisely that repentance was unnecessary. It may be that one took refuge in texts such as Genesis 18, but Jonah shows a whole city relenting. Moreover, it would be a strange blunder to make Jonah refuse to speak of destruction to Nineveh-Jerusalem while hinting simultaneously that Jonah is indeed Jeremiah or Ezekiel!

A slightly different version of the preceding historical thesis focuses on the character of Jonah himself. It is assumed that he may have been a nationalistic prophet of the North who backed up even such a wicked king as Jeroboam II because of his policy of expansion.[11] This version is a variant of the one mentioned earlier. Here it is not Jeroboam II who passes through conversion but the prophet himself, hence the epithets of praise, "prophet" and "servant," in the text of 2 Kings. The two versions have, in fact, a single meaning. The tale found in the book of Jonah would involve a shift from wickedness to righteousness by means of a dramatic conversion. Either way a negative note would be followed by a positive one. A refinement of the theory sees the eighth-century prophet speaking to Jeroboam II in order to bring him to repentance even though he himself was displeased both by his commission and by the outcome of his message to the king. Much later, the author of the book of Jonah transposed the historical situation into a fictional one in which a prophet of Israel was sent to the wicked Ninevites to proclaim their doom. Unexpectedly, however, he brought them to their knees and they turned to the living God, but in this the storyteller radically altered the nature of his model. Leaving history behind, he resorted to the story—indeed to a parable with symbolic meaning. Even the name Jonah leaves the realm of actuality and enters the universe of symbols.

With this point, however, our inquiry has gone one step farther. If it is taken for granted now that Jonah is no historical report, are we permitted then to read the tale as symbolic and even as allegorical?[12] In the latter case, Jonah would represent Israel and Nineveh the world, while the fish would be the symbol of the exile in Babylon.[13] We shall take exception to this reading on several counts, but it seems to us incontestable that there are a certain number of symbols or metaphors in Jonah, while the book as a whole is a metaphor or parable in itself. We shall discuss this point more fully below. This view is not new; the Rabbis saw in Jonah a personification of Israel; for example, the Hebrew *yônāh* is such a symbol in Song of Solomon. In the Talmud the same symbolism is found in *Shabbat* 130a.[14] This and other textual evidence of the metaphoric meaning of the name Jonah, point in a direction that is worthy of exploration.

A certain number of biblical texts elaborate upon the figurative meaning of *yônāh,* "the dove"; however, they represent different points of view. The dove is noted for its plaintive cooing (Isa. 38:14, 59:11), for its foolishness (Hos. 7:11), for its power of flight (Ps. 55:6) and for its loyalty to its mate and its gentleness (Song of Sol. 2:14; 5:2; 6:9). In general it is a "clean" animal mentioned with affection, and in many cases it designates

metaphorically the people of Israel (Ps. 68:14; 74:19; Hos. 7:11; 11:11).
One finds that the "Jonah" is a symbol of innocence and gentleness. In *Tg.
Song of Songs* 2:12 "the voice of the turtle dove" is understood as meaning
"the voice of the holy spirit of redemption" (cf. Matt. 3:16). George A. F.
Knight goes even farther and renders the whole name "Jonah b. Amittai"
as the Dove Son of Truth.[15] Jonah is Israel (see especially Hos. 11:11; in
Pss. 55:6 and 56:1 the MT has *yônāh,* but the Septuagint translates "con-
gregation" or "people") and the Truth is the Torah (see Ps. 119). Thus the
dove filled with truth is invited to share the Torah with the nations, but
she refuses. She is punished by exile to Babylon (Jer. 51:34, 44 show
clearly that the fish in Jonah represents just that).

Provocative as these suggestions are, we shall go beyond them to propose another reason why the author chose the name Jonah when we turn
to the question of the literary genre (see Chapter II).

The unity of composition of the book has been disputed in the recent
past. W. Boehme feels that it is a mixture of four main sources—in many
respects on the model of the Pentateuch—namely J, E, an addition to J, and
a redaction of JE.[16] Hans Schmidt, also sees a series of additions, as for instance in the psalm of 2:3–10 (inserted there because the shift from the
prayer in vs. 2 to the Lord's pardon in vs. 11 was deemed too abrupt); in
3:6–9 (on the king of Nineveh); in 1:4a, 5a, 9b, 13–14 and all the details
concerning Jonah's sleep and his dialogue with the skipper.[17]

Today, however, only the psalm in chapter 2 is thought to be a later addition; we call attention to the absence of Aramaisms there in comparison with
the rest of the book. Moreover, there are in the Psalter close parallels to that
psalm of thanksgiving, and the occasion of the parallels is often an escape
from fatal danger. In the course of our commentary we shall defend another
stance, convinced as we are that the psalm has been inserted where it now
stands by the author himself. The differences in style and vocabulary are owing to the difference of genre (from prose to poetry with many loans from
older psalms).

The book of Jonah presents, indeed, a remarkably balanced structure,
which makes it "a model of literary artistry, marked by symmetry and balance."[18] We adopt here the outline of the tale proposed by Leslie C.
Allen:

I. A Hebrew sinner is saved (1:1–2:end)
   A. Jonah's disobedience (1:1–3)
   B. Jonah's punishment; heathens' homage (1:4–16)
   C. Jonah's rescue (1:17—2:10 [Hebrew 2:1–11])
      1. God's grace (1:17)
      2. Jonah's praise (2:1–9)
      3. God's last work (2:10)

II. Heathen sinners are saved (3:1—4:11)
    A. Jonah's disobedience (3:1 –4)
    B. Nineveh's repentance (3:5 –9)
    C. Jonah's rebuke (3:10—4:11)
       1. God's grace (3:10)
       2. Jonah's plaint (4:1 –3)
       3. God's last word (4:4 –11)

Moreover the leitmotif of the book is found in all of its parts, with the notable exception of the psalm in chapter 2 for obvious reasons. So, for example, we read "Nineveh the great city" in 1:2; 3:2, 3; 4:11, while the attribute "great" is used about other things: wind (1:4); storm (1:4, 12); fish (2:1); fear (1:10, 16); wickedness (4:1); joy (4:6); see also 3:5, 7; 4:10. One finds paronomasia in 1:16; 3:2; 4:6; 3:10—4:1; repetition in 1:7, 12; 1:11, 12; 3:10; 4:5; cf. 2:1 –11; etc. Even the divine names as used in the book contribute to the cohesion of the whole, and Boehme proved to be very short-sighted. In association with Jonah, God appears always as YHWH (with the exception of 4:6 –9; see below). In relation to the sailors, God is Elohim (1:6), but after being presented to them by Jonah, he becomes YHWH (1:14 –15). In relation to Nineveh, he is, of course, Elohim (3:5 –10), and the condemnation is made on the basis of general ethical crimes, i.e., wicked relations between people and their neighbors. As we said above, 4:6 –9 constitute an exception; there God appears to Jonah as Elohim. It is noteworthy, however, that the context is one of nature. As God of nature, God is Elohim (as in the book of Job chapters 38—42 for instance).[19] He becomes YHWH again when nature is replaced by history and when God's mercy is again emphasized (4:10).

The unexpected coupling of YHWH and Elohim as a composite name occurs, on the model of Genesis 2:4 ff., in Jonah 1:9; 2:2; and 4:6. There is no problem with 1:9 and 2:2; in 4:6 it is both the God of nature, Elohim, and the covenantal God of Jonah, YHWH, who permits a $q\hat{i}q\bar{a}y\hat{o}n$ tree to grow in order to test Jonah.[20]

The book is thus a whole and, following the lead of Gabriël H. Cohn, we shall speak of "aspects" of a holistic work rather than "parts" or "elements" or even "layers." [21] Is it possible to fix the date of composition of this tale? Indeed, the question can be answered with a comfortable degree of certainty. There are, as a matter of fact, enough clues for assigning it a fifth century B.C.E. setting. Nineveh is described in terms that seem to be mythical rather than historical, indicating that the city had been destroyed long before Jonah was written. The size of Nineveh according to Jonah 3:3 does not correspond with the relatively modest measurements proposed by archaeologists. Nineveh, which was utterly destroyed in the seventh century (612, by Cyaxarus), did not exceed eight miles in circumference. However, André Parrot has suggested that Nineveh as described in the book of Jonah may have designated a triangular territory with an uninterrupted succession of cities from Chorsabad in the North to Nimrud in the South on a stretch of forty kilometers. In this case 120,000 human beings would not be an exaggerated estimate of population.[22] We must therefore turn to other evidence in order to determine the date of Jonah.

More decisive are arguments based on vocabulary and style. The book presents numerous examples of late Hebrew and of Aramaic forms of Hebrew words. For example, in Jonah 1:4 the term translated "to be thought to" (+ verb) is used in classical Hebrew strictly for persons, never for inanimate objects. In 1:9 the expression "God of Heavens" is typical of the Persian empire. The expression is coined on the model of Zoroastrian formulas and its use is confined mainly to texts written in Persian times and after[23] (see Neh. 1:4–5; 2:5; Ezra 1:2; 5:11–12; 6:9–10; 7:21, 23; Dan. 2:18, 37, 44; 4:34; 5:23; 2 Chron. 36:23). In 4:2 the preposition translated by "when" or by "while" is a Hebrew preposition with an Aramaic meaning absent in classical Hebrew. In 1:5 the term translated "mariner" or "sailor" appears elsewhere only in Ezekiel 27. The term translated "vessel" (1:5) is a *hapax legomenon* in Hebrew but is common in Aramaic and Arabic. In 1:6 the verb translated "to care" or "to think upon" is found with this meaning only in Daniel 6:3. In 2:1 the verb "to prepare" is found only in late Hebrew and Aramaic. As a final and quite convincing example, we note 3:7 where the verb "to cause" or "to command" is found only here in a Hebrew text, while it is frequent in the Aramaic of Ezra and Daniel (Ezra 4:19, 21; 5:3, 9, 13, 17; 6:1, 3, 8, 11, 12; 7:13, 21; Dan. 3:10, 29; 4:3; 6:27).

From a grammatical point of view one notices the use of the particle *še* (1:7, 12; 4:10), which comes from Syriac and Aramaic. In 4:6 the verb "to save" is followed by a preposition with the dative instead of the accusative as in classical Hebrew.

It has recently been suggested that some of these peculiarities are owing to Phoenician influence rather than Aramaic because of the sea setting of the story,[24] but this explanation does not help in dating Jonah. In some respects this argument recalls the Rabbinic opinion according to which Jonah was from Zebulun (see 2 Kings 14:25 [Gath-Hepher]; cf. Josh. 19:10, 13 [Zebulun]). So believed R. Levi (d. ca. C.E. 300). R. Johanan preferred to think of the tribe of Asher.[25] But in order for the linguistic argument to hold, the Phoenician influence should be felt only where the story has a sea setting, i.e., chapters 1—2. Why would it also be the case in chapters 3—4, which are set in Mesopotamia? Moreover, it seems wrong to view Jonah as a Phoenician tale adapted to Israelite conditions, since Jonah is too typical a Jewish story, understandable only within a Jewish *Weltanschauung*.

Linguistic information is not the only evidence to be considered with re-

spect to the question of the date of the book of Jonah. We have noted before
the expression "God of Heavens," which makes the reader think of Persia
rather than of Assyria (see Neh. 1:4; 2:5, 20; Ezra 1:2; 5:11 –12; 6:9 –10;
etc.). Another clue is provided by the participation of animals in mourning
rites, which recalls what Herodotus said about the Persians (*Hist.* IX, 24).
Furthermore, the association of the nobles with the king's decision is a typically Persian procedure hitherto unknown in the histories of Israel or Assyria (see Ezra 7:4; Dan. 6:17; Esther 1:13).

More importantly, the anthological character of the book of Jonah contributes to the solution of the problem of dating the work. The parallel with
the books of Kings has been noted, and we referred to 2 Kings 14:25, which
introduces the eighth-century prophet Jonah ben Amittai. There are, moreover, parallels between the prophet Jonah of the fifth-century and the
prophet Elijah. Some of those parallels may appear to be accidental, such as
Jonah 4:5, 6 in parallel with 1 Kings 19:9, 4. But others seem to be inten-
tional and carry an ironic tone that is hard to miss. So Jonah 4:2, 3 parallels 1
Kings 19:4, and Jonah 4:9 parallels 1 Kings 19:14. That connection is all the
more interesting in that Elijah and Elisha are the only prophets who were
sent to pagans, according to 2 Kings 7 ff. (cf. 8:7 –15, Elisha in Damascus).

The parallelism with the book of Jeremiah is still more impressive. Besides the fact that Jeremiah is called "prophet of the nations" (1:5), and that
he appears as one of those prophets who try to escape their mission (see 9:1;
20:9; etc.), the parallel between Jonah 3 and Jeremiah 36 is especially striking. The two texts envision the possibility of the nonfulfillment of divine oracles in the case of conversion (Jer. 36:2, 3; Jon. 3:8, 9). Moreover, the very
pattern of events in the two texts is parallel. To the threat expressed in
Jeremiah 36:7b and Jonah 3:4 corresponds a fast in Jeremiah 36:9 and Jonah
3:5, where the same expression is used (whereas Joel, for instance, uses another one; see 1:14 and 2:15); the king with his court is addressed in both
texts (Jer. 36:12, 20; Jon. 3:6); and the response of the King of Nineveh in
Jonah 3:6 –8 and that of Jehoiakim in Jeremiah 36:24 stand in ¹·-ect opposition to each other (Jon. 3:10; and Jer. 36:29 –31).

On the literary level also, the parallels between Jonah and Jeremiah are
numerous. "Make the proclamation" of Jonah 3:2 (cf. 1:2) is in parallel with
Jeremiah 2:2; 4:5; 7:2; 11:6; 19:2; and 20:8. The expression in Jonah 3:5
"from the greatest of them even to the least of them" is found in the reverse
order in Jeremiah 6:13; 8:10; 42:1; 42:8; 42:12. The expression "man and
beast" of Jonah 3:7, 8 and 4:11 has textual parallels in Jeremiah 7:20; 21:6;
27:5; 31:27; 32:43; 33:10 –12; 36:29. The expression of Jonah 3:8, "let
them turn every one from his evil way," appears also in Jeremiah 25:5; 26:3;
36:3, 7, and almost so in 18:11; 23:22; 35:15. The expression of Jonah 3:9
"who knows?" corresponds to similar expressions in Jeremiah 21:2; 26:3;

36:3–7; 51:8 ("perhaps," cf. Jon. 1:6). The expression of Jonah 3:9 "his fierce anger" occurs in Jeremiah 4:8, 26; 12:13; 25:37, 38; 30:24; 49:37; 51:45. The expression "Nineveh the great city" in Jonah 1:2; 3:2; 4:11 stands in parallel with Jeremiah 22:8, which speaks of Jerusalem. The expression of Jonah 1:14 "lay not upon us innocent blood" finds its parallel in Jeremiah 26:15 "if you put me to death, you will bring innocent blood upon yourselves, and upon this city, and upon the inhabitants thereof." Thus, in the conclusion of a detailed study of the sources of the book of Jonah, André Feuillet can state: "Jeremiah, the prophet of the nations, constitutes the main source for the author of Jonah." [26]

The book of Jonah also borrows from Ezekiel. In the Prime Testament there are only two shipwreck narratives besides Jonah 1 (Ps. 107:23–32 and Ezek. 27). Chapters 26—28 of Ezekiel forecast the fall of the city of Tyre through the allegory of a splendid ship armed by all nations, which eventually wrecks "in the midst of the seas." From this passage in Ezekiel, Jonah has borrowed several words and expressions. The term "mariners" of Jonah 1:5 is found elsewhere only in Ezekiel 27:9, 27, 29. The word "pilot" of Jonah 1:6 is found elsewhere only in Ezekiel 27:8, 27, 28, 29. Ezekiel 27:25–28 especially seems to have been used by the author of the book of Jonah. In both places we find expressions such as "Tarshish," "an east wind" (cf. Jon. 4:8), "to be broken" (cf. Jon. 1:4), or "cries" (cf. Jon. 1:5, "and they cried"), or again "in the heart of the seas" which recurs no fewer than six times in Ezekiel 27 and 28 (cf. Jon. 2:4). André Feuillet is correct, however, in calling attention to the sharp contrast introduced by the author of Jonah. Whereas Ezekiel described the fate of the foreign and adverse city of Tyre, here it is the Israelite hero himself who is lost in the "heart of the seas." (This reversal of situation is a feature that will come up again in the discussion below of the *Sitz im Leben* of the book of Jonah.)

There is probably no conclusion to be drawn from the textual parallels between Jonah and Joel (compare Jon. 3:9a with Joel 2:14a; Jon. 4:2 with Joel 2:13); the common expressions are liturgical and can be found in a number of other texts (see Exod. 34:6; Ps. 86:15; 103:8; Neh. 9:17). However, we have left unmentioned until now the parallel that seems to be the most important one, although it has never been invoked by critics so far as we know. It is an oracle of Third Isaiah, which will also clarify the symbolic meaning of the name "Jonah." Isaiah 60 proleptically celebrates all nations with their kings, their riches, and their animals coming to the light of Jerusalem. They come like doves (*yôn îm*, vs. 8) and at their head are ships (*on îyôth*, cf. Jon. 1:3) of Tarshish (vs. 9)!

The borrowing goes much farther. It implies at times what Albert Lord calls "compositional themes," i.e., recurring elements with a high degree of similarity in wording. At times also the parallels fall rather in the category of "type-scenes," i.e., repeated elements or details that are not always found in the same order nor to the same extent as their duplicates "but enough of which are present to make the scene a recognizable one."[27] Each of the imperatives in Isaiah 60:1 ("arise," "shine") belongs to one of these categories. "Arise" is used also in Jonah 1:1, so that both texts have the same beginning. "Shine" is clearly reminiscent of Second Isaiah's "light of the nations" (42:6; 49:6) and is here illustrated by the prophet Jonah's going to Nineveh. Isaiah 60:2 describes how darkness and gloom cover the earth; this theme in Jonah 1:2 becomes the doom of Nineveh. In Isaiah 60:3 the nations go toward the light, i.e., toward Jerusalem. Jonah reverses the formula: the prophet goes toward the darkness of Nineveh. Isaiah 60:4 is definitely centripetal; Jonah is centrifugal. Isaiah 60:5 is about the joy of Jerusalem, Jonah about the bitterness of the prophet. As hinted at above, Isaiah 60:8 provides the key for understanding the symbolism of the name Jonah. It is ironic; the nations fly like "Jonahs" (yônîm) to Jerusalem, and Jonah is ordered to fly like a yônāh from Jerusalem to Nineveh. But if he stands up as ordered, it is to flee away and go down (1:3), while the wickedness of Nineveh is going up to God. Jonah goes even deeper into the ship's and eventually into the fish's entrails. The "dove" has become a crouching dog!

Isaiah 60:10 mentions the bĕnê-nēkār ("strangers") among those who come to Jerusalem and then "their kings" in that order. Jonah 3 also mentions the Ninevites, then their king. "For in my wrath (qeṣep) I smite them," says God, according to Isaiah; Jonah 4:1, 9 use another word to describe Jonah's anger (ḥārāh, 3 times) but the parallel is unmistakable. Isaiah 60:19, 20 was the inspiration for Jonah 4:8, and "the days of your mourning shall be ended," for Jonah 3:5 ff. Isaiah 60:21 reads "your people ... shall be a branch of my planting"; it becomes a "qîqayôn-tree" in Jonah 4:6. At the end, Isaiah 60:22 uses metaphorically the term "a little one" and "a young one," whereas Jonah 4:11 ends the book with a kind of reification of those words: the little and young ones are such because "they cannot discern their right hand from their left hand"!

Third Isaiah is, right after the return from Babylon, a witness of the underground struggle in Jerusalem against the theocratic party of Zerubbabel, Ezra, Nehemiah, the Chronicler. If it was the case that for these leaders in Jerusalem the kingdom of God had come on earth and was visibly present in the building of the Second Temple, per contra, the Hasidim were unable to read history the same way. The twelve tribes had not been reunited, national independence was a long way off, economic conditions were disastrous, and the nations had never displayed more contemptuous indifference to God's city and to his Lordship. To ignore the situation in Jerusalem was only delusion. Far from being without importance, the nations were expected to come and pledge their allegiance to YHWH; this would indeed constitute the eschatological event, the crowning of history. All claims to exclusive election on the part of the Temple "establishment" were of no avail. Rather run to Nineveh and witness there the God-given gracious reversal of the course of history, the changing of wolves into lambs, than to stay arrogantly with one's head in the sand and pretend not to see the world out there. The book of Jonah, like the opposition literature of that epoch, puts its stock in miracle, the only alternative to foolish complacency and blind triumphalism. God will have mercy and spare Nineveh, and thus also Jerusalem!

All of this points in one direction. The *terminus a quo* is the return from the Exile in the second half of the sixth century B.C.E. As Jonah seems to have been in existence in the time of Ben Sirah (see Ecclus. 49:10; Tob. 14:4, 8 [codex S]), the *terminus ad quem* is the second century B.C.E. Between 538 and the time of Ben Sirah it is possible to propose a more precise chronology for the book, but in order to do this we must consider its setting in life *(Sitz im Leben)*.

The examination of the book's terminology has led us to conclude comfortably in favor of a post-exilic date. What were the main problems in Jerusalem immediately following the return from Babylon? No doubt the most vexing question was the apparent nonfulfillment of exilic prophecies. Instead of being a messianic era, the times were hard and the readjustment to Judaean conditions difficult. Specific promises of an Isaiah, a Jeremiah, or an Ezekiel could not be reconciled with the dire reality. One case in point is the fixation of seventy years duration for the Exile in Jeremiah 25:11; 29:10. Even in the second century B.C.E. a text like Daniel 9 still finds this to be a problem and explains that, contrary to what is said in the Chronicler's work (see 2 Chron. 36:21), the prophetic text should be understood as referring to seventy weeks of years. But it is not necessary to propose a date as late as the second century B.C.E. Already during the Exile in Babylon, an oracle of Ezekiel against Tyre (Chapters 26—28) had to be completed some sixteen years later by the prophet in a more realistic way (29:17 ff.). Contrary to what Ezekiel had first predicted, the Phoenician city resisted a siege of thirty years by Nebuchadnezzar! Such wavering in the oracles did of course aggravate the post-exilic discomfort as to their fulfillment.

In general terms, the problem of the former exiles consisted in the fact that instead of Zion's being restored as promised, the nations were triumphant. How could this be explained? Third Isaiah, for one, showed in several texts that the promises of the prophets needed to be understood as referring to things still to come (see 59:1, 9–15; 63:1–6; 63:7—64:11). Already during the Exile, the principle had emerged that the prophetic oracles had to be divided into promises of doom and promises of bliss. For Jeremiah only the latter needed confirmation in history. In this the prophet is in accord with Hosea 6:5 or Isaiah 55:10–11; the question had to be dealt with in

a broader context—namely that of true versus false prophecies (see Deut.
18:21, 22; Amos 7:17; Isa. 7:16; 37:30; 38:1 ff.; Jer. 28:15–17; 44:28–30;
but especially Jer. 28:8–9).

Crossan has shown Jonah's response to this particular question.[28] Jonah
establishes a parallel on the model of the opposition in Jeremiah between
oracles of bliss and oracles of doom. The bliss of the return is absent; neither
does the "doom" of the nations (here Nineveh) occur. Hence we have the
following schema:

This chart clearly indicates that the prophecy of bliss which is normally directed to Israel is now directed to Nineveh, and the prophecy which should
normally be for Nineveh is by implication addressed to Jonah's people, i.e.,
Israel.

One can thus wonder whether Bickerman's position is not vindicated,
namely, that Jonah was opposed to Jeremiah and Ezekiel (see Jer. 18:7–10;
Ezek. 3:16; 33:1–9; cf. above the stance of Hans Schmidt). Whereas the exilic prophets had declared that the impending destruction would be suspended by God on the condition that the people repent, did the prophet
Jonah personally believe that such a relenting on the part of God was scan-
dalous and inopportune? A comparison of the text of Jonah 3:8 with Jeremian texts shows that this is not the case. Jonah 3:8 is reminiscent of several
Jeremian passages which could lead one to draw the same conclusion as does
Bickerman. Jeremiah 25:5 or 26:3; 36:3, 7; 23:22; 35:15; and especially
18:11, emphasize the rule: "it may be they will hearken and turn every man
from his evil way; that I repent of the evil which I purpose to do unto them
because of the evil of their doings" (26:3).

In light of this, therefore, the attitude of Jonah looks like a step back-
wards in taking exception to the stance of Jeremiah and Ezekiel. But a closer
study shows that in theory the whole argument of the exilic prophets was
that any nation could be an example of God's readiness to relent, but in fact
the nation to which such a promise is addressed is invariably Israel. In all the
texts quoted above, it is specified that Judah is the object of the promise.
This is especially clear in Jeremiah 18:11: "now therefore speak to the men
of Judah and to the inhabitants of Jerusalem saying . . . ." The rule is thus
valid only for God's people. When the problem of a foreign nation is tackled
in Jonah, it becomes a new problem. For Jeremiah and Ezekiel it was a question of comforting the Jews in Exile, explaining that they were not the victims of the determinism of punishment. In God's economy, if "a nation"
(meaning they themselves) repents, God also will relent and forgive. In

short, the restoration is possible and at hand. On the contrary, at the time of Jonah it is a question of the success of the nations and the lack of success of the Jews who returned to Zion. Does this situation then show that Jeremiah's principle applies also to the arch-wicked city of Nineveh, for example? The prophet Jonah's response is passionately negative. This cannot be; it would be too unjust. Israel has been put down by the wickedness of the nations in the past—would she now be put down by their repentance?

One can take this a step farther. Jeremiah 36:12 –20 served as a model for Jonah 3:6. From such a connection however, emerges a taut paradox. Where no one appears receptive to the oracle of Jeremiah in chapter 36 that human beings and beasts would be destroyed (see vss. 29 –31), the terse prediction of Jonah to the Ninevites stirs a general repentance that means for them salvation, not only of human beings but also of beasts (see Jon. 3:6 –8, 10; 4:11). We can, therefore, draw a second schema:

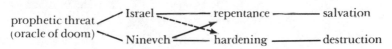

prophetic threat / Israel ——— repentance ——— salvation
(oracle of doom) \ Nineveh ——— hardening ——— destruction

The chart is read as follows: While the prophetic threat normally brings Israel to repentance and hence to salvation, the same oracle of doom should harden the heart of the Ninevites and bring them to destruction. But instead, the book of Jonah shows that the prophetic threat brings the Ninevites to repentance and hence to salvation. The implication is that if addressed to Israel, the same oracle would harden their hearts and bring about their destruction.

In other words, there is no theoretical opposition of Jonah to Ezekiel or Jeremiah, but the author of Jonah uses irony and contrast.[29] Jonah 3 contrasts with Jeremiah 36 because the individual Jehoiakim refuses to repent after a lengthy exhortation of the exilic prophet, whereas all the Ninevites repent after a few words uttered by Jonah. As for Nineveh, it is "the great city," like Jerusalem in Jeremiah 22:8 –9 (cf. Neh. 9:26 –35; Ezra. 9:7 –11; Mal. 3:6, 7). Also on the point of the theology of God's forgiveness, Jonah is an ironic contrast to Jeremiah. In Jonah 1:14, which stands in parallel with Jeremiah 26:15, the sailors are better than the Jerusalemites in the time of Jeremiah (cf. Jon. 1:16; 2:10). And in Jonah 4, the conversion of the Ninevites is of the type advocated by the exilic prophets to their fellow Jews—namely, penance, fasting, prayer, avoidance of sin. Furthermore, Jonah 4:2—the veritable center of gravity of the whole book—presents a liturgical formula which is normally reserved for the relations between God and his people exclusively (see Exod. 34:6; Ps. 103:8; etc.). In Jonah, however, we find it used within a universalistic framework in sharp contrast to the former usage in the Israelite liturgy. This very point allows us to date more precisely the book of Jonah. A comparison of the universalism of the book with earlier and later texts will show where to place Jonah in time. For Micah and First Isaiah, for example, the universalism is centralized in Zion. It is only during the Exile that we find a decentralized universalism in Jeremiah and in Isaiah 40–55. Both prophets make requisite a general conversion of the heart. With the return from Exile, however, there is a new attempt at recentralizing the universalism in Haggai, Zechariah, and Third Isaiah. An exceptional note is struck by Malachi 1:10, 11, which go very far in the interpretation of God's universal kingship. Finally, in Hellenistic times, one returns to a more conservative universalism in reaction to the temptation of compromise with paganism (see Ecclus. 36:1–17; 33:7–14; 1:25, 26).

The book of Jonah is clearly to be situated between the decentralized universalism advocated by Jeremiah and Second Isaiah and the recentralization of universalism as advocated by Haggai and Zechariah. In other words, with the book of Jonah we are in the fifth century B.C.E. This is also the most appropriate period for the problematic put forward by the book of Jonah. We now turn to this point.

* * * * * * * *

The fifth century saw the birth of two major developments in Judaism that had a long-lasting influence on its future: on the one hand, the Chronicler's work, which came into existence between 450 and 300 B.C.E., and on the other hand, Jewish apocalypticism, which "dawned" in the fifth century and lasted until the first century C.E. The Chronicler's work follows the so-called Priestly Document (P) in the Pentateuch, one aim of which had been to depict Moses as creator of the Temple in Jerusalem and of the Israelite cultus (the Tent in the desert has oversized dimensions which make it nonportable; it is in fact, a miniaturized Temple). For the Chronicler, the Second Temple under Zerubbabel and the restoration of the cult in Jerusalem constitute the fulfillment of prophetic promises, namely, that the return from Exile would initiate a blessed era of God's presence in the world. The Temple in Jerusalem is the kingdom of God on earth and the present king or governor actually sits on the throne of David, which is also the throne of YHWH (see 1 Chron. 28:5; 29:23; 2 Chron. 9:8; 13:8). Similarly, the present people of Israel embody the theocratic ideal. In other words, the Chronicler hails a messianic time without eschatology. In this conception, Israel has passed from the stage of people to that of Church. Cyrus's restoration of 538 had made eschatological expectations pointless.

This last point about Cyrus's edict is crucial. Seen by some as inaugurating the fulfillment of exilic oracles, it was considered by others as not even worthy of mention, for the restoration was still an object of hope. This latter position is the one of the so-called apocalyptic movement, which started immediately after the return of the exiles to Zion.[30] From this point of view (exemplified by Third Isaiah), the well-to-do people who centered around the Temple and enjoyed a relative but concrete power were not only wrong in their theocratic ideology but they were precisely those who were preventing the restoration from occurring. In order to bring it about, all exclusivism and triumphalism had to be eradicated. That is why, in their protest, "even the royal symbols are democratized and applied to the people." [31] Isaiah 62:3 reads, "you will be a glorious crown in the Lord's hand, a kingly diadem in the hand of your God." The good news is for the humble, the broken hearted, the captive, the prisoners, the mourners (Isa. 61:1 –2).

The division between the two parties is made especially clear in regard to the question of the Temple. For those who in time would become the Sadducees, the Temple is the establishment of God's kingship. For the visionary, on the contrary, the Temple is none other than the people themselves. Isaiah 66:1, 2 read

> The Lord says this: "the heavens are my throne and the earth my footstool. What is this house which you would build for me, and what is this throne dais? All these my hand has made and all of these are mine. Upon this one I will look, the humble, who is broken in spirit and trembles at my word."

This perspective continues for generations. On the one hand, one can cite the books of Haggai; First Zechariah; Ezra; Nehemiah; Chronicles, and on the other, Third Isaiah; Second Zechariah; Ruth; Jonah; Daniel. We cannot here provide a detailed account of a situation that became more and more complex and eventually resulted in the separation of the party of the "establishment" from the party of Hasidim characterized by the concept of radical eschatology. For our purposes it is more important to underline the radical measures taken by those in power in Jerusalem to ensure the purity of the kingdom of God on earth. Thus, Nehemiah and Ezra demanded divorce from foreign women and constructed, so to speak, a wall of separation between Israel in Jerusalem and the rest of the nations. Such a splendid isolation could in the long run save Judaism from extinction, but the price was enormous. On the contrary, the party of opposition, which expected an event that would completely change the course of history, viewed the relationship of God and the non-Jews on the one hand and of Israel and the nations on the other hand as crucial to the eventual coming of the kingdom of God. Far from condoning the isolation as it was implemented by the governors Nehemiah and Ezra, the Hasidim demanded that the relationship with non-Jews be part and parcel of a reassessment of Israel's identity. Their stance expresses itself in popular tales such as that about Ruth, the Moabite,[32] or Jonah, who in an unparalleled move goes to the arch-enemy of Israel, the Ninevites, to utter a word of God. All the nations, announce Third Isaiah and Second Zechariah, will soon come to Jerusalem and worship the living God with the Israelites. They will even become priests and Levites (Isa. 66:21) or celebrate the Festival of the Booths in the Temple (Zech. 14).

From this perspective the book of Jonah is a book of protest against the "ghettoization" of the Judaeans in and around Jerusalem. It is from that vantage point only that the book is intelligible and that the thesis as we shall track it in our reading of the book becomes clear. Already at this point our thesis allows us to escape the quicksand of the anti-Semitic reading of Jonah. For the hero of the tale is no petty, narrow-minded character, as so many Christians did or do believe. In fact, Jonah raises again the problem of election. Only Israel is elected or else election would be meaningless (see Num. 23:9; Deut. 7:7, 8; 10:15; Amos 3:2). Israel has been called to live separated from the nations (Lev. 20:26; 18:3, 4; 20:23; Isa. 48:20; 52:11; Jer. 51:6, 45). Nineveh is the antipode of Jerusalem, the non-elected, the foil of election, because she is what Jerusalem has chosen not to be. In a negative way Nineveh is the justification of Jerusalem's choice. She is the night over against which the daylight has meaning. Jonah cannot accept that the night might also be called to become day. At the very least it would relativize Israel's election. The refusal of Jonah (1:3) is not based so much on his aversion to the Ninevites as it is on his incomprehension of God's word and attitude (4:2). Such an incomprehension is characteristic of the party of the "ideologists" in Jerusalem for whom there is no opening to the nations. Jonah's problem is their own. For either God in his dealing with the Gentiles is by his own nature merciful (cf. Jon. 4:2)—in which case the prophetic forecast of utter destruction of Nineveh is pointless; or Nineveh will be irrevocably annihilated—but then why bother to say so in advance? It too is pointless. If, however, God plans to offer pardon—should Nineveh repent—and to save the wicked city, why did he not show the same compassion towards his own people, and why did he stir up successively the Assyrians and Babylonians in order to chastize Israel and Judah beyond reasonable measure? The problem is without solution. From that point of view, whatever God does necessarily amounts to nothing more than injustice and fickleness.[33]

The author of Jonah replies with a fictional narrative but one which does not lack some verisimilitude. Although it is most unusual that a prophet be sent to a nation other than his own, the case falls in parallel with the Elijah story, and many prophets in Israel did utter oracles against foreign nations. Moreover, the message that Jonah is to deliver to Nineveh is, expectedly, one of doom. In the words of Allen: "The audience is asked to ponder a theological riddle: what would have happened if no less a den of foreign devils than Nineveh had repented? God's primary providential concern is to preserve life, human and animal, not to destroy." [34] By the same token, the author of Jonah turns his back to the triumphalism of the party in power in Jerusalem, whose expectation entailed the annihilation of the nations. Jonah's book is written after the Exile as a pamphlet directed against the theocratic party in Jerusalem and against their complacent isolationism; but if he has recourse to irony, he refrains from caricaturing his opponents [35] He knows that their theological position is far from being stupid or even petty. He presents his hero (or antihero) Jonah as holding firm the promise of God to his people. Jonah is so far from being a narrow-minded bigot without breadth that he dares oppose God when he thinks that God's designs are wrong or unjust. That God is all that Jonah says he is as far as Israel is concerned does not raise any question in his mind. The irony and the scandal are that God is also all of these things vis-à-vis barbarian killers of Israel's children.[36]

With this remark, we indicate already that in the opinion of this essay's authors the book of Jonah must be read with the vivid consciousness that the issue is both theological and psychological. This is why in what follows Jonah will be read both as a theological pamphlet and as a folk tale directly bearing upon human psychology in general. This crossfertilization of two of the main sciences of human nature will prove, we believe, particularly fruitful. For interestingly enough, the author of the fifth century B.C.E. book of Jonah had intuited the basic and universal human struggle to find meaning in one's life and destiny. The book was written in reaction to the provincialism and bigotry of some in the Israel of old. As such it advocates the view that to be a Jew is in fact tantamount to taking a fully human attitude towards life rather than a membership in a select club or coterie. The tension between the particular and the universal is fundamental, and the modern reader is expected to respect the integrity of these two components in polarity. For the book of Jonah operates on two levels: it is a Jewish book for Israel with a definite position within a particular geographical and historical "setting in life," and it is also a universal message addressed to all people. Its very form, the haggadic narrative or folk tale, is one of the most universal literary genres in existence. For the folk tale, while it is not necessarily a myth, has the same universal exemplary meaning. Behind the uniqueness of its heroes one has no difficulty in understanding that *humanity* is at stake, coming from any land and any time.[37] Psychoanalysis has utilized primarily Greco-Roman symbolism to describe the fundamental means, strivings, and fantasies of humanity (Oedipus, Thanatos, Electra, Narcissus, and so on). It is our contention that the book of Jonah lends itself no less than does Greek tragedy to psychological or psychoanalytical interpretation. Moreover, as the vision of

Jerusalem is profoundly different from that of Athens, one can expect the symbolic patterns of the Israelites to reveal *other* human dimensions and images. Athens and Jerusalem are speaking of and to humanity. This simple fact bridges their respective conceptions. But once this has been said, very little unites the two anthropologies. One is heroic and tragic, i.e., deterministic; in it the human being is a pathetic pawn in fate's chess game. The other presents an antihero whose "tragedy" is transcended by a dialogue with the divine, in which Jonah is fully involved and to which he contributes either negatively or positively. From such a perspective, the issue with Jonah is not whether or not he will succeed in becoming what he can be,[38] but rather, whether he will become what he actually is.

We thus return to the decisive question of the literary genre of Jonah, which will by the subject of the next chapter.

Chapter II

JONAH AS SYMBOLIC NARRATIVE

Symbolic language is language in which the world outside is a symbol of the world inside, a symbol for our souls and our minds . . . The story [of Jonah] is told as if these events had actually happened. However, it is written in symbolic language and all the realistic events described are symbols for the inner experiences of the hero.

—Erich Fromm, *The Forgotten Language*
(New York: Grove Press, 1951), pp. 12, 22.

The main characteristic of narrative according to Paul Ricoeur[1] is that, like a proverb for instance, it *disorients* and *reorients* our imaginations. The *disorientation* occurs because the message conveyed by narratives—or by events before they are narrated—is a demonstration that we have misinterpreted the given. The *reorientation* is putting our attentiveness to the unfulfilled creation back on the track. It constitutes a real breakthrough in the circularity of our existence because the message, heard in reality for the first time, indicates a direction, an orientation, to our life movement. With such a direction, one leaves the rut in which the same phenomenon is perpetually interpreted by the same person according to the same rules with the same unsatisfactory result. In other words, the message lifts one up from the oppression of distributive justice, for example (for which Job looked in vain in nature), or of unchecked natural compulsions (*à la* Eli's sons, according to 1 Sam. 2:12 ff.). The narrative reorients as it proclaims the irruption of the unexpected grace of God which is a "how much more" (see Gen. 7:17 ff.; 8:13 ff.; Matt. 5:38 ff.; Rom. 5:6 ff.), the disconcerting superabundance of God's word which brings about what it says (Isa. 55).

Now the message is multiform. It is the creator of an endless literary tradition if only because of the ineptness of each attempt to encompass the incredible, the extravagant (we borrow both terms from Ricoeur). In the concert of those attempts, however, no literary genre is better suited to reshaping the imagination than the parable. As events follow events, and recalls by the unfulfilled creation are sent forth time and again, so also sagas are piled upon sagas to make sure that the message can be heard. In a way the same event is ceaselessly reinterpreted, and the same saga reshaped without end; but the parable reaches forthwith the ultimate dimension of the event in tracing for us the movement that leads from the apparent triviality of the surface message to the transcendence of its deep meaning. Ezekiel, Daniel, the apocalyptic literature, the parables of Jesus, for instance, tell us what the kingdom of God (the referent) is *like.* The concentration is not on the terms of the metaphor but on the movement, on the *likeness* which reveals the gestation of eternity in human time, the emergence of the ultimate in the contingent.

Jonah is a parable, i.e., according to Crossan, a "story subverting the world," for the structure of expression on the part of the speaker lies in diametrical opposition to the structure of expectation on the part of the hearer.[2] The critic continues, "it is clear that parable is really a *story event* and not just a story. One can tell oneself a story, but not a parable. One cannot really do so just as one cannot really beat oneself at chess or fool oneself completely with a riddle one has just invented. It takes two to parable."

If we remember (following Robert Scholes and Robert Kellogg[3]) the two main characteristics of narrative—namely, that it is a *story* told by a *storyteller*—we need add that, in contrast to pure oral tradition, the author of Jonah, although ever present in his tale, stays a certain distance from the narrative. He thus identifies himself with Jonah and studies Jonah from outside, adopting a stance which evolves only from his characters' viewpoints (the mariners, the Ninevites) and, more subtly, from his readers' opinions.[4] The narrative of Jonah, is meant to *apprehend* reality; it does this *through* the interrelation of character and incident, a characteristic of epic. But the genre of epos is broken. First, the epos that demands a reciter and an actual audience is replaced here by fiction, although representational in character rather than illustrative, mimetic rather than contemplative. Second, as we have seen, the author keeps some distance from his tale. Finally, a resolution of the tension in the narrative never comes, so that we could call Jonah's plot a "non-plot"! Similarly its hero is a picaresque "non-hero"! Not meant simply to amuse, Jonah is more than an "imaginative folk tale"; not claiming simply to be true, it is more than "legend"; mimetic, it is antithetic to myth, for myth is cyclical and dualistic. The quest of Jonah is for identity, not for the Grail! Jonah belongs to ". . . the great realistic narratives [which] combine the tragic concern for the individual with the comic concern for society . . . inserting . . . tragic characters in comic situations."[5]

So far we have called Jonah a parable and, with specific qualifications, an epic; it is an epic in the form of a parable. The present mix of tragedy and comedy in the narrative must now be studied more closely. Crossan suggests that "Jonah is a parabolic lampoon, a parody directed at the very heart of the Bible. It converts into paradox the prophetic traditions themselves." [6] Stereotyped characters and scenes in biblical literature at large are here given exaggerated features so as to mix comedy with tragedy. For instance, it is a recurring theme in the Bible that the charismatic person offers resistance to the divine call (so Moses, Gideon, Isaiah, Jeremiah), but Jonah overdoes it. He sails in the opposite direction of the call and instead of arguing like the others, he remains obstinately silent.[7] He even pursues that attitudinal line in sleeping during the God-made tempest. And when at last he resorts to speaking he sings a psalm whose language, normally metaphorical (as in Ps. 130), is now to be understood literally. Similarly, in parallel with Elijah's complaint about his failure before Achab (1 Kings 19:4 –5), Jonah requests to die, but now it is after his resounding victory before the King of Nineveh!

In parody everyone is an object of laughter. Here the Israelites are mocked for their excessive nationalism, and the nations for their stupidity (see Jon. 1:5 ff.; 4:11).[8] From such a situation it is tempting to draw purely literary or humanistic conclusions. But we have seen that the book of Jonah is not meant to entertain; it is a parable, a "story subverting the world." Neither is it a timeless lesson for the betterment of humanity but a protest against a well-to-do party in Jerusalem in the fifth century B.C.E. which abused its power in order to "ghettoize" Judaism. The only possible conclusion, therefore, is that this light-spirited parody is only the surface of a message full of gravity.

Perhaps the main reason for the complex mixing of the realistic "with the extraordinary and the improbable"[9] is that, in Israel, history is never really dismissed from narrative. The tale may well be—here as in a "Greek" parallel—in discontinuity with our present and actual situation, but it is spoken *in* situation. Thus the historicity of a Hebrew narrative is to be assessed not in terms of "Historie" (sequence of recordable events) but in terms of "Geschichte" (real or fictional events receiving their orientation from outside, for their referent is not to be found within them or their records). Now, in the book of Jonah, as in Ruth or Esther, the contact with the real does not depend upon the materiality of specific happenings, but upon the unbroken fidelity of God who "reaches out" to us in the actuality of events or in a folk tale, the one and the other being encompassed in "Geschichte."[10]

Donald G. Miller is reported to have called Jonah "the high point of the Old Testament . . . the peak of Old Testament revelation."[11] The statement is striking and it might well represent the truth. It is all the more interesting that such a profound theological achievement adopted the form of a tale. Its brevity and unassumingness did not prevent it from becoming very well known, yea, probably the best known story in the Bible. For even though "one of the smallest strands in the mighty cable of the Scriptures"—as Herman Melville's Father Mapple says[12]—the book is one of the most puzzling and intriguing of the entire Prime Testament. It is quite revealing that the theme of Jonah and the fish[13] with all its psychological and emotional dynamism is repeated in so many popular folk tales.

It is fascinating to realize that a tale like Jonah's, even though told in the language and ideas of a particular epoch, has managed to survive throughout the centuries and to remain one of the most exciting short stories of our time. To limit ourselves to modern literature, Jules Verne's Captain Nemo (1877) in his submarine, the Nautilus, lives in the depth of the seas away from all civilization; Collodi's Pinocchio (1883) is swallowed by a "dogfish" after disobeying the fairy and his "father"; Herman Melville's Captain Ahab (1851) strives for vengeance against the whale Moby Dick; Daniel Defoe's Robinson Crusoe (1719) displays a real kinship with the traveler Jonah. Perhaps the fact that the biblical tale ends with such a striking lack of resolution sparked the exceptional imaginations. Psychology knows of the "Zeigarnik Effect,"[14] according to which completed tasks tend to be more easily forgotten than uncompleted ones because in the former case the motivation to perform is satisfied "while the drive persists and enhances memory when (the tasks) are uncompleted."[15] We all feel the urge to take over Jonah's uncompleted task. Whether we want it or not, when we allow the narrative to grasp us, we become Jonah. His unfinished business with life painfully reminds us of our own daily struggle with meaning. No wonder, therefore, that the book has received various psychological interpretations. Bruno Bettelheim, for one, has shown that different personal meanings are found in the same story, depending upon the emotional maturity of the reader.[16] These symbolic stories, we feel, reflect universal unresolved conflicts deeply rooted within the human psyche, so that they must be dealt with ever anew and at every stage of a person's emotional growth. Bettelheim sees Jonah's struggle from a psychoanalytic point of view. For him the key to the narrative lies in Jonah 2 where the prophet discovers his "higher morality" and is "wondrously reborn." The acknowledgment of his "higher self" helps him to go to Nineveh. This he was able to do only when he reached "full humanity" (i.e., when he was no longer able to depend on his Id or Pleasure Principle, which had urged him to run away to Tarshish).

But, it is Hyman Fingert who presents the first detailed Freudian analysis of the prophet's inner anguish.[17] Fingert sees Jonah's character and behavior as revealing an emotionally disturbed person who actually lived centuries ago. The main theme of this historical parable is that Jonah is angry at his mother for preferring his father over him. This injustice "could be the wickedness of Nineveh that Jonah feels called upon to denounce."[18] At this point, the "prophet" of the story receives from his Ego the command to rebel against his parents' preference for each other. The saving of Nineveh symbolizes his renunciation of his sexual longing "and wishes for the mother and her destruction."[19]

Besides seeing mother symbols in practically all events in the story (e.g., Tarshish, the ship, the fish, Nineveh or the king), Fingert comes up with interpretations still more difficult to follow. For example, with regard to the worm that ate the gourd (Jon. 4:7) he has this to say:

> It seems indicated that the worm responsible for the gourd's destruction represents Jonah's fantasy of the destructiveness of the penis in intercourse. . . . Preoccupation with pregnancy or birth is also indicated. . . . It would appear possible to surmise that Jonah's wife may have died following, or during, pregnancy or from a disorder of the female organs he could relate to intercourse.[20]

The analyst did not take into consideration any of the historical, conceptual, or existential issues facing Israel at the time that the narrative was written. The result is a far-fetched unwarranted interpretation. Jonah's fantasies are less apparent than are Fingert's.[21]

The only other psychoanalytic study of the Jonah narrative is by Joseph More.[22] For him the tale has no connection with a real person, contrary to Fingert's opinion. More understands the book as a "myth of Biblical man, his character and its vicissitudes."[23] He sees the prophet Jonah experiencing resentment and jealousy towards the Ninevites: "God, Jonah's father-figure is the God of Nineveh too, and thus the father of the people of Nineveh, who thereby become Jonah's brothers."[24] In biblical times, the author argues, large families and strong sibling rivalries were not uncommon. The stories of Cain and Abel or of Joseph and his brothers depict well such situations.

What Jonah wants is to get the love of God all for himself. Nineveh represents "the bad mother whom (he) wants to destroy because she mothers others."[25] The issue for Jonah is not, however, Oedipal. He does not want to get rid of his father in order to get his mother's undivided love and attention, as Fingert believed. Rather, he is jealous of his siblings because of the love they also receive from his parents. That is why, afraid of his death fantasies as regards his brothers in Nineveh, the prophet decides to run away to Tarshish. Moved by his fear to destroy those he loves in Nineveh, he runs away lest his murderous wishes (Id impulses) be fulfilled should he go eastward to the Assyrians.[26]

So goes More's psychological abstraction. No better than Fingert does he take in consideration the historical context of the book of Jonah. This omission entails the oversight of crucial points of the tale and consequently its tendentious reading.

Of particular relevance to our study are the contributions of Carl G. Jung and Erich Fromm. In studying universal myths and fairy tales, Jung in particular noticed that a "hero" must go through a rite of passage before being recognized as "divine." A typical challenge to the hero is to battle a monster, usually representing the unconscious.[27] In some instances—as in the case of Jonah—the hero is swallowed by a sea monster or Leviathan. Inside the belly, the "hero" begins to settle accounts with the creature while it swims eastward toward the rising sun, which symbolizes rebirth.[28] Using inner resources of courage and creativity the hero typically finds a way out (rebirth) by cutting essential and vital organs of the monster.[29]

Within the unconscious—symbolized here by the "monster"—lies one's fear of being destroyed by the mother and all she represents. Jung designated such a phobia by different names: "fear of fate," "fear of self," "fear of life," or even the "Jonah-and-the-whale complex." [30] All of these labels are used to describe the *universal* struggle that each and every one of us faces in asserting oneself as unique and separate from others *in spite of* the desperate temptation to withdraw into womb-like (non-responsible) states.[31] For Jung, then, as also for Rollo May, a hero is one who resists morbid dependency on security and status quo (symbols of the mother's womb) by "cutting the psychological umbilical cord."[32] Such a battle for deliverance from the maternal grip is endless. Rebirth, Jung concludes, is the ability to free the ego consciousness from the "deadly grip of the unconscious and its confusing energy."[33]

Even though he connected the book of Jonah with other myths, Jung did not in fact study the prophet. Such an interest is found in Fromm's work. Unlike Fingert or More who saw Jonah struggling with his incest taboos, Oedipal complex or sibling rivalry, Fromm's approach is more pscyho-social in orientation. All the events of the narrative, he explains, are symbols of the prophet's inner experiences (e.g., going aboard the ship and down to its inner parts, falling asleep, being in the ocean or inside the fish). These guaranteed him a condition of "safe withdrawal from communication with other human beings. They represent what could be represented in another symbol, the fetus in the mother's womb."[34]

Jonah runs away from God because he is afraid that the people in Nineveh will repent and be forgiven. The prophet differs from other prophets in the Hebrew Bible in that he is not prompted by love of and solidarity with his fellow human beings (here the Ninevites).[35] In fact, Fromm argues, "he wanted 'justice' to be done, not mercy."[36]

These several psychological references to Jonah, be they direct or indirect, are interesting. We intend, however, to point out their shortcomings and to propose a hermeneutical approach that takes into account the fact that the book of Jonah is bi-dimensional, namely, psychological *and* spiritual. The confrontation of psychology and spirituality in the same short story contributes to making the book a profoundly human document. Jonah combines in his person a quite average "layperson," immediately analyzable by psychologists, and a prophet, a religious holy man of sorts, less easily "exhaustible" by psychological explanations. Both aspects meet in Jonah's very human reluctance, or outright refusal to obey, for there is evident here more than the sheer dictates of human survival.

Similarly, there is also ambivalence in God's own orders, for God decides to destroy wicked Nineveh yet hopes to spare it as he expects the city to pass through repentance. Here again the psychological and the theological dimensions are intertwined. Furthermore, Jonah knows that his mission is a reflection of God's ambivalence and that, in a way, he is only a secondary personage in the drama between God and a human partner symbolized by "Nineveh," with whom he, Jonah, cannot identify himself.

That is why his expressions about this unfairness are not reducible to feelings, because what is at stake is not just a wounded self-esteem but the very principle of one's calling, one's vocation on behalf of others. But then, when the problem is considered on a level that transcends the inner psychology of Jonah, acknowledging the dimension of responsibility toward others, Jonah is universal, not so much because of his inner drives—Oedipal or otherwise—but inasmuch as persons are responsible not only for themselves but also for their "people," for the community in which they live and with which they share a historical destiny.

Israel's tradition painstakingly shows the conflicting aspect of the phenomenon called "vocation." Moses must go back to Egypt for the sake of his "brethren," not because he wants to but because such is the imperative of the Ground of Being. Jeremiah says that he is but a child; Ezekiel remains obstinately silent, stubbornly up-tight; Isaiah is crushed under his commission to plead before people who are walled in by their obstinate refusal. All of them are afraid of the immensity of a task they have not chosen, not even fathomed, but which takes them by surprise and staggers the routine of their existence. Furthermore, all of them are frightened in the face of a task that cannot really succeed, for the nature of the message is such that it is the antipode of demagogy. This element, by the way, is decisive in distinguishing true from false prophets, for the "success" of prophecy is perfectly ambiguous. What the prophet can humanly expect is in most cases the undesirable—for instance, that the oracle of doom finds its fulfillment while there is no message of hope for his people. Isaiah will render his people blind, deaf, stupid; he will create by his speech the very conditions for lack of understanding, of conversion, of healing. Jeremiah furnishes a perfect example; he is compelled to preach the very opposite of what he wishes. From the outset he knows that he will be torn between the desires of his heart and the excruciating divine mandate to condemn those he loves. He knows that he is sent "to root out, to pull down, to destroy, to throw down" (1:10), but no excuse is accepted by God. On the contrary, Jeremiah is warned that should he "be dismayed before them [his adversaries], [God] would confound [him] before them" (1:17). In other words, if Jeremiah allows fear to paralyze him and to prevent him from announcing the impending destruction of Jerusalem, God will make him recede into the ranks of the mediocre ones who tremble before their superego.

There is thus a biting irony in the fact that Jonah is presented in the tale as desiring the fulfillment of his prophecy and being displeased by the relenting of God. But one must realize that Jonah's situation is unique in the annals of Israelite prophecy: his addressees are not his people but the archenemy of his people. The destruction of Nineveh corresponds in Jonah's mind to the salvation of Jerusalem. The paradox of a prophet looking forward to the accomplishment of his message of doom is therefore counterbalanced by the fact that, according to Jonah's logic, it is ultimately Jerusalem's fate that is at stake. There is thus a profound agreement between Jonah and the rest of the Hebrew prophets, but the unusual character of the situation exacerbates the clash between the psychological and the theological aspects of Jonah. The prophet sent to Nineveh sets the "psyche" and its imperatives on the one hand against the "soul" with its demands on the other hand. Psychologically there is no doubt that Jonah stands in the right against God; he has been deceived by God[37] into working against the survival of his own nation and for the prosperity of Israel's tormentors. There is in God an intolerable lack of justice in dealing with human problems. Theologically, however, the situation presented in Jonah's story is much more complex. On the one hand, there is congruence with a long history of "the Lord's acts of justice" in God's being "gracious, merciful, slow to anger, of great kindness, and relentful" (Jon. 4:2). But on the other hand, all those divine qualities have been displayed up until now on behalf of God's people, not a foreign nation.

It is precisely that conflict on the psychological as well as on the theological level that is called here the "Jonah complex." It is the outcome of a clash between what one would choose for oneself or, in Maslow's words, what one feels good about, and what one is under commission to do. Jonah is thus torn between his desire for the status quo, an undisturbed enjoyment of his personal potentialities and accumulated possessions and the fulfillment of a vocation which inevitably does not fall in line with the search for happiness. Albert Schweitzer, in order to become Albert Schweitzer, had to leave behind the organs of Gunsbach and the exercise of his musical genius and become the director of an obscure hospital in the jungle of Africa. True, there is only one Albert Schweitzer in human history, but the particularity of his vocation is inserted in the generality of the being-called-for-a-task.

Israel has constantly encountered that indispensable crossing over the brook of Jabbok which transcends vital necessities and psychological comforts. As Saint-Cyran once said about the ill abbot of Singlin: "It is necessary that he go [and visit a parishioner], it is not necessary that he live." The question concerns which "master" we choose to obey. True, there is no eradication or denial of the existential realities which Freud called our superego, but Israel adds to Freud's analysis: this is not *yet* it! For "if anyone . . . does not hate his father and mother, wife and children, brothers and sisters, even life," he cannot fulfill the ultimate vocation of the human person as the image of God (Luke 14:26).

The "logotherapy" conceived by Viktor Frankl acknowledges that much. "Existence falters unless it is lived in terms of transcendence towards something beyond itself."[38] This must be understood not in the sense of Pindarus's *genoio hoios essi* (become what you *can* be), i.e., in the actualizing of one's potential, in the fulfillment of the greatest number of imminent possibilities, but in the sense of Frankl's statement: "Human existence is essentially self-transcendent . . . integration of the subject presupposes direction towards an object." For the question is not ultimately what we expect from life but what life expects from us.[39] In the case of Jonah it is not what Jonah expects from his prophecy or his God that is important but what God expects from him. Israel is precisely a community subjected to that discipline, a discipline (or a law, a commandment, a Torah) that makes Israel different from the nations not because of her intrinsic qualities or potentials but because of her willingness to transcend those potentials she has in common with all the nations.

Chapter III

ANONYMITY AND CALLING (JONAH 1)

"Why does man accept to live a trivial life? Because of the danger of a full horizon of experience, of course. . . . freedom is dangerous."

—Ernest Becker, *The Denial of Death*
(New York: The Free Press, 1973), p. 74.

The book of Jonah opens with a commandment. In its individual and collective dimensions the commandment is a call to go "beyond," that is, an exhortation to have the courage to be separated from the crowd. It is the call from status quo to dynamism. Ultimately, however, this is not a divorce from society but, on the contrary, the true contribution to society, for a person's true life in the world consists not in protecting the status quo but in the choice to go farther in the quest for transcendent truth. We shall deal with this issue more fully later (see Chapter VII), but it should be made clear from the outset that the problematic of Jonah is not one of "happiness" but of liberation. This is why Jonah starts to be Jonah the very moment he hears God's call. Before, he is anonymous and, so to speak, motionless. Afterwards, his name is Jonah and his *raison d'être* is to go toward the ultimate, i.e., the surpassing of the self toward that which is both impossible and necessary. Frankl writes: ". . . it is my conviction that man should not, indeed cannot, struggle for identity in a direct way; he rather finds identity to the extent to which he commits himself to something beyond himself, to a cause greater than himself." [1]

The construction of vs. 1 appears frequently in the Bible (see 2 Sam. 7:4; 1 Kings 17:2, 8; Jer. 1:4, 11; etc.), even at the beginning of a book (Hos. 1:1; Joel 1:1; Mich. 1:1; Zeph. 1:1; Hag. 1:1; Zech. 1:1). The copula "and" at the start of the narrative indicates that the beginning is not absolute. Jonah is not yet Jonah before the call is heard, but he is already living in expectation of what will happen to him. When it occurs, however, the irrevocability of the phenomenon is threatening.

Intuition tells Jonah that no matter what he is going to do about his situation, something is changing within him. From now on everything in his life depends upon how he will handle this existential conflict. What he assuredly cannot do is to ignore the call. He has become the living illustration of a psychological complex common to all, or at least to many, but singularly exemplified in his destiny. Abraham Maslow spoke, as we shall review later, of the "Jonah syndrome," i.e., the fear of standing alone, the escape from greatness, and the unwillingness to face the necessary obstacle on the way to one's fulfillment:

> . . . to discover in oneself a great talent can certainly bring exhilaration but it also brings a fear of the dangers and responsibilities and duties of being a leader and of being all alone. Responsibility can be seen as a heavy burden and evaded as long as possible.[2]

> . . . [The Jonah Syndrome] is partly a justified fear of being torn apart, of losing control, of being shattered and disintegrated, even of being killed by the experience.[3]

It is therefore normal that we react to such a situation with regret that the commandment has been given in the first place. Without the commandment, Jonah has no feeling of guilt and is even quite satisfied with himself.[4] As Paul says in the New Testament, there is no sin without commandment. Jonah experiences the commandment of God as the imposition of the impossible upon him and he develops a feeling of culpability that will eventually bring him to flee to Tarshish, in the direction contrary to that given in his orders.

The revolt of Jonah is in the name of an idea; it is inconceivable, objectively speaking, that he be called to do the impossible. No "God" would logically make such a demand. The commission to go to Nineveh and to proclaim the doom of the city is simply not reasonable. If there is any "God" capable of such insane calling, one must flee as quickly as possible. In the name of sanity Jonah sails west instead of riding east; and anyone who would claim to be sensible would approve of Jonah's decision. The whole of international wisdom literature agrees with Jonah, for what it abhors above all is a lack of moderation.

But what is required of Jonah (and of humanity in general) is to go *beyond* his own limits ("towards the land I shall show you"), because he has been chosen (like all other human beings created in the image of God) by one who is beyond all limits. While the calling does not make Jonah a superhero, one could say that it makes him leave his condition of subhumanity to become—in the image of his commissioner—bondless, liberated, and free. The paradox is that Jonah, before he receives God's commandment and while fleeing from the commandment, is *not* free. Only when one assumes responsibility for the commandment is one free, for the simple reason that it enunciates for the first time the *project* of a person, one's *raison d'être*, one's ultimate meaning. Theoretically—and legitimately—one can affirm that Jonah, son of Amittai, faced an unlimited number of existential possibilities throughout his life. Between the Yes-response and the No-response there is of course a limitless range of possible choices. Practically, however, and once the commandment is uttered (i.e., since the beginning of human existence), only *one* choice is capable of making Jonah the man he actually is: the decision to fulfill his vocation by going to Nineveh and there proclaiming his message. That is why the story of chapter 1 of the book, which seems self-contained, is in fact open-ended. As long as Jonah refuses to go to Nineveh—indeed, as long as he refuses to be Jonah—the story of Jonah cannot end.

One could say without stretching the evidence that he himself brings about the sea storm; he is at the same time author and victim. He *cannot* have a safe trip because the turmoil of his soul must necessarily find an echo in the turmoil of his environment. He cannot contain the whirlwind of excitement, passion, or remorse within his chest. Jonah is guilt-stricken and, contrary to the statements of simplistic psychological schools, guilt is in itself not a flaw of the personality. As Maslow said,

> . . . it is good, even *necessary*, for a person's development to have intrinsic guilt when he deserves to. It is not just a symptom to be avoided at any cost but is rather an inner guide for growth toward actualization of the real self, and of its potentialities.[5]

Martin Buber offers the following insight:

> True guilt does not reside in the human person but in his failure to respond to the legitimate claims and address of the world.[6]

Similarly, the sea tempest, the mirror of Jonah's soul, has more than a one-sided value. It is not just a punishment of Jonah's stubbornness but also an appeal, an opportunity offered him to respond to the call (as Jon. 2 will make clear). In the meantime, Jonah is at an impasse; he is seized by the crippling feeling of being empty and lost. For Frederick Perls, this constitutes the third stage of neurosis.[7] In the terminology of Rollo May, it is an experience of "inner vacuousness-vacuity," and for Frankl, "an existential vacuum."[8]

Verse 3 introduces the first escape of Jonah (for there are more than one in the tale). Jonah is conscious of the fact that he is about to discover something about himself that scares him. Hence he returns to anonymity or to a substitute identity by delving into commonality with others. He denies what has been revealed to him about himself and chooses to belong to something external rather than internal. Paradoxically, his running away demonstrates that the vocation he has heard is relevant for him. Had the call been hollow and meaningless, Jonah would have simply remained untouched and unconcerned. But ". . . it is well known that we are susceptible only to those suggestions with which we are already secretly in accord."[9]

Jonah delves into the crowd, not only to leave behind his particularity in the wake of general indifference but also, being the only Jew on the ship, to try to obliterate his Judaism. It is interesting to note that it is not a matter of indifference, when a Jew leaves Israel and goes into the diaspora, whether he turns to Tarshish or to Nineveh. In other words, the lands of the *gôlāh* ("exile," "dispersion") are not uniform. Only Zion, the point of departure, the center, remains identical to itself; the concentric circles around it are more or less in the image of their "omphalos" (see below).

Paradoxically, this has nothing to do with geographical distance or proximity, not even with the relative goodness or wickedness of the foreign peoples involved. It is clear that Tarshish is not any less "worthwhile" than Nineveh. If anything, that city of Spain is to be preferred at the time of Jonah to the capital of the Assyrians at whose hands Israel suffered so much. But Jonah must go to Nineveh and not to Tarshish. There is now a message to be deliverd to the Ninevites; tomorrow, perhaps, there will be a message also for the Tarshishians. Thus, in turning his back on Nineveh Jonah "profanes," so to speak, the *gālût* ("exile"); he empties it of its content and reduces it to a mere escape. Jonah is in fact not respectful of the environment he pretends to choose for himself, for he uses it as an object for his own gratification. That is what psychology knows as manipulation of the milieu. Jonah has understood perfectly well that the vocation he has received will make him face the unknown—and maybe even death, nothingness. He therefore resorts to a sheer instinct of survival. Who could blame him for doing so? Ironically, however, he does not know that his choice is deadly.

In short, part of the struggle of Jonah lies in his realization that his vocation is so extraordinary that it defies the common stance of any human being. He feels threatened by an appeal that singles him out so completely that it makes him a being of exception in the world. As a matter of fact, one must realize that Nineveh constitutes the very opposite of all that Israel held as valuable and worthy of praise. To go to Nineveh means, for Jonah, to go to Hell. No one, he thinks, can demand this from him, nor for that matter from anyone in the world.[10]

As R. E. Clements, among others, has noticed, there is in the book no presentation of the Ninevites "as arch-enemies and oppressors of Israel,"[11] but such a characterization would have been totally superfluous. (None of our contemporaries would expect an explication of the term "Auschwitz" each time it is used by an author.) More serious is the question, why Nineveh? Why not Babylon, for example? One must remember that in the late Hebrew literature, "Assur" designates the Persian empire. Jonah, being written at that time, naturally chooses the name of the Assyrian capital as the setting for its narrative.[12] In the background therefore is the whole problem of Persian prosperity representing the nations' welfare in contrast to Jerusalem's destitution. Jonah brings us right to the middle of the post-exilic problematic and its struggle with the nonfulfillment of exilic prophetic oracles. From that perspective, Jonah represents the Janus-faced Jewish community of Jerusalem. As the one who refuses to go to Nineveh, he embodies the stance of the theocratic party and its withdrawal into itself; but as the one who goes to Nineveh, he is a sign of the opening of the unexpected miracle of the conversion of the nations after the proclamation of God's word by a Jewish prophet. In other words, the author of Jonah sees at the core of the nonfulfillment of eschatological expectations in Jerusalem a lack of consciousness of being called for a specific and universal task.

The topology of vocation is completed by the nonillustrious identity of Jonah, son of Amittai, who is, as we have seen, a little-known prophet of 2 Kings 14:25. Jonah is an inconspicuous member of his people. And this is another way for the author to emphasize that vocation is addressed to anyone and not necessarily to the elite. Jonah becomes what he is through the commandment, which is addressed to him as well as to any Israelite, and for that matter to any human being. Of course, each vocation is unique; what is universal is the fact of being called.[13]

The singularity of individual vocation provides a *comic* dimension to the narrative. This feature, so important in the tale of Jonah, rests on several contrasting elements. One thinks, for instance, of the little Jonah sent to the immense city of Nineveh, of his very name which means "dove," standing in opposition to the wickedness of the Ninevites. But there is still another element, probably the most important one, to which we turn now.

Throughout the book, Jonah appears as an antihero who can never live up to the grandeur of his task. This is the result of choice, not a character flaw, and one can readily recognize in it the antideterminism that is so characteristic of Hebrew thinking. Jonah has every reason not to become heroic and he exercises this freedom to express his unwillingness to become a hero. The task entrusted to him remains throughout the story an unbearable burden, a coercion, an assault upon his desires. Until the end, he expresses it in the plainest manner possible. If he could have his way, Jonah would not go to Nineveh but would lead another kind of existence in Palestine. This antiheroism often provokes some sneering among the "bourgeois" readers of the tale (when it is not the occassion for some to give vent to their anti-Semitism). They do not realize that it is precisely that human trait which allows readers to feel at home with the story, never smothered by heroic actions with which they cannot identify. In this way, the author underlines the universal character of the human condition. People hardly feel called to imitate a Greek hero, but all know that they are called to tasks that are both within their reach and yet transcend them. Moreover, if Jonah does not become a hero in the tale, he becomes, at the very least, a free man. No document has shown better than has the *Iliad* the impossibility of immortality through heroism, [14] but Jonah is not looking for immortality. His quest is for life—not only his own but also, as he will learn in due time, the life of others, even the Ninevites. *The Hebrew Scripture posits that the human vocation involves a certain quality of life, a becoming which brings human beings to be themselves by means of an ongoing dialogue with the source of life, i.e., God.*

The problem is therefore not how to become divine as in the Gilgamesh epic[15] or in the *Iliad* but how to become fully human. The "heroes" try to steal liberty from those who, by their very nature, are the sole possessors of freedom, i.e., the gods, but Jonah is not after divine prerogatives or natural human rights. As Maimonides once wrote, "Man has not been created free, he has received the commandment to be free." "Heroism" here requires that the human being choose to be free, i.e., to transcend the self and reach out to the impossible, to holiness, which makes humanity like God (see, e.g., Lev. 19:2).[16]

Were this a Greek tale, the author would take delight in showing that his main character chooses the ideal. Jonah, from that perspective, would jump into the extraordinary, and his story would become for us entertainment—a way in which we might escape our limitations. On the contrary, Jonah reacts most prosaically like every "normal" human being; he resorts to a defense mechanism in order to preserve his own self. Thus, Jonah easily becomes for the reader an "alter ego." We all sympathize with him, feeling that we would probably have acted as he did, or rather that we are actually doing just as he did.

Furthermore, like Jonah, we too seem to share the illusion that life can be lived in avoiding death, in avoiding the obstacles on life's way. For this is exactly what Jonah is doing; he flees from failure and death with all his strength.[17] It is therefore perfectly appropriate that the tale continues with a demonstration of biting irony as to how mistaken the prophet has been in thinking that he was escaping death. The wreckage of the ship, the "drowning" of Jonah, and his burial in the belly of the fish are together the response of life to his deadly choice. Amos, as early as the eighth century, gave expression to this kind of ironic retributive justice when he said, "as if a man did flee from a lion, and a bear met him; he went in the house and leaned his hand on the wall, and a serpent bit him" (5:19).[18]

The book of Jonah also shows what existential damage is wrought by the illusion that life is equivalent to the avoidance of obstacles. Jonah moves from alienation from the past, which he empties of vocation and becoming, to alienation from the future, which he keeps devoid of project. The present cannot, of course, be salvaged from such a desert-making process. The Greek philosopher Democritus (fifth century B.C.E.) put it well when he said that this is "not exactly hardly living, but rather slowly dying" (frgt. 160).[19] It is, said Jung, a "partial suicide." [20]

The text makes sure that we do not miss that point. Tarshish marks the western boundary of the inhabited world (Isa. 60:9; 66:19; Ps. 72:10). One thinks of Spain or of Sardinia. Josephus prefers Cilicia (*Antiquities* 9:10.2). It is in any case the symbol of the ultima Thule, which does not know the word of God (see Isa. 66:19), in accordance with the popular motif of concentric circles around Jerusalem, the center of the universe.[21] "YHWH, the God of heaven, has made the sea and the dry land" (Jon. 1:9), but the more remote one is from the Center, the less directly is God's presence felt. There is thus on the part of Jonah no naive belief that he can escape God anywhere in the world. In the words of George M. Landes, it is an escape from "Yahweh's *cultic* presence where the prophetic oracle is vouchsafed." [22] The expression used here, "to flee from the Face of YHWH and he went down," is the very opposite of the formula "to stand before the face of YHWH" which is the sign of prophetic receptivity (1 Kings 17:1; 18:15; 2 Kings 3:14; 5:16; Jer. 15:19). Wilhelm Rudolph labels Jonah's movement here as "desertieren." [23]

As to Jonah's motivation, Rudolph's warning is again praiseworthy. He recalls that the reason why Jonah fled is clearly expressed in 4:2 and that one should not therefore look for other motives such as the fear of pagans, the dangers of the journey, etc.[24] Jonah flees from his mission, but traditional Jewish literature, as we noticed earlier, empathizes with his move! Jonah is credited for not putting Israel to shame with the repentance of Gentiles (cf. *j. Sanhedrin* 11, 30b, 45; *Mekilta on Exodus* 12:1 [2a]; *Pirqe de Rabbi Eliezer* 10 [beg.]). He was like an escaped servant of a priest, who decides to go into a cemetery where his master cannot follow. But the master said: "I have your peers who can go after you!" So God "sent out a great wind into the sea, etc." (Jon. 1:4) (*Mekilta on Exodus* 12:1 [1b]).[25]

The interpretation is attractive. It does not lack depth, for what is indeed intimated here by the Rabbis is that God's command has an unethical ring. Jonah is right to resist. In order to obey God, Jonah would have to violate an ethical principle that clashes with other religious values. Søren Kierkegaard, in his homily on the "Aqedah" (the "binding" of Isaac in Gen. 22), speaks of a "teleological suspension of the ethical." And this is precisely what transcends Abraham's and Jonah's theological and ethical standards. Jonah cannot just ignore his commission, because he intuits that God is asking him to go beyond his love for his people in order to love even his enemy. Meanwhile, his running away from the commandment implicitly raises the question of whether Abraham, for example, did well in consenting to sacrifice Isaac. Perhaps, secretly, God wanted the patriarch to refuse the order in the name of ethical norms. Anyway, according to the Rabbis, Jonah saw a sign of approval for his decision to flee to Tarshish in the fact that he found a ship ready to go from Joppa. This made him so glad that he paid in advance for the trip rather than afterwards, as was customary! (*Pirqe de Rabbi Eliezer* 10). He thus decided to face the most terrible danger for a Jew, namely, the ocean—the abyss of Genesis 1:2—rather than obey God's call. In Psalm 48:8 "the ships of Tarshish" are those which dare to face the deep seas (cf. 1 Kings 10:22). The emphasis of the text is surely not on Jonah's cowardice; if anything, Jonah is ready to die for his convictions. One can therefore speak of a death wish "with the intention of ending decisively and irrevocably any possibility of God's renewing his commission." [26] But, as the narrative will ironically show, if one flees from the place of theophany where God expresses his exigencies, the theophanic exigencies will then be manifested in the belly of a big fish!

In concluding this analysis of verse 3, let us note (along with other exegetes) its impressive structure:[27]

a. Jonah rose . . . from YHWH's presence
b. and he went down to Joppa
c. and he found a ship
d. going to Tarshish
c'. and he paid the fare thereof
b'. and he went down into it
a'. to go . . . from YHWH'S presence.

(In vss. 4-16 the structure also revolves around the nucleus of vss. 9-10a.)

Raphael Weiss[28] has shown that the sea is the central theme, as if everything pertaining to the commission of God would lead into the sea. God's action within nature is somewhat surprising here in that Hebrew literature is generally more interested in history, in "Heilsgeschichte." There are in Jonah strong wisdom trends,[29] which, it is interesting to note, are also present in the post-exilic protest literature such as Job or Ruth. Both of these, we recall, also introduce foreigners to Israel's concern. It was therefore appropriate to explore the realm of "natural theology" and to send the reader back to the "Noachian covenant" between God and the whole universe. However, in doing so, these works were at least implicitly relativizing Israel's exclusive election, and this they did purposely. By the same token, they stepped onto the ground of universal folklore, while never relinquishing the particular *Weltanschauung* of their people. That is why there is nothing wrong in seeing sea and fish as symbols of death and rebirth—the tale itself supplies the proof as it continues. Although wind, sea, and fish are for Israel neutral creations, totally dependent upon God's orders, in contradistinction to heroic legends in which the natural elements are powerful adversaries of the divinity of the cosmic order, there is a remnant of mythological conceptions in the synonymity of sea and monster in Israel.[30] The sea is a symbol of darkness, of violence and destructive power (Ps. 88:7), but as the motif of the fish here shows its sense retains a literal component. One hesitates to characterize the "whale" as a monster of chaos or as a saving "sea taxi" for the prophet. Cohn displays prudence, therefore, when he refrains from an attempt to locate influences on the archetypal images used by the author of Jonah. More important, he says, is the question of how those motifs are experienced in the book of Jonah.[31]

Similarly, Jonah's flight to the west is probably to be interpreted in parallel with many popular legends as a plunging into darkness. One can compare other biblical reports of flights by land (e.g., Moses in Exod. 2:15 or Elijah in 1 Kings 17:3), and it should be noted that the awakening of Jonah's conscience begins at *dawn* (4:7), while he sits to the *east* of Nineveh (4:5) under the blowing of an *east* wind (4:8)! [32]

The motif of the storm is far from exhausted, both in the book itself and in this essay, but the flow of the narrative is interrupted by the mention of a curious situation: while sea and wind are raging, Jonah is asleep! Verse 5 takes us to a second aspect of the survival impulse. Jonah goes to sleep in the bottom of the ship. First Jonah fled for his life. Now he chooses to ignore the storm and regresses to an embryo-like state of immobility. He leaves responsibility to others. He willingly "deserts" (Rudolph). He "goes down into the bottom" (vs. 5), a little-veiled symbol for the motherly womb. Jonah seeks a state of "selective inattention," an expression which means "that one overlooks, or is inattentive to, that which has provoked anxiety . . ." [33]

As we have seen in Chapter I of our essay, the ship—and later the sea monster—may represent the exile of the Judaeans to Babylon. In accordance with a general prophetic stance about the catastrophe that befell Jerusalem in 587 B.C.E., the book of Jonah intimates that Jonah-Israel have themselves provoked their own exile. The victory of the Babylonian monster (cf. Dan. 7:4) did not result from an arbitrary decision of God and was certainly not accidental. The prophets cancelled all shreds of historical determinism and affirmed the people's full responsibility for their destiny. Hence, Israel could have avoided the exile to Babylon, and Jonah the sea storm and his subsequent "death" in "the belly of the nether world" (2:3). How? By fulfilling their call. It is important to realize that in revealing Israel's shortcomings and bringing to the level of conscience a lot of repressed feelings of culpability, the prophets made clear to their fellow Jews, however paradoxically, that they could bring about their own salvation just as they had provoked their own condemnation. The same applies here; Jonah is no toy in the hands of fate. Nor is the sea storm in Jonah 1:4 ff. a purely natural phenomenon. Nothing happens by chance or according to mechanistic cause and effect relations.[34] The storm does not remain on a meaningless level, independent of human existential problems. Although it could be a voiceless cataclysm, Jonah has gathered all the prerequisite elements for making the event meaningful, and now he is living it through as such. This is so clear that nobody on the ship is fooled by the "anonymity" of the phenomenon. On the contrary, all try to say its name, to discover its veiled sense, to translate its message into an intelligible language. Their intuition proves entirely correct, for as soon as the message is received the storm recedes.

We cannot insist strongly enough on the fact that Jonah has by now reached the point of no return. He has symbolically retrieved the fetus-like condition within the motherly womb. In the words of Fromm:

> The story is told as if these events had actually happened. However, it is written in symbolic language and all the realistic events described are symbols for the inner experiences of the hero. We find a sequence of symbols which follow one another: going into the ship, going into the ship's belly, falling asleep, being in the ocean, and being in the fish's belly. All these symbols stand for the same inner experience: for a condition of being protected and isolated, of safe withdrawal from communication with other human beings. They represent what could be represented in another symbol, the fetus in the mother's womb. Different as the ship's belly, deep sleep, the ocean, and a fish's belly are realistically, they are expressive of the same inner experience, of the blending between protection and isolation.[35]

That Fromm is right is shown, for example, by parallel passages in the Bible where a storm gives expression to an inner experience of a hero (2 Kings 2:1, 11 [Elijah]; Job 38:1; Jer. 23:19, 30:23). It is also demonstrated by the use of the same verb *ṭwl* in Jonah 1 for the stirring up of the wind (vs. 4) and the casting forth of the freight (vs. 5) *or of the prophet* (vss. 12, 15). By the same token, Jonah and his shipmates are not so powerless vis-à-vis the storm as it might seem. The sequence of events is not accidental. They are not senseless, and they are not even unequivocal. Theirs is an ambivalence that provides the opportunity for exercising liberty. Jonah can grant them either a positive or a negative significance. They are equivocal because they are an invitation to choose between good and evil, life and death (cf. Deut. 30). Jonah's new flight—into the "uterus"[36]—is, at the same time, the very condition for his "rebirth." One thinks of the words of the Nazarene to Nicodemus in John 3:3: "Unless a man has been born over again he cannot see the kingdom of God."

Parallel to the inner transformation of the hero, the sailors "clean up" the boat and thereby open the place to new possiblities. The situation is clearly one of transition, already beyond the former condition but not yet yielding the new. That is why the action of the sailors is itself ambiguous; one might understand it as a repression of the awareness of reality. Not having resolved the problem of the storm on the spiritual level, they face an unusual obstacle for which their training had not adequately prepared them. They are fearful because the tempest demands an approach different from the usual, and hence they must themselves be different. But they are on equal footing with Jonah in their deep existential unpreparedness. They trust the untrustworthy: the gods do not answer, either because they themselves are paralyzed by the storm or because they were only illusory human self-projections in the first place. Between Jonah and the sailors is a yawning chasm in terms of their respective religious beliefs, intellectual formations, sophistications, professions, etc., but the human predicament is the same, be it in Israel or on a cosmopolitan sea vessel. The only difference is on the cognitive level. What Jonah has identified as God's calling, the sailors intuit and unconsciously detect as a potentially transforming power which forces their choice. Paradoxically, however, the sailors who are unable to pinpoint the source of their anxiety are closer to the truth than the sleeping Jonah! At least they are awake and searching. At this point it is appropriate to remember that the book of Jonah is a fifth-century polemical work written to denounce the indifference of some in Jerusalem to the nations' fate, thereby monopolizing for themselves the concern and the blessing of God.[37]

Crisis demands relief, and Jonah tries to obtain it by sleeping. The sailors, after attempting everything else, eventually find relief by throwing Jonah into the sea, "bundled" with their fears. (On this more will be said later.) Jonah's "sleep" is not itself a sign of unusual faith and serenity, as is Jesus' sleep in the boat during a storm on the lake of Galilee (Luke 8:22 ff.). The term used in Jonah indicates a catalepsy rather than a sleep. That is why R. B. Y. Scott translates "in a stupor," and refers to Psalm 76 where the term can be rendered "to be stunned."[38] Similarly, W. Vischer speaks of "autohypnose de l'église."[39] It is a numbness but not an unprovoked one (cf. vs. 6: *mah lĕkā nirdām?*). Once again, the Rabbis were not at fault; Jonah slept, they said, "because of the anguish of his soul."[40]

It would be a mistake to reduce Jonah's numbness to the dimension of a mere episode. In fact, the Jew who fled the center of creation is now presented as paralyzed in the midst of an endangered universe.[41] The scene of verse 5 is unmistakably parallel to 1 Kings 18, the confrontation of Elijah with the prophets of Baal on Mount Carmel (see vss. 26–29). This connection is also made by Rabbi Hananiah in *Pirqe de Rabbi Eliezer.* On the ship, he says pointedly, there were seventy languages (= the whole world), and each one, with his idol in his hand, was calling to his god with the idea that the god who would save them is the true god. So much for R. Hananiah. But, contrary to the scene on Carmel, it seems that here the prophet is not in the picture, for to be is also to be seen, to be exposed to the others' "look," as Jean-Paul Sartre puts it. Thus, the pessimistic reading of Hananiah regarding the sailors is counterbalanced by the remark of Fromm to the effect that by now the mariners are showing an unexpected sense of humanity in trying everything to avoid the irreparable.[42] They invite Jonah to join them in their quest (vs. 6). The skipper even uses the same words as those of God in 1:2: "arise . . . call." Allen compares this repetition to what happens during a nightmare.[43]

It is not one of the least surprising features of the book that the narrative constantly deals first with the effects of the events on the Gentiles and only afterwards with Jonah himself. One finds the same phenomenon in Chapters 3 and 4, where the order is as follows: (1) the population, (2) the king (3:5, 6 –9) and (3) Jonah (4:1 –4).[44] The text is already preparing for the second part of the tale. To the "perhaps" of the skipper will correspond the "who knows?" of the king in 3:9. This way of keeping the future open to the divine grace is deeply moving.

We do not know what Jonah answered the mariners, for verse 7 brings us to a situation comparable to that of verse 5. In fact, the sailors have concluded in the meantime that someone on the boat is causing the common evil. Will that person become a scapegoat? It does not seem so, since Jonah is considered equal to all others in the casting of lots. There is no plot against the Jew here. (We, however, had the optimal conditions gathered for the eruption of anti-Semitism in all its ugliness. Most of the pogroms in history occurred under circumstances more tentative than these.) It is thus again made clear that the author of the book of Jonah had the definite purpose of portraying the non-Jews in a favorable light. At the outset the sailors are ignorant of Jonah's origins (vs. 8), but even when they find out, they do not jump to conclusions, nor do they plot against his life despite the tie they have discovered between his crime and their destiny. On the contrary, they try to save him even when he has told them to throw him into the sea! Their moderation is exemplary, their humanity is a model. They take it upon themselves to increase their efforts and they row even harder (vs. 13). Only as a last resort do they appeal to Jonah's God and beg that the responsibility for Jonah's death rest not upon them but upon God himself, since he and only he demands the capital punishment of his reluctant servant. In short, there is a remarkable absence among the sailors of bigotry and ethnocentricity. If the lot "fell upon Jonah," it is not owing to any prejudice. It is forthwith understood as God's acting because Jonah effectively *is* responsible for the storm.

On a deeper level of understanding, of course, the Jewishness of Jonah is not played down in the least. The sailors' discovery does in fact mean more than they themselves can fathom. All Jewish readers of the tale understand immediately that the real issue is Jonah's unwillingness to perform his priestly vocation in the world. This is precisely what endangers the whole world, for the whole of humanity has embarked on the same boat. The very first to acknowledge this is Jonah himself, so when the lot falls upon him, it does not come at all as a surprise. He was expecting it all along; he was looking for it like a magnet attracting iron filings. He is the only one in touch with the real issue and the only one able to make sense of it. However, the others are not sidetracked, for in the end, when Jonah-Israel is sacrificed and "all is accomplished" as far as he is concerned, the "nations" gathered on the ship realize that God was present with them in the person of the Jew. They fear YHWH, offer a sacrifice, and make vows (vs. 16).

In the meantime they have recourse to casting lots, a process with which the modern reader feels uncomfortable because of its strong flavor of superstition. It is found elsewhere in the Bible (Josh. 7:14; 1 Sam. 10:20–21; Prov. 16:33). The focus of Jonah 1:7 is not on the *ex opere operato* power of the lot, although the Bible does not generally shrink from giving credit to numinous manifestations even when they are wrought by pagan magicians or sorcerers. What is at stake here is something similar to what we described when discussing the meaning of the sea storm. As the tempest was Jonah's tempest, the casting of lots is the external manifestation of an "inner experience." The "magnetic" Jonah attracts to himself his own condemnation. It is not—let us emphasize the point again—that Jonah is a tragic hero comparable with the fateful Atrides. Though at times life takes on aspects resembling those depicted in Greek tragedy, the book of Jonah as a whole makes clear that determinism does not ultimately prevail. According to determinism, "yet forty days and Nineveh shall be overthrown." According to God's graciousness and long-suffering, however (cf. 4:2), Nineveh shall be spared. According to determinism also, Jonah would die for his disobedience to the divine will but he emerges alive from the fish's belly. The mariners, however, never knew. Not any more than the Greek philosophers envisioned the transcendence of Necessity. In short, Jonah appears as a tragic hero only to those who do not go beyond chapter 1 of the book. To those who continue he is a man who encountered tragedy but transformed it into a human drama.

We anticipate. For now, the narrative artfully lets Jonah come out of his incognito condition. The process by which others recognize the exceptional man as decribed in the text—here, the Jew Jonah—is strikingly realistic. At first he appeared inconspicuous; he was one of their group and nothing distinguished him from the average. Then, Jonah's attitude caught their attention, and soon enough provoked their suspicion. Eventually, they concluded that Jonah was different.[45] Now this pattern is so significant in its universal recurrence that one can wonder whether the former inconspicuousness of Jonah was not owing to the others' deliberate refusal to see. *Jonah wanted to hide, and it pleased everyone.* If the exceptional being, if the free person, if the Jew remains anonymous, no one is sorry. On the contrary, the "assimilation" of such a man means the disappearance of the threat he represents to the mediocre others (see below Chapter VII).[46]

Jonah intuits that this is indeed the universal norm. He is therefore confident that his presence on the ship "to flee unto Tarshish from the presence of the Lord" will remain unnoticed. His will for anonymity corresponds to the unwillingness of others to confront the Problem that Jonah poses—giving a face, as it were, to the faceless. This is why the "miracle" in this instance lies not so much in the sea being stirred by the storm as it does in the event of human consciousness being compelled to acknowledge reality instead of fleeing from it. At exactly this point, Jonah's flight is stopped and with it the human impulse to self-imposed blindness. Jonah goes far beyond what was demanded of him. He not only answers the mariners' question but adds a response of his own which reveals his full identity; he confesses: "I am a Hebrew and I fear the Lord, the God of heaven, *who has made the sea and the dry land*" (vs. 9).[47] Everything is stamped with a mark of identity as creature of the God of heaven. In an entirely personalized world where every object bears a name, Jonah cannot remain nameless. Conformity, "the great destroyer of selfhood," [48] is defeated. Jonah is forced to emerge from the crowd. He is "Hebrew and he fears the Lord." [49]

Whether the mariners indeed understand the whole of Jonah's confession or not, this much they know: the diffuse causes of their general troubles have been condensed into one particular man with his particular problems. Such a discovery inspires fear in them, but surprisingly no one of them wonders why one culprit among them effects such a collective chastisement. Modern readers, however, feel less inclined to accept this fact. They cannot but find somewhat revolting the fact that a whole ship is threatened with destruction because of the sin of one passenger. The historian of religion responds to this problem with the concept of the so-called "corporate personality." According to this idea, the individual is inconceivable apart from a group, whose "personality" transcends individual limits. Clearly, this refers primarily to kinships, and beyond, to covenantal communities. But there is also a more general category to which all people belong, i.e., to which they are properly responsible, namely, humankind.[50] Such a unity of all human beings has been emphasized in both the heathen origin-myths and in Israel's concept of a common human ancestor. "We are all responsible for all" (Dostoyevsky). What this implies is that every person has a particular vocation to fulfill within the collective unit for the betterment of the latter. The refusal by one to answer the call brings a threat to the whole group. In the words of Becker, "This . . . is the only real problem of life, the only worthwhile preoccupation of man: What is one's true talent, his secret gift, his authentic vocation? . . . How can the person take . . . the great mystery that he feels at the heart of himself, . . . to enrich both himself and mankind with the peculiar quality of his talent?" [51]

Here, the lot falls upon Jonah just as in Joshua 7 it fell upon Akhan. And, as Akhan was stoned to death by the community as a sign of dissociation from his crime, so also must Jonah eventually be rejected lest he be taken as representative of the collective personality of the ship, and so draw the whole group along with him into death. The attitude of the sailors here is particularly interesting insofar as it involves not hate but rather fear and paralysis before the unknown. Fear and the absence of hate: let us reflect on these elements.

As far as the mariners are concerned, something has occurred that has displaced the dramatic center. The mariners' cosmic anxiety has become fear directed toward a specific object, Jonah. From this point the sea storm bears a name; it has a cause and a project.[52] We recall here Maslow's analysis of the need to know and the fear of knowing.[53] The sailors realize that some step must be taken (for the sea grows more and more tempestuous), but they want the move to be Jonah's and not their own. They prefer to play blind and pretend not to see Jonah's despicable plight. As May wrote, ". . . the reason we do not see truth is . . . that we do not have enough courage . . . . For to seek truth is always to run the risk of discovering what one would hate to see." [54]

But what do the mariners so carefully avoid? Why do they display such "selective inattention?" The answer lies in the numinous aspect which accompanies Jonah and which makes of him an unusual human being. His difference, as we saw, is the threat. It evokes a feeling of anxiety in the crowd because it demonstrates that there are other games that are played by other rules, while we had thought all along that our game was the only possible one. No system, no highly structured society can afford the presence of the unique in its midst. When Nebuchadnezzar erects the statue, the symbol of his regime, it becomes intolerable that one man in the vast empire might go to his room and pray to the God of Israel. Similarly, the sailors are those "one-dimensional men," of whom Becker speaks, who are "totally immersed in the fictional games being played in their society, unable to transcend their social conditioning." [55]

Verse 12 shifts our attention from the sailors to Jonah. Strikingly, Jonah displays here the full depth of his desperation. Against all expectation, he does not intercede for God's forgiveness; such a prayer would have implied a radical change in himself, and he knows that the tempest is "the reflection of (his) own turmoil and anger." [56] Instead, he prefers to die. We have already said that it is wrong to speak of Jonah in terms of cowardice. Here again the Rabbis interpret the episode in the most favorable light. For

R. Johanan (ca. 140 C.E.) Jonah fled precisely in order to be sent to the nether world in the train of the patriarchs and prophets who gave themselves up as oblations on behalf of their people; so Moses (Exod. 32:32; Num. 11:15), David (2 Sam. 24:17) etc. (*Mekilta on Exodus* 12:1[2a]).

For *Pirqe de Rabbi Eliezer*, "the ship is a type of the world which only can find its salvation through the willing martyrdom of the Hebrew, who, although inoffensive in his conduct with his fellow-men of all nationalities, is nevertheless quite willing to allow himself to be doomed to destruction in order to relieve his fellow-men of their threatened ruin." [57]

Jerome calls the sea storm here "the storms of this world" (*tempestas mundi*), and he sees in Jonah the one "who slew thee [death]" (*ille te vincit*), for he "surrenderd his dear life into the hands of those that sought it" (*dedit dilectam animam suam in manus quaerentium eam*).[58]

Be that as it may,[59] from a psychological vantage point, Jonah behaves like an acutely depressed person—hopeless, helpless, and feeling as if he were carrying a contagious disease. His injunction to the sailors to dispose of him is a gesture of suicide. "Despair expresses the feeling that time is short, too short for the attempt to start another life and to try alternate roads to integrity." [60]

Ultimately, the mariners have to throw Jonah overboard, and so put an end to a historical episode. As soon as they do so, however, not only does Jonah disappear from their sight, but they themselves fall into oblivion. They never come back into the story; they pursue a purposeless voyage on an anonymous ship. For all, both writer and readers, they have fulfilled their role. For a while, they had emerged from darkness and had been in the spotlight. They now return to their former obscurity. We cannot but feel that they have missed a golden opportunity. For a short time they were making history; now they are swallowed up in the mist. Their sacrifice to YHWH has been no doubt a grand event, but it has no far-reaching effect. In short, in throwing Jonah into the ocean ("bundled" with their fears, as we said above), did not the sailors also throw themselves? Are not they too sinking with him to the bottom of the "shapeless and void?" In this sense it could be said that Jonah is their scapegoat, i.e., the vicarious victim of their collective escape from their vocations!

Jonah continues to represent more than just himself. He symbolizes the return to the pre-formal, to chaos. He is "loaded" with the cowardice and the treason of all. His descent into the nether world is a sign of condemnation for the general human failure to comply with the divine entreaty. His "death" is significant because humanity sinks with him as a result of similar panic in the face of vocation, responsibility, and authenticity. That is also why the story must follow him in his fall. To remain on the deck of the boat means, paradoxically, to leave history and adopt the phantasms of a ghost ship.

We must follow Jonah into the sea because he is all of us. True, we are unable to imagine how it is that history continues beyond the hero's drowning, beyond the seemingly final fact of death. But *it is not necessary to imagine an impossible future in order to question the finality of the present.* Jonah cannot be simply blotted out or annihilated. The return to *Urzeit* (primeval ages) is also the condition for the coming of *Endzeit* (ultimate ages). That is why Daniel 7 and 4 Esdras 13 in particular describe the enthronement of the human being *(Homo)* emerging from the ocean, as if these mystics were re-writing the story of Jonah after chapter 1!

But if our analysis is correct, we must go farther. Jonah, swallowed by the sea monster and eventually spewed out onto the land, also represents the sailors' crew! In retrospect, Jonah's gloomy injunction that the sailors get rid of him may have a motive other than suicide. Twice, in fact, he expresses altruistic motivation in the words "for you" (vs. 12). Such generosity gains its full import from the perspective outlined above.

Where are the "resurrected" sailors for the remainder of the story? They are not to be found if we look narrowly for a ship and its crew. But once we realize what it is that they stood for in the first place, namely, the non-Jews, those to whom the prophet Jonah is sent, they appear again on the horizon. Finally, they are not lost adrift on a Flying Dutchman; they are now in Nineveh, unaware that they await someone they both know and do not know, as is always the case when arrives He That Cometh.

Chapter IV

FROM NUMBNESS TO MEANING (JONAH 2)

. . . initiation lies at the core of any genuine human life. And this is true for two reasons. The first is that any genuine human life implies profound crises, ordeals, suffering, loss and reconquest of self, "death and resurrection." The second is that, whatever degree of fulfillment it may have brought him, at a certain moment every man sees his life as a failure. This vision does not arise from a moral judgment made on his past, but from an obscure feeling that he has missed his vocation; that he has betrayed the best that was in him. In such moments of total crisis, only one hope seems to offer any issue—the hope of beginning life over again. This means, in short, that the man undergoing such a crisis dreams of new, regenerated life, fully realized and significant. This is something other and far more than the obscure desire of every human soul to renew itself periodically, as the cosmos is renewed. The hope and dream of these moments of total crisis are to obtain a definitive and total renovatio, a renewal capable of transmuting life. Such a renewal is the result of every genuine religious conversion . . . . Death prepares the new, purely spiritual birth, access to a mode of being not subject to the destroying action of Time.

—Mircea Eliade, *Birth and Rebirth*
(New York: Harper & Brothers, 1958), pp. 135-136.

"Salvation lies in Remembrance," said the Baal Shem Tov, father of eighteenth-century Eastern European Hasidism. In this context, it is interesting to note that one of the most striking features of Jonah 2 is the use of the past tense. Jonah remembers, i.e., he rewrites the past,[1] providing it, as it were, with new "members." He reorganizes or, better, organizes for the first time material for which he had previously surrendered responsibility. This he does through *interpretation,* i.e., in deciphering its *meaning,* "taking the story of a life which was experienced as shaped by circumstance and which was recounted as such, and retelling it in terms of choice and responsibility." [2]

In this process of reminiscence, we regain the present. Jonah's ultimate goal is to find meaning in his present condition which, in and of itself, is a radical negation of sense and of life. Invariably, any human being who is caught in the absurd dimension of existence must come to terms with the past. When the Judaeans were exiled to Babylon and their holy Temple in Jerusalem was destroyed, their existential problem surpassed their present circumstance of being in a foreign country and having to adapt to conditions that were totally alien to them. In fact, the most profound question had to do with the validity or invalidity of their past. Had the foundation of their history so far resisted the new crisis? Had they lived for something reliable or for naught? Had it been worth living up until now by the values of yesterday? Were these values still viable?

We draw this parallel between Jonah's plight in chapter 2 and the exile of the nation to Babylon not only because of similarities in the two situations but also because, as we noticed earlier, scholars have seen in the story of Jonah being swallowed by the fish a typology of the exile on the model of Jeremiah 51:34, 44. So, for example, James D. Smart writes that we have here "a symbolic representation of the Exile and the return."[3] Perhaps we should not stress this point. We may have here merely a discrete allusion to rather than a "symbolic representation" of that traumatic event in the history of the people. But this much remains: it raises the fundamental question of the values of yesterday. The problem cannot be ignored in the present circumstances, and it must not be smothered by the substitution of "modern" standards for old ones. It is a mistake to believe that there are substitute values available when the former ones are questioned. Only the inexperienced and the gullible can be persuaded by demagogues that a new world order will spring from the vacuum left by the rejection of the old order. On the contrary, the wise and the prophets know that a society or an individual does not change values as one changes clothes. As the Talmudic story goes, in order that Rabbi Eliezer and his family will not suffer hunger anymore, God must recreate the world, another world. But is it certain that Eliezer will not be hungry in the new world? "Perhaps!" says God. Eliezer then exclaims: "All that for a 'perhaps'!" (*Ta'anit* 28a). Yes, perhaps. For another *raison d'être* means another history, another past. What is now offered to Jonah is not a past that lacks the call to go to Nineveh. Rather, Jonah is offered the possibility of a transfigured existence. In some way, it remains the same existence, but it is endowed now with another meaning; it is integrated rather than disoriented; the present, up until now characterized by emptiness, takes on profound significance. Life prevails over death, resurrection over decay and rot.

That is why chapter 2 of Jonah dwells upon the different elements of a prayer which critics often reject as later accretions. Even if the critics were correct (but they are not; see below), the insertion of the prayer into the book at this point would be a stroke of genius on the part of the final redactor. It allows us to follow Jonah's movement from numbness to meaningfulness. Integral to this movement, paradoxically, is the deliberate suspension of the plot. At last, Jonah takes time to reflect upon his experience.[4]

This is a kind of musical pause, although it is a pause that has a melody of its own and becomes, in fact, a psalm. If the psalm were not present at this point in the narrative, the tempo of the story as well as its configuration and meaning would be transformed. We would be left with the wrong impression that the swallowing of Jonah by the fish was only an episodic accident, an almost casual obstacle on the road to success. Jonah would then be a toy in the hands of God, tossed hither and thither by the capricious waves and billows of the divine mood. The proper accent, on the contrary, falls upon the decisive importance of Jonah's sense of failure. There is no element here that serves to minimize it. The prayer of Jonah, that is, the sense-giving, creative, celebrative "name" by which the prophet speaks of his experience and by which he transfigures chaos into meaning (and thus "Good Friday" into

"Easter"), is uttered *in* the fish's belly, not *after* Jonah finds the security of dry land.

The following quotation from May seems to have been written with Jonah in mind:

> A dynamic struggle goes on within a person between what he or she consciously thinks on the one hand and, on the other, some insight, some perspective that is struggling to be born. The insight is then born with anxiety, guilt, and the joy and gratification that is inseparable from the actualizing of a new idea or vision. . . . the insight must destroy something.[5]

In biblical language this experience is called resurrection. And does not the whole message of the book of Jonah lie in the fact that when everything seems to be lost (in the case of Jonah, of the sailors, of the Ninevites), everything becomes possible? For life is an endless start, a continuous creation of meaning, a leap of faith says Kierkegaard, a passage from darkness to light, from non-being to being. What this means is that a new world can be shaped from the nether world, from non-being (in exile or in the heart of the seas) being can emerge. In the midst of confusion, despair and death, Jonah mysteriously chooses to let an insight be born and to give it substance.[6] He turns to the "source of life" (Ps. 36:10) and, as the Jonah text puts it, "prays unto the Lord" (2:2); he restores the channel of communication with the Other. When the circumstances are so terribly overwhelming that it would seem only natural for Jonah to think only of himself and of the incomprehensible arbitrariness of his fate ("Why me?"), precisely then Jonah breaks through the wall and reaches out toward another One.[7] He passes from a state of complacency to one of generosity, from the narcissistic sentiment of feeling sorry for himself to loving self-oblation.[8] This, according to Israelite understanding, is indeed the passage from death to life, a fact that verse 11 confirms.

Thus, those who deny the "authenticity" of the psalm, on the ground that Jonah "is not a creature of gratitude and thanksgiving" are mistaken.[9] Theodore Robinson says that the psalm is "sicher nicht ursprünglich,"[10] but he makes his assumption primarily on the false ground that the fish is a saving device and does not properly belong to the awfulness of the sea (see below).[11]

Of course the psalm has a cultic origin.[12] It is even a kind of psalmic potpourri of themes that are present in the biblical Psalms (vs. 3, cf. Ps. 120:1; 18:6; vs. 4, cf. Ps. 42:7; vs. 6, cf. Ps. 69:2; vs. 7, cf. Ps. 18:16; 30:3; vs. 8, cf. Ps. 142:3; 143:4). It has been borrowed by the author and inserted into the place it now occupies in the tale. It is no ornament, however, but rather an indispensable link in the narrative without which the tale would be crippled. With it, the reader witnesses the dynamic transformation that takes place within Jonah, namely his repentance, a theme that would be absent were it not for the prayer.

Repentance, says Paul Tillich,

> is the act of the whole person in which he separates himself from elements of his being, discarding them into the past as something that no longer has any power over the present.[13]

And we quote also this statement from a rich article by Max Scheler:

> Repenting is equivalent to re-appraising part of one's past life and shaping for it a mint-new worth and significance.[14]

Prior to the incidence of the psalm in the tale, Jonah is that average man (of whom Kierkegaard speaks) who is his own shaper, so to speak, in the unauthentic universe in order that he may forget his own nothingness. Repentance, then, requires that one transform the meaning of one's nothingness, in order that it be no longer a provocation of God but rather an invocation of God. Before, the human being was nothing; but in the course of the dialogue, the nothingness is filled with the substance of the discovered Thou.

> One goes down into the belly of a giant or a monster in order to learn *science* or *wisdom*. . . . No initiation is possible without the ritual of an agony, a death, and a resurrection.[15]

Jonah, as we said, can now look at his resurrection in the past tense—as St. Paul will later do (1 Cor. 15)—and address his prayer to God as if all were already accomplished for him. The whole of Jonah's previous existence is transformed by the very fact that he is understood, that someone else shares the same perspective and sympathizes. For despair may well consist in a person's discovery of being the only one of a kind, that communication is blocked, that one is at an impasse from which there is no escape for no one has been there before. Hope is born while facing the unknown and discovering that one is not alone,[16] and surely enough, Jonah has Company in the fish's belly! All the difference lies here. He is the same man with the same existence and the same commission, but he is filled now with hope instead of despair. Nothing magical has occurred, no *deus ex machina* has come down from heaven, no angelic trumpet has resounded, no lightning has rent the skies. Jonah experiences not triumph but, if anything, the ultimate worsening of his predicament (see the discussion on the fish below). All the conditions are set for Jonah's disappearance, and the prayer shows that indeed he could die now, for, from a spiritual point of view, he has gained the insight, he has reached the peak. What must follow can only be commentary upon the event he has witnessed. Hence, Jonah's death would not be the sterile end of a worthless existence, a "death by accident" in the words of Sartre.

Jonah's death would be a death *for something*. The waves and the billows that surround him are not simply what they appear to be; rather, they are "Your billows and Your waves"! Jonah faces not nothingness but God, i.e., not death but life. This happens mysteriously enough through Jonah's gestation in the womb of a new "mother." He discovers his authentic father and mother. The Nazarene asks, "who is my mother, who are my brothers? . . . Whoever does God's will, this one is my brother, my sister, and my mother" (Mark 3:33, 35).

At this point at least, the book of Jonah touches the realm of myth. It is a well-known mythological theme that the hero must descend into the nether world in order to overcome chaotic forces. The motif is highly ambivalent as it reflects both the natural drive in all human beings toward non-being (Thanatos) and also the courage to confront the unknown, however terrible it may be, in order to extract being from non-being. The major dimension of the myth, however, is the return of the hero to the mother's womb, i.e., to the undetermined, the shapeless and nameless, but all the same, to the efficaciously protective environment.[17] For this is *the* environment *par excellence*—primal, natural, nurturing, supporting, self-contained, undisturbed, "virgin."

The symbolism is thus double-edged. The hero, swallowed by a monster or a giant, experiences both death and a "re-entry into a pre-formal, embryonic state of being. . . . which precedes all forms and every temporal existence. Upon the cosmological plane, this double symbolism refers to the *Urzeit* and the *Endzeit*." [18]

In the story of Jonah, the myth is compounded by the highly symbolic element of the sea. The symbolism of water, recalls Eliade, has to do with the pre-formal.[19] It is first and foremost the water inside the womb, yet simultaneously it is a sign of nondevelopment and to a certain extent of non-being. Nevertheless, it is also the promising primordial milieu where life begins. The ambiguity of the symbol becomes clear once again; life and death neighbor each other. Moreover, the fish with its connotation of life and fecundity adds to the analogy in representing the motherly womb and takes on a significance that is rooted in the mysterious origins of life. Thrown into the ocean by the sailors, Jonah returns to the very source of his existence.

Although G. Campbell Morgan is right when he says, "Men have been looking so hard at the great fish, that they have failed to see the great God," [20] we cannot neglect to say a few words about the "whale." Some scholars have insisted that it has a wholly positive significance as the providential means of salvation for the prophet. Jonah therefore finds a harbor in its entrails, and the psalm of thanksgiving makes sense, coming as it does from a man who realizes that he is alive and well after all. There is some confirmation of this understanding in Jewish tradition. For instance, R.

Tarphon, in *Pirqe de Rabbi Eliezer* on Jonah 2:1, says that the fish had been prepared by God "from the six days of Creation." Jonah entered the fish's mouth "just as a man enters the great synagogue . . . . The two eyes of the fish were like windows of glass giving light to Jonah." [21] Furthermore, the fish carrying Jonah inside is itself about to be devoured by Leviathan. It is thus clearly distinguished from the latter, with the motive of presenting Jonah as a savior (even a Messiah[22]); for Jonah saves the fish, which takes the prophet to the bottom of the abyss. Jonah says, "On thy account have I descended to see thy abode in the sea." He then witnesses the bottom of all waters (including the primordial ones, the Reed Sea, the Sheol; see *Pirqe de Rabbi Eliezer* 10). With this in mind, we read J. Steinmann's statement, "It was necessary that the prophet know the trial of going down into hell in order that he have the courage to preach salvation to the heathens." [23]

But the Rabbis are not unanimous on this point. For R. Judan (ca. 350 C.E.), God has saved Jonah *from* the guts of the fish (*j. Berakot* 9, 13a, 42). In parallel with this, the use of the image provided by Jonah 2:1 in Matthew 12:40 ("three days and three nights at the heart of the earth") shows that the fish is not to be construed as "a salt-water taxi," [24] but as a primeval chaos-monster "tamed" for particular purposes. Landes is right when he writes: "It is to be noted that Jonah's being devoured by the sea monster was not a providential intervention to save him from drowning but was the penultimate act of his destruction. This seems clear from Amos 9:3 and Jeremiah 51:34." [25]

The problem is more important than meets the eye. If one were to follow the parallelism that exists between chapters 1 and 2 on the one hand and chapters 3 and 4 on the other, then a "friendly" fish in chapter 2 would correspond to a "friendly" Nineveh in part 2. Nothing is farther from the truth. The whole parable pivots around the wickedness of the pagan city and also the terrible nature of the sea monster in chapter 2. Nineveh is the nest of cruelty, inhumanity, and bloodthirstiness (cf. Nah. 3:1 and passim). Hence, to present Jonah as a "reluctant missionary" is to resort to a false cliché, insensitive to the real purpose of the tale. The truth of the matter is that Jonah's theology cannot reconcile a God who stands in covenant with Israel with a God who stands on the side of the SS. For Nineveh is as "gemütlich" (nice and cute) as a Gestapo torture-chamber, and the fish of Jonah 2 can be dubbed a "sea taxi" only by a wishful-thinking "eisegete." The fish is a monster, just as Nineveh is a monster. In the one case as in the other, salvation occurs at the very heart of chaos.[26] To miss this point is to miss the very "apocalyptic" kind of thinking which gives to the tale its highly dramatic dimension (see below, Chapter VI).

Clearly, Jonah could not have been made to cut his way through the flesh of the fish, as did Herakles, a motif that finds endless repetition in the fairy tales. Moreover, Nineveh shall not be destroyed, but neither shall it remain intact. Nineveh is spared, although it does not deserve to live, and the sea-monster lives because it did not annihilate its prey. Jonah's psalm itself is the substitute motif for the hacking through from inside. Jonah "cuts" away from darkness and thus becomes a foreign body inside the fish. The monster becomes sick with the prophet and vomits him out.

It was supremely important for the author of the tale to take his full distance from the myth. There is here no descent of the hero into the nether world with the intent to prove himself to the world. Jonah does nothing to please or to overwhelm the crowds; he needs neither the approval nor the applause of the throngs. The monster is not hacked into pieces, thus avenging the people for their fear of death. Jonah's dirge becomes a hymn of thanksgiving—a phenomenon observed often in Israel's psalms. One could say that everything happens *inside* Jonah. He is the one who, in remembering that God's grace endures forever (cf. 4:2), courageously gives a decisive twist to his complaint and transforms it into a cry of victory.

It is paradoxical that Jonah, swallowed as he is by natural elements, realizes that he must go beyond nature. Like the obedience of a good soldier whose new "family" supersedes his natural family and who has left behind current laws and feelings—even conscience and self, so that he is indeed someone else—Jonah's obedience goes beyond all limits. His prayer is properly "impossible" and its outcome (not its recompense, see below) unbelievable. But it is no more impossible and unbelievable than the moral transformation of Jonah. In the depth of the abyss, swallowed by the fish, he has torn himself away from introversion and has turned toward *another*, thus discovering love.

Such is the realization of Jonah, once any escape from the existential question becomes impossible. Many in his stead would indeed succumb to the abyss of nothingness and oblivion, but Jonah, on the contrary, transcends the abyss in a move toward life. Even before the text states that he is spewed out by the fish, Jonah has overcome meaninglessness and absurdity. Through his existential choice, he stands on the "dry land" (cf. Jon. 2:11 with Gen. 1:9; 2:7 –8) instead of lying forever in the entrails of the chaos-monster. "(Man) can exercise selectivity toward his history," says May; "(he) can adapt himself to parts of it, can change other parts, and, within limits, can mold history in self-chosen directions." [27]

What this last quote fails to convey, however, is the dialogical character of Jonah's redemption. The history which the prophet "molds" is an I-Thou relationship in which he, Jonah, reaches out to another. The story-teller skillfully expresses this in several ways, one of which is to contrast it with Jonah's attempt (in 1:5) to regress, and to repress reality by sleeping "in the innermost parts of the ship." Now, *mirabile dictu*, Jonah is led not only to the innermost parts of the fish, but also to the innermost part of his being, where, paradoxically, he hears the Voice from Without. Now he does not sleep—a Jewish metaphor for death (Gen. 47:30; Jer. 51:39; John 11:11)— rather he is fully awake and searching, an attitude which in Jonah 1 was proper to the mariners. If anything, the situation is at its lowest ebb, but for the author of the book, the events follow a course from which God is not absent.

This is an important corrective to our pervasive feeling that the hero is totally alone throughout the story.[28] For Jonah is a kind of third term that binds together past nothingness and future uncertainty. The storyteller symbolizes this triad in the "three days and three nights" that represent the duration of Jonah's term in the fish's belly. How could one not feel alone under such conditions? Time itself appears to be frozen, as at "midnight," when it is no longer yesterday but not yet today; when the question concerns the night but the response speaks of morning: "Watchman what is left of the night? . . . Morning comes . . ." (Isa. 21:11-12). The resolution of the tension comes not when one of the terms—today/yesterday; morning/night— swallows the other, but when both meet in the "between" which constitutes the firm ground of their reaching out from their respective spheres.[29] Thus, Jonah becomes here the terrain on which converge past and future, and he transcends both in an attitude that Buber calls "acceptance, affirmation and confirmation" of the purposefulness of existence. *This he does precisely in addressing himself to Someone who was present from the first.* Jonah reaches out, he breaks out of his isolation and the former pattern of his behavior. He painfully gives birth to himself, which is another way of saying that he passes from death to life.[30]

For, what is of greatest import is not speculation upon the state of resurrection but rather involvement in *the process of resurrection* itself. Typical of Israel's way of thinking is the attempt to capture a movement in its process rather than in its outcome. Whereas a physicist assesses a movement between two points by taking into account the distance covered and the velocity of the object, Israel chooses to focus upon the process itself.[31] Jonah's movement from zero to the infinite takes place in the "in-between" field where simultaneously the point of arrival is *already* reached while the point of departure is *not yet* fully left! Jonah is in the belly of the chaos-monster, in the depth of the abyss, in the valley of death and absurdity, yet he holds a dialogue with the Ground of Being and Meaning. In the words of Emil Fackenheim, he puts "sanity in the midst of insanity, hope in the midst of despair, life in the midst of death." [32] Jonah's action "in the midst of," is the cathartic collapse of the negative into the positive; it is the climactic point of the dialogue with God. Therein lies the full meaning of the prayer of Jonah. In the grave of his lost illusions, Jonah "remembers" (vs. 8), and the grave is emptied by his decision to transform absurdity and death into meaning and life.

For the victory that really counts does not come once the battle is over and there is no danger of relapse, but *in* the battle itself when one confronts the enemies face to face and fully recognizes them for what they are and the nature of the danger they pose. When such enemies are effectively changed into friends,[33] when Jonah's phantasms are tamed and integrated, when the suicidal drives are transformed into the humble love of God, then the chaos-monster becomes a fish-belly that truly harbors Jonah for his protection and survival.

We now have Jonah and his God in view, but what has become of other men and women? The author makes them as present as possible without destroying the verisimilitude of the situation into which he has placed the hero, namely, into the entrails of the fish. Jonah's fellow human beings are indirectly included in his prayer. As a matter of fact, at "the bottoms of the mountains," he still finds himself in God's "holy Temple" (2:8). In other words, Jonah returns to the living context in which his people experience God's historical continuous presence. Jonah's praying in the Temple means not only that Jonah faces his God in a private I-Thou dialogue, but also that he rediscovers the "cloud of witnesses" who bridge all the generations of his people.

We now come close to one of those taut paradoxes that only Israel could maintain. In the abyss, in the belly of the chaos-monster, Jonah prays face to face with the Living God! For this he did not have to become a "Guru," abstracting himself from the prison of his flesh. Nor did he have to become somehow ubiquitous, for the Temple itself has come to him and stands exactly where stands the holy man. The Temple is as much in the fish's belly as it is in Zion. God and his host meet Jonah in his "exile."

But if God's presence is there, then surely it is also in Nineveh! For nothing is by nature or creation more "foreign" to God's celestial abode than the *tĕhôm* (Gen. 1:2) where Jonah now finds himself. Nothing is more "deprived" of the divine presence. Nothing speaks more clearly of death and nothingness. Even Nineveh cannot compete with *tĕhôm*. Jonah's experience, therefore, has far-reaching consequences, which he himself draws in the sequel of the tale. They have universal dimensions. Indeed, Jonah relives the age-old experience of his people in history. He has now gained the ultimate human capacity to envision the divine where it is least logical, least imaginable.

The immediate context makes clear that Jonah is unable to *hold* the mystery of life; the vision of God cannot be anything but a flash in the darkness. Besides, it would be too much for one to integrate, were it not caught in a gracious glimpse as, for instance, Moses was allowed to see God's back, while His "face shall not be seen" (Exod. 33:23). Precarious as it is, however, the vision of God in Jewish tradition is the very meaning of life. Paradoxically noncontemplative in its essence, vision here means participation in God's doing.[34] Truth here is a *Way,* in contradistinction to the static Ideals of Greek philosophy and Far-Eastern mysticism. Existence is a perpetual beginning from the ashes of the past.[35] It is so because life consists of the ceaseless attempt to utter the ineffable Name.

The vision, therefore, is here also a hearing![36] Jonah finds the answer to his search only in dialoguing with someone else. Only in the direct relation with a particular and unique "Thou" can his plight be transcended. For only in singling out one partner can Jonah truly reach out to all other partners, including the Ninevites. As Fromm writes, "If I truly love one person I love all persons, I love the world, I love life. If I can say to somebody else 'I love you,' I must be able to say 'I love in you everybody, I love through you the world . . . .' " [37]

The parallel with modern psychotherapies is striking. The aim of nearly all psychological schools is precisely to help patients discover the roots of their sufferings. The patients find out, often to their own amazement, that in reaching out to other human beings by sharing their concerns, they are able to break the cyclical patterns from which any escape was previously impossible.[38] This is not to say that there is a radical break in the personality (or in the Jonah narrative). Jonah does not leave a sinful condition to adopt a saintly one. There is here no Ovidian "metamorphosis" from a formerly stiffnecked, stubborn, and hardhearted sinner, into a broadminded, radiant, and successful "P.R.-person." For it is the same Jonah of chapter 1 who now prays in chapter 2. It is he who, even in the depth of the bottomless ocean, stands face to face with God. The "reborn" Jonah has in no way discarded his human nature and temperament. He is the Jonah of always, replete with both flaws and virtues, who shows occasional good will and frequent short temper and is capable of untold courage and some all too specific acts of cowardice. This Jonah, the story tells us, went to Nineveh and delivered his unbelievable message, but he also expressed anger at the sparing of the city. Thus the "resurrected" Jonah "accepts, affirms, and confirms . . . the work which [the soul] is destined to perform upon the world," [39] but Jonah's "core" remains the same.

But whatever the throngs of others do to deceive themselves in "regarding lying vanities" (vs. 9), Jonah now affirms and confirms his uniqueness and vocation (vs. 10). This offers a stark contrast to his former attitude (in chapter 1) when he wished to remain anonymous. He displays a concrete sign of self-abnegation: he offers a sacrifice and says his vows (vs. 10). It is scarcely the same Jonah as in chapter 1, who narcissistically used others as mirrors of himself. He has now passed from *eros* to *agape,* i.e, to the love of the Ground of Being in the person of the human "Thou." This is made clear by the fact that sacrifice in Israel is a totally gratuitous and disinterested act. It is not a bargain with a moody god or a bloodthirsty demon. Verse 11 here emphasizes that Jonah's salvation is no *quid pro quo* offered in recompense for the gift of the sacrificer. Jonah's move toward God finds a response, but not a recompense. Jonah is restored to life at the very moment when all seems to be over for the prophet, at the moment that he accepts death, not as a supreme act of injustice and absurdity but as an act of God, and he greets it with thanksgiving.[40] Because Jonah ran a risk without the least speculation about its outcome, because he fully trusted the goodness of his partner in the dialogue, because he lost his life in a pure oblation on behalf of the Other; because of this, he found his life! "Real sacrifice occurs only when we run the risk of having sacrificed in vain" says Frankl.[41] He adds: ". . . only insofar as a person is capable of ignoring and forgetting himself is he able to recognize anything in and of the world." [42]

Does this actually mean that the self is annihilated in the process? Of course not, for on the contrary Jonah does not remain in the grave. But the question deserves further reflection. When one breaks the monologue with the self and acknowledges a "Thou," one passes from "death" to "life" (see below Chapter VII, on the Voice from Without), but as the sequel of the tale shows "the worst is not death, but the rebirth itself. . . . It means *for the first time to be subjected* to the terrifying paradox of the human condition, since one must be born not as a god, but as a man . . . " [43] Of this, chapter 3 of Jonah is an illustration.

Chapter V

FAITH
AND
DOUBT
The Ambiguity
of Commitment
(Jonah 3)

*Man's struggle for his self and his identity is
doomed to failure unless it is enacted as dedication and devotion to something beyond his self, to
something above his self.*

—Viktor Frankl, *Psychotherapy and Existentialism*
(New York: Washington Square Press, 1967), p. 82.

The book of Jonah could have ended with chapter 2.[1] Its content would then approximate that of a Greek myth and its message would concern a rigid uncompassionate God, to whom a person has no choice other than to surrender. Or, the book could have begun with chapter 3 in epic fashion and ended like a tragedy. We would then have something like the following: As soon as he receives God's commission, the prophet, like a Greek hero, shows his readiness to fulfill it. Triumphantly he proclaims the message to the Ninevites and brings them to their knees. But his victory is no more than a Pyrrhic one, and he addresses a complaint to God about his radical reversal of intentions.

But the book of Jonah does not end with chapter 2 nor does it begin with chapter 3. Once again, God calls the antihero, Jonah, despite his unwillingness to go. This receives considerable stress at this point of the story and recalls the very commandment that appears in chapter 1. That is why the text says that God spoke to Jonah "a second time," a statement which raises a problem, for is there really a second chance in a person's life? Life does not go in circles; an opportunity missed is an opportunity lost. We never swim in the same river, as Heraclitus has said. Then does Jonah actually receive the word of his calling a second time? The answer is No. But he finds himself confronted once again with the same vocation after his "death" in the fish's belly. In fact, the content of Jonah 3:2 is exactly the same as that of Jonah 1:2. Jonah is the one who "hears" it "a second time." "The Lord" does not need to open his mouth a second time. We are not dealing here with a myth or a fairy tale, where a calling might well remain inconsequential and the hero unaltered, owing to the more or less oneiric relation that exists between characters and events.[2]

"The word of the Lord came to Jonah" from within. The choice which he

makes in the fish's belly implies that from now on he will not allow the
events he has just experienced to remain voiceless. Were the tale a myth, the
second divine order issued to the hero might be construed as blackmail, i.e.,
now that you know that God's will is inescapable and how fatal it is for one to
resist it, hear once more the call, but this time don't be stubborn! [3] But in
the case of Jonah nothing of the kind happens. Jonah remains totally free;
free to say yes or no, free to obey, but also to give vent to his anger and dis-
appointment (cf. Jon. 4). Jonah's personality we see once again is not
crushed by what has happened at sea.[4] One should always bear in mind the
dialectic that we stressed in the preceding chapter between the change that
occurs in Jonah and the integrity of his person. Too often modern readers of
the tale short-change this tension. Rudolph, for example, projects elements
of chapter 4 onto Jonah 3 in order to show that Jonah has not changed his
mind in the fish's belly. In this way Rudolph unwillingly makes the psalm of
chapter 2 appear to be a hoax, and he consciously belittles Jonah's compliance with God's order in chapter 3. He even uses the term "sabotage" to
describe the prophet's restricting himself to the letter of his commission so
as to be blameless before God (see the discussion below on this point). Such
a stance becomes all the more suspect when he falls into the trap of equating
the narrow-minded Jew Jonah with the whole of his people.[5]

At the basis of this misunderstanding is a "static" conception of liberty in
which revolt would be a state of mind and freedom its opposite. Both would
be absolute, and the choice between them would elude all relativism. Furthermore, the choice itself would be a situation rather than a movement. On
the contrary, verse 3 here states: "so Jonah arose and went to Nineveh according to the word of the Lord." Here is the dynamic freedom of Jonah: a
historical move—not a natural virtue. For Rudolph, Jonah's obedience
comes only out of panic, while the text makes clear that the prophet does
not crawl at the feet of a tyrant. On the contrary, he "stands up (arises)," as a
free man and responds in obedience to the call of the liberator. He realizes
that he had had a misconception of freedom when he pretended to take his
destiny into his own hands and to be responsible only to himself. That led
nowhere but to choas, to the shark's jaws, to "closed bars" (2:7). For liberty
is not solipsistic. It cannot be achieved through self-alienation or through
navel-gazing isolation. Humanity is gerundive; it *is* not free; rather it *becomes*
free. The bipolar character of the word *šēnît* ("*a second* time") suggests that
no one becomes a person without *first* going into the entrails of "hades."
Abraham must leave Ur in Chaldea and raise a murderous arm against his
son. Isaac must live through the unforgettable and perhaps unforgivable
trauma of becoming "the lamb for the burnt offering" of his own father
(Gen. 22:7). Jacob must struggle the whole night with the angel and emerge
crippled—but still standing. There is no escape from that crucible of liberty.

"A second time," therefore, is no mere repetition. It is the living rhythm of an act which is thwarted by one's solipsistic instinct of survival (the "Jonah complex") but which is followed by its fulfillment when the call is heard "a second time." This, then, is freedom, the liberation from the inhibitions that bog a person down in the quicksand of complacency.

When Jonah hears the word "a second time," he has in the interval (which might be either a split second or an eternity) passed from infancy to maturity, from inauthenticity to authenticity. To illustrate this, the tale employs a polyphony of sounds that deserves our attention here. While Jonah is in the sea (chapter 2) surrounded by the cruel elements, he has to realize that the waves and billows are only deafening just as the roars of the crowds at home or in Tarshish are only stunning. Jonah discovers that the way to his own sanity lies in rediscovering his own "voice" (2:3). This is not to say that he would trust a response coming from himself, for on the contrary he raises his voice in order to beg for a response from someone else: "Out of the belly of the nether world, cried I, and Thou heardest my voice." In the preceding chapter, we stressed Jonah's reaching out, which serves to break his cocoon and make him pass from "death" to "life." Now chapter 3 of Jonah introduces a totally unexpected element to the concert of sounds that takes place between God and the prophet. At first Jonah hears nothing! Indeed, the response of God to Jonah's prayer is not what it should be. If we were dealing with a myth, it would be easy to imagine a fitting reaction to Jonah's discourse.[6] Surely the god or the fairy would express a mixture of anger and benevolence. But here, instead of speaking to Jonah, God speaks to the fish!; "and it vomited out Jonah upon the dry land." Moreover, when God speaks to Jonah, it is neither anger not benevolence that Jonah hears but the very same commandment as in the beginning. The benevolence of the fairy would obliterate past unsuccessful experience with one stroke. Time would be cyclical and the expression "a second time" would not carry the tension it has here. In myth, the second time would represent mere repetition, and Jonah's voyage to the bottom of the sea would be radically meaningless because it would not bear on history, his own or that of anyone else.

In this case, however, the commandment honors Jonah's experience in its fullness. Jonah is addressed as a responsible man; hence he is given an order, a call, a vocation. The one who speaks to him does not see him as empty, worthless, and helpless, nor even as a weakling exhausted by three days and three nights in the depths of the sea. He is a command-able person. Moreover, the demands of the caller have not lessened. If anything, they are even more strict now. Obedience to the call remains today as foolish as before, for circumstances have not made the commandment more reasonable. Jonah's decision to go to Nineveh does not level with reason. Jonah does something *extravagant* in "going out of the usual path, . . . roving beyond just limits or prescribed methods." [7]

As if to emphasize the prophet's folly, the text presents Nineveh as having monstrous proportions. It is "an exceedingly great city of three days'
journey." And not only is it an insurmountable obstacle before Jonah, but its
magnitude is commensurate only with its deceptiveness. As Herman Melville's Father Mapple says in *Moby Dick:* "Jonah did the Almighty's bidding.
And what was that, shipmates? To preach the Truth to the face of Falsehood!
That was it!" [8] It is striking that the book of Jonah repeats no fewer than four
times the phrase "that great city" (1:2; 3:2, 3; 4:11). The number "four" is
symbolic of the world. [9] Nineveh is thus a microcosm of all the falsehood,
the crime, the conformism, the solipsism, and the uniform anonymity of the
human race. She deserves to be utterly destroyed within forty days because
of her "evil way and the violence (*ḥāmās*) in their hands" (vs. 8). Now *ḥāmās*
is precisely what was condemned by the prophets as regards Assyrian behavior towards the nations (Isa. 10:13 –14; Nah. 2:11 –12 and esp. 3:1; Joel
2:12 –14; see also Job 16:17).

The text attempts so little to exonerate the Assyrian city that in verse
4 it implies that Nineveh is but another name for Sodom and Gomorrah. [10] In fact, the Hebrew verb *hāpak* is specifically used in connection
with the total destruction of the two ancient cities along the shore of the
Dead Sea (cf. Gen. 19:21, 25; Deut. 29:22; Amos 4:11; Jer. 20:16; Lam.
4:6). [11]

It is to such a nest of human turpitude that Jonah is sent. He now appears
as the antitype of Lot, who left the condemned cities without looking back,
thus leaving them to their fate. Jonah's action, on the contrary, will eventually save Nineveh, and the prophet's initial refusal to go contrasts further with
Lot, who was so much attracted to the riches of the valley's towns. [12] That the
comparison with the Genesis narratives about Abraham and Lot is no accident is confirmed by the wording of verse 5, where the Ninevites are
credited with the same insight of faith as Abraham himself (Gen. 15:6) or
the people of Israel (Exod. 14:31)! In the three texts under consideration
(Jonah, Genesis, and Exodus) we have the same verb "he/they believed"
with the same syntactic construction. The main difference, and an important
one, is that Abraham and Israel believe in YHWH, whereas the Ninevites
believe in *Elohim.* [13]

One can also contrast Sodom, where not even ten righteous people
could be found (Gen. 18:32), with Nineveh, where everyone "from the
greatest to the least" (vs. 5) passes through repentance. Moreover, Sodom
and Gomorrah had only the time from dawn to dusk to reper., while Nineveh has forty days. The swiftness of God's action, which is provoked by the
enormity of Sodom's crime, has been sacrificed in Jonah for the sake of the

"forty days" motif with the clear purpose of including Nineveh in Israelite destiny (see note 9, above).

The parallel between Jonah 3 and Genesis 19 is therefore not without ambiguity. In contrast, Jonah fulfills his commission in Nineveh unequivocally. The commandment of God is literally fulfilled (cf. vss. 2 and 4). The prophet conveys the oracle exactly as God gave it, in keeping with the rabbinic insistence upon literalism in the transmission of a divine message. They call attention, for example, to how Adam abused his role as mediator by forbidding Eve to *touch* the tree of the knowledge of good and evil, whereas God had laid injunction only against its fruit.[14] We can thus understand Jonah's exactitude in complying with God's intent.

But human acts are always open to more than one interpretation; they are never the result of one simple motivation.[15] Jonah, as is shown by 4:2, is not without his own understanding. The very transmission of the message in unaltered form is already an interpretation of it as being unconditionally binding. "Yet forty days and Nineveh shall be overthrown" is in fact the expression of how Jonah understands the divine commission. This is probably the reason why the text does not say that God uttered that message (cf. vs. 2). It is on the basis of this interpretation that Jonah resolves to go to Mesopotamia. Though there is within him, in his innermost being, a devastating doubt as to the real bearing of the message (cf. 4:2), he readily smothers any other "translation" of the will of God. He does not even relate to the Ninevites the source of the wrath that hovers over them, nor does he suggest what attitude the Assyrians should take in response to the message.

But how can Jonah proclaim anything other than sheer condemnation to the city of wickedness? The "logic" of faith itself indicates that if there is a message for Nineveh it can only be one of doom, for it is that cursed pit of snakes which has attempted to destroy Jerusalem and burn the Temple.[16] Any other alternative is insane. It is forbidden to add to Jerusalem's martyrdom by granting immunity to the chaos-monster.

Thus, the only justification in Jonah's eyes for going to the archenemy of his people and preaching there the word of God lies in the fact that it will seal the doom of Nineveh. Jonah has no taste for playing the role of a Cassandra whose words are never believed. Not only does Jonah want his words to be believed but also he is prepared to rejoice in the anticipated ruin of Nineveh. When the city burned in 612, Nahum the prophet exulted. Unless one excludes the latter book from the biblical canon, there is no reason to be surprised when one reads Jonah here.

But the sequel of the tale shows that Jonah is wrong and that his interpretation of God's message is abusively one-sided. Why this is so must be left unanswered for the moment, but at any rate it is clear that the ground collapses under Jonah's feet. God's repentance in forgiving the Ninevites means that God's "justice" is equivalent to flagrant injustice. Indeed, Jonah has feared all along that God is too tender, too compassionate, too easily moved by his creatures. He is too quick to forget the crimes of the murderer, thus disregarding the fact that those crimes have crippled Israel. Who is God that he should be so prompt to overlook the infamy of his people's enemy—of his own enemy—but so slow and even reluctant to bind up his people's "wounds, bruises, and festering sores," to "mollify with oil" the injuries he inflicted? It is with good reason that Jonah wonders whether it would not be better for him to be among the torturers rather than among the tortured. His existential choice to take sides (cf. Albert Camus, *La Peste*) with the victims, "les vaincus," is radically questioned. What "profit"—to use a term of Qohelet—is there in being among the friends of God rather than among his enemies? As in the book of Job, with which Jonah has much in common (including a final divine discourse that conceals as much as it reveals), the issue is one of *justice.* For if God himself is not just, there is absolutely no justice in time or eternity. Justice is a myth, an opiate, a balloon as big as it is empty. And God, who presented himself as the champion of justice, the God who taught humanity the concept and the content of justice, is himself a balloon, for he stands or falls with justice.

When Jonah wants to die (chapter 4), it is no childish whim. For where is the one who would blindly choose to entertain relations which are so disastrous to oneself and to one's people? Who would opt for leaving one's city in shambles and mourning its dead in order to become, in the very city that committed the crime, the instrument of its forgiveness and salvation? Where is the Auschwitz survivor who would go to Berchtesgaden or Berlin carrying God's salvation? Qohelet could not find any trace of justice in the world. Job and Jonah go still farther, for they wonder whether there is justice in God himself, but then, "it is better for me to die than live" (4:3, 8).

But we are anticipating, for the paradox consists of the fact that although the prophet was interpreting God's commission as being unconditional, the Ninevites understand it differently. They introduce a "perhaps," which Jonah had refused to entertain (cf. vs. 9, and our Chapter IV). Now those who change the meaning of the apodictic pronouncement are not casuists but the very inhabitants of Nineveh, "where are more than six score thousand persons that cannot discern between their right hand and their left hand"! Despite the absence of any conditional clause in the oracle, the Ninevites are able to transform determinism into mere possibility. They bring a conclusion of their own to the prophetic sentence and make it say not only what Jonah actually proclaimed but also: "Who knows? The divinity might turn and repent. He might turn away from his fierce anger, and we shall not perish" (vs. 9). In other words, the Ninevites dare to understand the message as being entirely different from that carried in the messenger's interpretation. Hence, they are said to have believed *God,* not Jonah (vs. 5).

The text, one must say, becomes at this point both ironic and comic. Although Jonah speaks in a vengeful spirit (unless it is with indifference?) in sealing the deadly fate of Nineveh and utters his oracle without nuance, without pity, without love or affect, its very brutality unexpectedly brings the message home to the Ninevites and they repent! The whole thing looks really too easy. The reader of the tale is left unsatisfied. The dramatic confrontation seems to have been sidestepped by the author. It does not take much imagination to picture the intense dialogue that might have transpired between the prophet and the Ninevites on a public square of the city, perhaps "spiced" with a scornful rejoinder to the prophet's presumptuous and arrogant attitude of judgment. Such a dramatic debate among the inhabitants of the city on the issue raised by the prophet would not be out of place here, followed by a statement of the public repentance of all "from the greatest of them even to the least of them." But it does not occur in the actual book of Jonah. The theme of Nineveh's repentance is given short shrift. The point of the story clearly does not lie in the romantic description of the psychological debate of the soul with itself.

Perhaps the reason for this shortcut has been rightly intimated by Wolf Mankowitz, who argues that Jonah reveals to the Ninevites something they already know without admitting it to themselves: [17]

> *Jonah* (to the King of Nineveh): Oh, so *your* little bird tells *me* a hundred times nightly to come to Nineveh and inform *you* that in forty days from now *you* are completely in liquidation. And that's what *I'm* telling *you?* It's a madhouse here!

Be that as it may, the irony of the matter is that the Ninevites' interpretation of God's intent is more appropriate than that of the prophet. They "choose life in order to live," a staggering phenomenon about which we must say more. For the moment, however, a warning note must be struck: the conversion of Nineveh is *not* the goal of the book. If it were, there would be no reason for the tale to continue with the whole of chapter 4. In fact, the Ninevites' mourning rites only pave the way for something that is of greater importance to the storyteller and his original audience.

But neither is the conversion of Nineveh a small element in the book. As before in the case of the sailors, the Ninevites' attitude is integral to the progression of the story. It makes an ironic contrast with Israel's expected attitude toward heathens. Instead of passively waiting for forty days before undergoing their own death, instead of escaping the problem (as Jonah had done in chapter 1), instead of shedding sterile tears upon themselves, the Ninevites confront the issue head-on; they telescope the forty days and make present an event that is not due to come until the future. They mourn themselves as dead people. In a remarkable and highly unusual move, they choose not to spend the rest of their short existence in pleasure. Even though they are in the situation of one who is "condemned" by physicians with a diagnosis of terminal illness, they choose not to heed Horatius's exhortation *carpe diem* as long as it is still possible. They use the time before death to raise a question with determinism, saying: "Who knows?" And, since there are infinitely more chances to meet the catastrophe announced by the prophet or physician than there are to be granted a reprieve, they have at least enough imagination to see themselves already dead, and they proceed to their own interment.

It would be unwarranted to conclude that the mourning Ninevites have plotted to circumvent their own condemnation. It may well be, on the contrary and despite what we intimated above, that they have understood the prophet's oracle as being immutable, *fata denunciativa,* i.e., with a deterministic slant.[18] But instead of feeling helpless and ultimately unconcerned about an event over which they have no control, they reflect upon their past; they review their foul deeds; they unveil the image of their wicked soul, and they mourn. It might well be a gratuitous move that is essentially incapable, in their own eyes, of altering the course of their destiny, but at least the Ninevites choose to respond humanly to a situation that involves human beings and not robots. In other words, what is important to realize at this point is that however we name the reaction of the Ninevites, they do *respond* to a "sooth-saying", which they thereby transform into a *challenge*—to themselves, and beyond, to destiny.

It is a tremendous step, a formidable wager to say that perhaps all is not said in the prophet's oracle.[19] Maybe death is not the final divine word. "Yes, all *may* be, all is possible; nothing is either too atrocious to be impossible in the world and in history, nor too sublime to be impossible in human conscience and action. . . . At Nineveh's gates, saved by its repentance, this is the lesson taught by God to Jonah whose soul strived after automatic certainties. These are pulverized by the fiery fugue of *Perhaps*."[20]

The miracle is that the "perhaps" of the Ninevites corresponds to the secret desire of God to send his prophet to Nineveh in the first place. From the start, the oracle destined for the Ninevites was *not* unconditional prediction. The message could be interpreted as being of the same nature as "a law of the Medes and Persians which altereth not" (Dan. 6:10, 13, 16). Then indeed the Ninevites would have effectively granted to the prophet's oracle the character of a brazen law which no one can alter. In other words, it is up to the Ninevites to tip God's word one way or the other. Besides, the negative dimension of Jonah's omen is not altogether cancelled by Nineveh's repentance. Tobit 14:4, for example, intimates that God's pardon of Nineveh is to be understood as a temporary remission. "I believe," says Tobit, "in the word of God upon Nineveh which Jonah spoke." [21] The present episode thus falls in parallel with other remissions of penalty, as for instance that on behalf of David (2 Sam. 12), of King Hezekiah (Isa. 38), or of King Ahab (1 Kings 20). Nineveh is not spared forever; in fact, it was actually overthrown in 612, long before the book of Jonah was ever written. The tale, therefore, keeps that catastrophe suspended in the background of the narrative. Every reader knows that it is only a question of a temporary reprieve. Thus, God's grace is underlined; the threat to Nineveh has nothing to do with impotent or insufficiently grounded anger on the part of God. The fact that the Ninevites mourn shows that they made no mistake about it. They intuited that despite appearances, there was a way out of the impasse. Indeed, Jonah himself had been apprehensive that they would discover this "weakness" in his God (cf. 4:2). [22]

The repentance of the Ninevites displays a quality that corresponds to the nature of the call they have received. Their repentance is prophetic because it echoes the profound dimensions of the prophetic "provocation" of humanity by God. They have heard a word of God and now they speak his very language! For what they say could have been said by an Israelite; it is worthy of Daniel's companions (Dan. 3:17 –18), of the prophet Joel (2:14), or of the prophet Amos (5:15): "who knows whether God will not turn and repent and turn away from his fierce anger that we perish not?" Here, it is the nonspeculative "who knows?" that people of hope oppose to hopelessness. As Sartre would have it: the Ninevites bring into the realm of the "thinkable" an unthinkable situation so as to transcend it at least in spirit. The French philsopher writes in *The Flies,* "human life starts across the river of despair" (Orestes' reply).

But, if every aspect of the Ninevites' future is thereby changed, it also changes Jonah's whole universe. As far as he is concerned, the "contract" has not been respected by God. The prophet had come to Nineveh with a program, and the program is changed in the very course of its realization. Originally, God had so stubbornly clung to his intent for Nineveh that he stirred up the ocean to swallow Jonah. God was so sure that Nineveh had to be overthrown that nothing could prevent him from confronting the Ninevites with a proclamation of their doom. Even the cosmic "unalterable" laws were changed to ensure that Jonah would go and, on behalf of his Lord, spit in the face of the cursed city. But now that the time has come for its realization, God himself sides with the Ninevites and "repents from the evil that he said he would do unto them" (vs. 10).

We should pause at this point to recall that the book of Jonah is a satire that was written in the community of the restoration against the party in power in Jerusalem (see above, Chapter I). The author's protest against the isolationist policy of Zion's "ideologists" makes sense only if the nations' "conversion" is at all conceivable in the first place. Thus, the author appears to be saying that if only the community would open itself up to the world instead of withdrawing within itself as at present, a miracle would happen that would, in fact, usher in the much-awaited restoration. Even the hesitant or reluctant Jonah obtains resounding "success," although his conception of success becomes totally different when he goes out into the world.

If anything is logically unexpected, it is the repentance of Nineveh even though the prophet has done nothing to provoke it but on the contrary desires the city's destruction and considers the reprieve a terrible personal failure. All odds are against the possibility of the sinners' repentance, and this is exactly what the author wants to emphasize at this point. The book of Jonah is in no way a treatise upon missiology; its message is not "spread the good seed and it shall surely spring forth." That which the ideologists in Jerusalem refuse even to consider is that the seed might be thrown outside of Zion. Thus, the book is a plea for a radical change of their policy. The ground of the exhortation is that the restoration has not been realized, despite the proclamation of theocracy in the Temple by the priests. The restoration, says Jonah, will occur only *with* the nations, not without them. And if one asks by what unfathomable means such an event might be possible, one should first take the pain to "go to Nineveh"! Israel resists with all her might this offer to the historical enemy of the Chosen People, however indirect that offer may be. Jonah is repulsed by the sparing of Nineveh in the name of sacred principles; he refuses to be the instrument of what he considers God's betrayal of his covenant with Israel. But God "has his reasons that reason does not comprehend"! (Pascal).

One thing entails another. There occurs a chain-reaction as soon as one "impossibility" has become actual. The repentance of the Ninevites is extraordinary, but not so much as its sequel. God is "found by those who did not seek" him in the past (cf. Isa. 65:1, from roughly the same epoch as Jonah). The repentance of the wicked city stirs the repentance of God, and who knows how far this concatenation of cause and effect will go? Perhaps it will go as far as the celebration by all the nations of the feast of Sukkoth on Mount Zion as dreamed by Zechariah (Chapter 14). The dream is "impossible," but by the grace of God not unrealizable! [23] In the I-Thou relationship which Jonah indirectly restores between God and the Ninevites, there is a striking reciprocity of feelings and reactions. We said above that the Ninevites' move corresponded to God's secret desire in the first place. We must now go one step farther and reflect upon the verb used in Jonah 3 to describe God's repentance (vss. 9, 10; 4:2). As André Neher writes:

God's repentance is, assuredly, one of those biblical notions introducing the theme of failure in its sharpest form. . . . The Hebrew term which expresses this repentance is *nehama* which at the same time means repentance but also *consolation*. . . resilience in the face of failure, the will, the energy, the taking over again of the task, it is hope. Thus failure and hope are not two separate moments of the divine word, they inherently belong to each other as two facing poles. One single term expresses their concomitance so that, in the biblical text, failure and hope are read in the same word; they are seized in the same hinge of the biblical venture.[24]

God is consoled by Nineveh's repentance. It is now clear that, before the Ninevites bet on the possibility of escape from the impasse ("Who knows whether God will not turn and repent?" vs. 9), God had placed a wager upon the Ninevites, just as he had placed a wager upon Jonah when he called him to "cry against Nineveh" and upon Job according to the prologue of that book. The very fact that Jonah is sent to Nineveh in the first place, and with an oracle of doom which seems to leave no room for reprieve, is paradoxically the demonstration that the future is not foregone. For if it were, from the Jewish point of view, it would make absolutely no sense to go to Nineveh and to "cry against her." For Greek tragedy, it makes sense to confront human beings with *moira*, because they can intellectually conceive of a world from which humanity is absent. Their vision is cosmocentric, not anthropocentric as is the Hebrew conception. Greek "Truth" can exist without humanity and thus can be proclaimed for its own sake. Not so for Israel, for the "Truth" here is the truth of God *and* humanity in the making, not an Idea. In other words, "Yet forty days, and Nineveh shall be overthrown" can perhaps be conveniently called *fata denunciativa* by Bickerman, thus using a Greek category, but the category must be adapted to the new reality and not become a Procrustean bed for the Jewish conception! From the outset, Jonah's commission is *prophetic*, not just predictive. The prophet is not a soothsayer in Israel, and if his word is understood as operative, it is not because it is magical but because it participates in the history which it describes. [25]

We have already contrasted God's will with "the law of the Medes and Persians which altereth not," according to the testimony of the books of Esther and Daniel. The Rabbis broadened this perspective and opposed the human judges, who cannot revoke their sentence, to God who can. Philo sees here the divine attributes of omnipotence in practice,[26] which is correct enough, but it still needs qualification. For the "omnipotence" of God appears here, embarrassingly enough, as weakness! Jonah makes this point clear in his plea to God (4:2). From all we know of omnipotence, through our experience with human tyrants and despots, discretionary power is but another term for obduracy and capriciousness. But the unalterable aspect of omnipotence receives a fatal blow here, as the God of Israel paradoxically expresses his sovereign liberty to change his mind! As for the other aspect of omnipotence, namely, capriciousness, it too is out of the question here. God's decision to relent from "the evil which he said he would do unto them" (vs. 10) is no moody gesture but in fact corresponds to his original desire and expresses not his unreliability but his "graciousness, compassion, long-suffering, and abundance in mercy" (4:2).

We are thus confronted with an either/or alternative. Either the word omnipotence is misused by Philo (and also by the Rabbis, Calvin, etc.) [27] and so should be altogether withdrawn from Judeo-Christian theological vocabulary, or else the term is retained (as are *eros*, *metanoia*, *hamartia*, etc.) but with a meaning different from that which it has in secular contexts. Either way, God's thoughts and actions are not measurable by philosophical standards. No people are more aware than those living after Auschwitz of the impossibility of speaking without qualification of the "omnipotence" of God. As can be seen here, the book of Jonah already makes a *caveat* in this respect. God is compassionate (Jer. 15:6; Ps. 19:13; Judg. 2:18); he comforts himself in repentance (both his own and that of the Ninevites). For this indeed is his "omnipotence," that he can so totally change the hearts of human beings that their complicity in wickedness passes into unanimous penance.

Verse 5 insists on that point, showing that the mourning rites extend to include the leaders themselves (vs. 6). This order is important, for it shows that it was a spontaneous popular decision. They decide to mourn without first checking with the authorities as to whether they think such behavior is appropriate and timely. It is well-known in the field of mental health that an "internal locus of reference" (to use a Rogerian concept) is the basis for sound and mature decision making. [28]

The move initiated by the populous is nonetheless condoned and made official by the "King of Nineveh" who in the process sheds his attributes of kingship and at the same time all autocracy, totalitarianism and dictatorship. The "King of Nineveh" [29] was called the "king of kings," but he appears here to be extremely accessible, in contrast to the inhuman and cruel image given by the Assyrians. One of the results of repentance is the retrieval of one's humanity and the dropping of all pretentious roles.

At the other extreme of the social ladder, the reader is struck by the mention of the beasts' participation in the ritual (vss. 7, 8; cf. 4:11). This motif appears during the Persian era in Jewish literature (cf. Joel 1:20; Judith 4:10). It was apparently a Persian custom to include animals in funerals (Herodotus, *Hist.* IX, 24; Plutarch, *Alexander* 72; see also Vergil, *Fifth Eclogue* 24 ff.; some modern scholars call attention to the attire of horses during present-day funerals). The point is not only that the animals form a "topocosm," as Theodor H. Gaster notes,[30] but also that, along with the Ninevites' passage from a, so to speak, "non-kosher" state to a "kosher" one, all that belongs to them also passes into the realm of redemption. In other words, in the process of their repentance, the whole of nature is also transfigured. From the picture given in Isaiah 11:6 ff., it could be said that we have here a taste of paradise!

No wonder then, that human repentance has the extraordinary effect of changing God's mind. Such, in particular, had been the striking discovery of the Hebrew prophets during the Exile. This parallel introduces us to a crucial issue in the understanding of Jonah.

Although there are several texts of the sixth-century prophets which stress God's versatility, the *locus classicus* among them is Jeremiah 18:7–10, which Bickerman believes Jonah opposes because of the unconditional character of its prophetic declarations. Jonah "refused to accept the perspective of Jeremiah and Ezekiel, in which the prophet is no longer God's herald but a watchman who blows a horn to warn his people of coming danger (Ezek. 3:16; 33:1–9)."[31] But Bickerman's point is self-defeating. He fails to realize that the radical change of milieux from Jeremiah to Jonah makes their respective problematics entirely different from and even opposed to one another. Our thesis in contradistinction to that author's viewpoint can be summarized thus: Despite the generality of terms used by the prophets Jeremiah and Ezekiel, what they actually have in mind is strictly and exclusively the fate of *Judah* and not the fate of all the nations. Jonah, therefore, cannot take advantage of the "universalistic" statements of the prophets of the Exile and simply apply them to Nineveh. With Jonah, we are dealing with a *new* problem and the very least one can say about it is that it is far from evident that it has been "solved" by Jonah's predecessors.

Thus, when we realize that the invitation which is addressed to the Ninevites in Jonah 3:8, "Let them turn everyone from his evil way," is found verbatim in Jeremiah 25:5, we must be careful to stress the point that in Jeremiah it is addressed to Judah (cf. vs. 1). The same applies to Jeremiah 26:3 (cf. vs. 2) and to 36:3, 7 (which is all the more interesting as vs. 3 comes as a restrictive provision to vs. 2). Jeremiah 18:11 is still clearer; the message is for "the men of Judah and the inhabitants of Jerusalem," and the prophet says: "for you . . . against you," as if to indicate a very particular move of God on behalf of his people. We find the same phenomenon in 23:22 ("my people") and in 35:15 (cf. vs. 13), etc. We have already mentioned Jeremiah 36. This chapter has been taken as a model by the author of Jonah. "It is here and there the same course of events: divine threat (Jon. 3:4; Jer. 36:7b); publication of an extraordinary and general fasting with, here and there, the use of an expression unparalleled elsewhere *qârâh rôm* (Jon. 3:5; Jer. 36:9); the king and his court happen to hear the news (Jon. 3:6; Jer. 36:12–20)."[32]

But in Jeremiah's scene, nobody is impressed, including above all King Jehoiakim of Jerusalem (vss. 29–31). "Exposed to the same word of the Lord as Nineveh, Jerusalem, the king of Judah and his ministers do not relent from their evil ways so that the Lord may forgive them." [33] Consequently there will follow destruction of "man and beast;" whereas in Jonah there is general repentance, which entails the salvation of humans and beasts (3:6–8, 10; 4:11). But the trees must not conceal the forest. In Jeremiah the oracle is entirely conditioned by the particular covenantal relationship that exists between God and "the house of Judah" (vs. 3). In Jonah, on the contrary, we stand outside of that unique framework. There is nothing in Jeremiah or Ezekiel to make us extend that which is valid for God's people to God's foes!

St. Jerome is certainly correct when, in his explanation of Ezekiel, he says that the prophets foretell punishment in order to make it unnecessary. But again, it is Nineveh and not Jerusalem that is in question here and those who share in the storyteller's fiction of a Jewish prophet who is sent to the pagan city par excellence, are the contemporaries of the reformers Ezra and Nehemiah. Is it so evident, therefore, that Jeremiah's and Ezekiel's statements concerning *exceptional* divine actions that favor the Jewish exiles in Babylon are to be extended to include Nineveh? If indeed they are, it cannot be automatic but must follow a decision taken *de novo* by God himself. Further, the same divine action that was once the motive for Israel to rejoice and praise becomes here at the very least a cause of puzzlement. Are the Ninevites on the same plane with the Israelites? Does God's grace and compassion for his people in the dungeon create a precedent by which to extend that grace to the jailers?

It must be emphasized here that the author of Jonah does not think in terms of automatism or precedent (Jeremiah; Ezekiel). What his narrative does claim is that God can apply his gracious compassion to Nineveh just as he does to Jerusalem. That such a message is not easy for Jonah and the bourgeois of Jerusalem whom he represents to accept should not surprise us. We are surprised only when we do not comprehend the bearing of such a revolutionary conception.

For the paradox of the book of Jonah is compounded by a feature to which André Feuillet has called attention. Not only did the Ninevites repent, moved as they were by an extraordinary theological insight ("who knows. . .?"), but as we stressed earlier, they did so "from the greatest of them unto the least of them" (vs. 5). This expression, it is well-known, is "Jeremian" (cf. 5:4–5; 6:13; 8:10; 44:12). "In Jeremiah's book, it is only with the coming of the messianic era that all shall know YHWH from the least of them even to the greatest of them (31:34); in Nineveh, with Jonah's message that marvelous fulfillment is already at work!" [34] The point is important here. It recalls a Jewish tradition according to which, when a non-

Jew turns to God and repents, that non-Jew becomes immediately greater than Israel's high priest himself, while the day that this happens becomes greater than Yom Kippur, and the place that witnesses it holier than the holy of holies! [35] In this Gentile, Judaism sees the purest fruit of its preaching (cf. Matt. 8:10; 15:28). In the words of Jesus "there will be greater joy in heaven over one sinner who repents than over ninety-nine righteous people who do not need to repent" (Luke 15:7).

It is true that the Ninevites, even before they are given the benefit of the *covenantal* attributes of Israel's God,[36] display a disposition which is strikingly close to a Jewish attitude in similar situations. Our preceding review of the parallels that exist between Jonah 3 and the book of Jeremiah has shown this clearly. The Ninevites' fasting and repentance closely follow the model of Jewish repentance and mourning rites. What is said in Jonah 3 concerning the Ninevites could be said without the slightest alteration—except perhaps for the use of YHWH instead of Elohim—about Israelites. This is not a lack of imagination on the part of the author of the tale, for what he intends to prove is that non-Jews can indeed become "greater than the high priest." The sailors of chapter 1 "offered a sacrifice to YHWH and made vows" (vs. 16; cf. Mal. 1:11); the Ninevites turn to God and repent, thereby inaugurating a messianic era not in Jerusalem but in Assyria!

Critics are generally at a loss to explain the presence of such so-called "universalistic" themes in Second Zechariah, Malachi, and Jonah. Feuillet, for example, writes, "Universalism comes suddenly to the fore, in contrast with the rather particularistic tone in the rest of those books. . . ." [37] What is forgotten is that "universalism" does not stand in contrast to "particularism." The sailors sacrifice *to YHWH*[38] and the Ninevites convert to Jonah's God because, in their contact with the Jew Jonah, they become *Israelites*. It is not a question of conformism with or adoption of "Judaism"—although, of course, this can be a sign of that too. *Israel* is the name given to the human relation-with-God. Israel's tie with the divine, Israel's election by God and election of God are precisely what make her universal, for these are what bind her to the human.[39] Nothing, in point of fact, is truly human without a divine dimension. Neither is anything divine without its human incorporation. As Bonhoeffer put it: "Einen Gott den es gibt, gibt es nicht" (a god which there is, is not at all). God is the one in relation-with-Israel. The contrast, therefore, is not between particularism and universalism but between election and paganism. The nations are barbarian, "Goy" in every respect, for they prevent the fulfillment of their humanity. E.M. Cioran wrote, "The common man is an unfulfilled Jew." [40] The Goy is a "spurious" person, an incomplete Jew.

The sailors and the Ninevites both realize this much, and they adhere to the community of Israel, throwing themselves (for a while or forever) into the stream of her history.

Chapter VI

A
MATTER
OF
JUSTICE
(JONAH 4)

. . . beyond justice and anger lies the mystery of compassion.

—Abraham Heschel, *The Prophets* (New York: Harper Torchbooks, 1962), Vol. II, p. 67.

In the preceding examination of Jonah 3 we remarked that, under certain conditions, the narrative could have started there. The book could also have ended with the conclusion of chapter 3. All seems to be said there, for the repentance of the Ninevites brings about the repentance of God. But after reaching this edifying peak, the author draws us again into the depths of despair. For, as far as Jonah is concerned, to accept the resolution of the tension of the narrative through the direct reconciliation of God and Nineveh would mean that he, the Israelite prophet, shares in another "Heilsgeschichte," that he can commit himself to a destiny other than that of his own community, that he can identify himself with Nineveh rather than with Jerusalem and lose his very personality, which has been until now so closely associated with his people's history.

But Jonah does not fall into this trap; the narrative at this point opens with the theme of his anger. The noun "anger" appears no fewer than three times in the chapter, and there is one occurrence of the verb "to be angry." Jonah, we are told, reacts with anger to God's forgiveness of Nineveh (vs. 1). Thus, God, who is "slow to anger" (vs. 2, but the Hebrew wording is different) raises an unexpected question about Jonah's anger (vss. 4, 9): "Does your anger become you?" That is: Does anger open up your understanding of what is happening?[1] It is clearly a didactic kind of question raised by God in the expectation of a negative answer. We have seen, however, that Jonah's logic must not be so easily dismissed. In the words of Allen:

> [Jonah] considers it intolerable that Israel's experience of Ex. 32 should be mirrored in Nineveh; he cannot stomach Yahweh's cheapening his mercy by offering it to all and sundry.[2]

The rabbis of old had sharp exegetical insight when they interpreted Jonah's reasoning in the following way: "since the heathens are nearer to repentance, I might be causing Israel to be condemned. Rather I would die (4:3, 8; cf. 1:12)." [3]

Jonah's anger is complex. In a way it does acknowledge the confrontation with God. The Lord is present here, as he was in chapter 2, where Jonah was transformed in the process. Here, however, the text stresses that the prophet's attitude is radically different. He does not like this new experience of the divine Presence. The rationale for such displeasure is also clearly stated. The whole issue, as Cohn has shown, pivots upon the term *ra'* ("evil") as it is used in the narrative.[4] Jonah began by addressing himself to *rā'ātām* of the Ninevites (1:2) and he brings them back *middarkām hārā'āh* from their evil way (3:10), thus averting their punishment for God repents of the *rā'āh* which he had intended to do to them (3:10). But this precisely is *rā'āh gedô-lāh* a great evil (4:1) in Jonah's eyes. And Cohn adds: "It is his very zeal *for* God that turns Jonah against God." [5] We have stressed this point all along. St. Jerome follows the Rabbis and states: "[Jonah's] despair is about Israel's salvation. . . . He is not saddened, as some think, by the salvation of pagan multitudes, but fears that Israel would perish." [6]

In other words, Jonah had clearly expected the literal fulfillment of his oracle of doom against Nineveh. He preached to the Ninevites, not in order to bring them to repentance but in a spirit of vengeance that is without parallel in Israelite prophecy, unless perhaps one invokes Isaiah 6: "Make the heart of this people fat . . . lest they see with their eyes, and hear with their ears, and understand with their heart, and return, and be healed" (vs. 10). But that which in Isaiah revealed a profound and painful lack of hope on the part of God and his prophet becomes in Jonah a mixture of rage and desire for justice (cf. Nah. 1:3, 7; 2:1; 3:4–7, 19).

For ancient Israel, being is inseparable from performing. Abraham *is* the one who leaves Ur and becomes the father of the faith; Jacob *is* the one who fights with the angel and deserves to be called Israel; Amalek *is* the wicked one who tries to thwart the fulfillment of Israel's destiny. Similarly, Nineveh is the destroyer of Jerusalem, the concentration camp for God's people, and God's decision to spare it perpetuates a fatal threat to Israel. One must always bear in mind the *historical* character of the reality about which the Bible speaks.

On the other hand, determinism is passionately rejected by Israel (all the more so if determinism implies the presence of an enemy to be overcome). The Nineveh of tomorrow is not necessarily the same as the Nineveh of yesterday. This, in part, is the lesson of the whole of Jonah. Only a miracle comparable to the "impossible" appearance of a Bethlehem's star can alter the steady course of events, and Jonah's "logic of faith" militates against such an hypothesis, not only because history is not made up of miracles, but when they do occur it is precisely in "Bethlehem." That they can actually happen in Nineveh is not warranted in Jonah's eyes and, in any case, this remote possibility cannot be taken for granted as if it were routine in history. For all practical purposes Nineveh is what it represents; it represents evil.

Jonah's anger does not, therefore, emerge from solipsism and parochialism. It is a righteous wrath for which Jonah feels no shame.

> Every man's anger is righteous indignation in his own eyes. Every man feels his anger is legitimate because it is due to a violation of his personal code of "how things ought to be." [7]

Moreover, the angry Jonah does not take a distance from God, nor even from the possibility of his own change of mind. The same critic adds: "A sense of indignation at unrighteousness is an indispensable first step in repentance"; this statement is complemented by Pederson's remark: "We often become angry at those we love the most." [8]

"Does your anger become you?" asks God. Jonah does not answer simply because he is not arrogant, but his attitude clearly shows that he believes in the legitimacy of his indignation.[9] His anger does indeed become the situation and it opens his eyes to the meaning of what is happening, but he sees only deception which makes him wish to die rather than to live.

At this point we recall Crossan's words ". . . the hearer expects prophets to obey God, and pagans such as the Ninevites, especially, to disobey God. But the speaker tells a story in which a prophet disobeys and the Ninevites obey beyond all belief." [10] It is divine extravagance that the city which was predicted to destroy Israel (according to Hos. 9:3; 11:5, 11; Amos 5:27; cf. Ps. 137:7 –9) is spared. Ostensibly, if Nineveh were destroyed, Israel would be safe (see Nahum 3 which rejoices in the downfall of Assyria). But through Jonah's mission the enemy of Israel is paradoxically spared, and is, so to speak, kept in reserve for further evil-doing against Jerusalem. It is in order to avoid this that Jonah proclaims the inevitable doom of the wicked city, on the model of Sodom in Genesis 19. But, in Jonah, Sodom is spared!

If Jonah is disappointed, however, he is not really surprised. From the beginning, as he himself confesses (4:2), he has suspected that his oracle would not come true. There is a conflict in his mind between the traditional affirmation that the Lord changes not (Isa. 45:23; Mal. 3:6; Num. 3:19; 2 Sam. 12) and a strong intuition that God wants to be defeated by his children in Nineveh. Has he not himself experienced the transformation of doom into the newness of life? Hence, Jonah's anger is a projection on God, as on a super ego, of a sentiment within himself with which he feels incapable of dealing.[11] From this perspective, there also arises the problem of unfulfilled prophecy. God's positive attitude in response to the repentance of the Ninevites effectively makes a liar out of Jonah (cf. Deut. 18).

Jonah is thus robbed of his vengeance, life appears to him as meaning-less, and he wishes to die. He despises the divine mercy, which he himself had enjoyed, when it is shown to Israel's foes. There is a striking contrast between chapter 2, in which Jonah relies upon the steadfast love of God and celebrates God's grace which endures forever, and his impatience now when the same grace is shown to the Ninevites. In chapter 2 he had transformed a dirge into a cry of victory, but now his voice becomes again a lamentation. His triumph had been premature. It would have been better for him to per-ish in the sea than to be thus flouted, not so much in his honor as in his profound theological convictions. Deuteronomy 18 provides the backdrop for the tale here together with Jeremiah, who becomes a laughing stock when his predictions are not immediately realized, so that he too curses the day on which he was born (20:14).

As we mentioned in Chapter V, the problem of God's forgiveness of the wicked city was not settled in the minds of Jonah's readers. A late text, Tobit 14:4 says: "I believe the word of God upon Nineveh which Jonah spoke"; Tobit clearly expects the utter destruction of Nineveh as announced by Jonah (cf. Josephus, *Antiquities* 9.10.2 §214). Philo tries to assuage Jonah's sharp feelings in the following imagined dialogue between Jonah and God: "Thou mayest say, O prophet, . . . from My humiliation didst thou receive honor." "If thou art perturbed about the falseness of thy proclamation, thy accusation is against Me and not thee, O prophet. For thou preached not what thou wished but what thou received" (6, 41, 48).[12] Philo's reasoning is a bit too neat. In the words of Sullivan, ". . . anger, in either its mild or se-vere grades, is one of the most common masking operations for anxiety." [13] Indeed, Jonah's anger appears to him to be more pleasant (or "becoming") than anxiety before God's display of power. Jonah dares to say to God: "it is unfair; all this for nought?" All the humiliation and danger, the descent into the nether world, the guilt feelings, the victory over himself, the confronta-tion with the Ninevite crowds, was for an empty result. Nothing will really change Nineveh; it will continue to be evil as before; repentance is weak and blind. It is as if you would bet on a bad horse which, in time, will change into "a beast dreadful and terrible . . . it will devour and break in pieces and stamp the residue with its feet" (Dan. 7:7).

Jonah's indignation is precisely what prevents him from choking to death. Rather than explode with dissatisfaction and actually die (for which he expresses the wish on several occasions in this chapter) it is better that Jonah vent his anger, even if he risks being blasted by God's thunder. His strength lies in the fact that his life is no longer his most precious good. After his near suicide in chapter 1, Jonah displays here quite a healthy defiance of his inclination toward death; he expresses that which weighs down his heart. Jonah expresses his readiness to die in this chapter (vss. 3, 8), but this is not the result of a natural psychological tendency. He is not tempted by self-destruction, but he is anxious not to be vulnerable to the accusation of complicity with the one who hurts him. God has become his enemy and Jonah says so loud and clear. He also knows that he is up against an insurmountable obstacle. His foe is absolutely invincible both physically and spiritually. Even under the most horrible circumstances, in the death camps of Nazi Germany, some rare exceptional people still believed that "Thoughts are free." [14] But in the case of Jonah, even his ideas do not escape his divine torturer. Even what he thinks and believes cannot pass unnoticed by the one who has become his adversary. But Jonah refuses to resort to mimicking his jailer—as did some camp inmates who behaved and even dressed like the Nazi SS. His refusal falls in line with Job's attitude to his deceitful "friends," and to the God of systematic theology. Jonah will not be subdued or manipulated; rather, he will be either a free man or a martyr for the right cause.

Jonah's theology is not one-sided, however; he cannot be accused of believing in an authoritarian God who lacks the attributes of mercy and compassion. He proves this in one of the most terse and pointed summaries of the whole Bible (vs. 2). Such a creed derives from a longer list of God's attributes in Exodus 34. One can also refer to Psalm 103:8, Nahum 1:3, or Joel 2:13, where we find the exact wording of Jonah 4:2. Jonah simply *chooses* to call into question the exercise of divine mercy towards Nineveh. This, he thinks, is tantamount to warming a snake on one's breast.

The dramatic tension in the tale is enhanced by the necessity, on the part of the reader, of acknowledging that God has been "right" all along: first of all, for sending Jonah to Nineveh with an oracle of doom against the city, and second for forgiving it after it repents (see 4:11). But Jonah's reluctance to obey may be still more correct! Clearly, the prophet does not seek to protect himself, and we argued earlier that his flight is not cowardly. His attitude on the ship demonstrates that he is no petty weakling. His bold argument with God here leads in the same direction. As a rebel with a cause, selfish survival is the last thing he has in mind. On the contrary, if his understanding of justice implies that he must die, so be it! For if it is necessary to relinquish the very principle of a meaningful existence in order to live, why prolong life?

The question now becomes: What must prevail when there is a conflict between God's truth, so to speak, and one's fidelity to and love for one's martyred people; or between the demands of loving one's enemy, and the imperative not to betray one's own flesh and blood, not to "waste" it in the crematoria of Bergen-Belsen or Nineveh? Jonah, for one, chooses not to relinquish his humanity in blind obedience to a debasing command. He does the *only* thing that is left to a *free* person: he refuses and so puts his life on the line. This is, properly speaking, the virtue of disobedience. If he had made no objection to God's command, he would have become a puppet, a straw man, a "quisling," not a prophet. Paradoxically, it is only the disobedient Jonah who deserves our attention; perhaps only the disobedient Jonah is truly obedient. And perhaps God, from the outset, does not wish to be obeyed. God was certainly "right" to "have pity on Nineveh, that great city wherein are more than six score thousand persons that cannot discern between their right hand and their left hand, and also much cattle." But Jonah may be still more right to refuse to consider the Ninevites' crime against his people a trifling matter. What is at stake in the book of Jonah is not the clash between an omniscient and all-wise God on the one hand, and a narrow-minded, petty, chauvinistic Jew on the other. This would indeed offer little of interest. The true opposition exists between two conceptions of justice and grace. As said in Jonah 4:2, the prophet "knew (from the beginning) that [God is] a gracious God and compassionate, long-suffering, and abundant in mercy. . . . *Therefore* [he fled beforehand] unto Tarshish." Precisely *this* justice, *this* grace, and *this* mercy Jonah cannot condone. Is there to be justice, grace, and mercy for the *Deutsche Christen?* Long-suffering and compassion in behalf of Julius Eichmann? What about the children in Jerusalem who were permanently crippled, both physically and emotionally, at the hand of the Ninevites? Cyril of Alexandria (PG LXXI) was indeed inspired when he stated that Jonah was sent to Nineveh and not, for example, to Tyre in order to show that God is merciful even towards the *worst* of all sinners.[15]

Some "Fathers" of the Church found it convenient to depict Jonah as a stiff-necked representative of the Jewish people, who considered the concept of the redemption of Gentiles to be repulsive. Such vicious slander should only demonstrate that the Spirit does not always blow where one might expect. Similarly, all the German professors of the Aufklärung who advocated rationality in religion and saw in Jonah a symbol of Jewish fanaticism not only missed the point of the tale but revealed their own arrogance and parochial anti-Semitism. They also demonstrated that rationality does not necessarily make one intelligent!

Jonah's flight to Tarshish is no blot on his reputation. On the contrary, we love him because he fled; we admire him because he put his life on the line rather than make God an accomplice of murderers. The Christian scholar Rupert of Deutz (twelfth century) was right when he stated that Jonah refused to obey God out of piety to his people and that is why God was not very angry at Jonah. Long before him, the difference of interpretation between Origen (A.D. 185–254) and Jerome (A.D. 347–420) on this issue brings us directly to the point. Origen insisted upon the full pardon of the repentent sinner; the Devil himself will be converted in the end. Jerome reacted to this opinion with indignation, rhetorically asking whether ultimately there will be no difference between the Virgin Mary and a prostitute, between the Angel Gabriel and the Devil, between the martyrs and their torturers.

The question is a perennial one. The Rabbis dared to say that even the *yēṣer hārā'* (the evil inclination) could be redeemed. Furthermore, it was said by the Creator to be "very good" (cf. *Genesis Rabbah* 14.4). This attempt to shatter the stronghold of the "ideologists" of Jerusalem, is precisely the aim of the book of Jonah. But let us stress once again the point that their position is far from being ludicrous. It is, on the contrary, as noble as that of the author of Jonah, whose stance was picked up by Jewish mysticism: evil itself can and must be redeemed, not annihilated. Nor did St. Augustine conceive of a definition of evil from which the term "good" is absent. Evil is "amissio boni," "privatio boni," etc. But after Auschwitz, can one seriously and without offense affirm that evil is but the reverse of good? Where are the "sparks" of the Spirit amongst the SS of Dachau?

It remains that for the author of Jonah and for the party he represents, Nineveh must be warned about its wickedness, and perhaps in this way, be brought to repentance and salvation. True, Jonah-Israel must fulfill his vocation towards the nations (the prophet's feelings and convictions are not the ultimate criteria for what is right and wrong), but following Jeremiah, Jonah is entitled to complain: "O, Lord, Thou hast enticed me, and I was enticed, Thou has overcome me, and hast prevailed. I am become a laughing stock all the day, everyone mocketh me" (Jer. 20:7). But Jonah is not compelled to debase himself; until the end, he maintains his liberty as a human being and rebukes God for the justice that he considers to be nothing more than injustice. In so doing, Jonah is not so much envious of the Ninevites' salvation as he is jealous on behalf of the honor of his people and, through his people, the vindication of the *innocent*.

At least on one point, however, the "visionaries" and the "ideologists" of Jerusalem agree. Whether or not the "missionary" is reluctant, it is only from him that the nations can hear a word of God at all. It is indeed striking that the Ninevites, although they are both physically and spiritually the antipode of Israel, must receive God's words for them from the mouth of an Israelite! The indispensable mouthpiece of God is the vicar of God on earth. It is Jonah-Israel and no one else, who must be given the credit for the salvation of Nineveh. For without Jonah, Nineveh is like a Sodom or a Gomorrah, which nothing can save.[16]

From this standpoint at least, Jonah is not to be confused with a psychologist. From a psychological point of view, it would make no sense to have a Sicilian come to New York to counsel the inhabitants of the megalopolis. Similarly, no one other than a Ninevite knows the psyche of his fellow citizens and how to speak effectively to them. Genuine counseling must include many guarantees, such as commonality of language between advisor and advisee, empathy, and interpersonal qualities that will facilitate communication. According to Carl Rogers, there are at least six basic conditions that are necessary if positive personality change is to occur in the therapeutic process: warmth, permissiveness, acceptance, genuineness, internal frame of reference, and unconditional positive regard (respect).[17] Strikingly enough, *all* of these features are *absent* in Jonah's relations with the Ninevites![18]

In short, there are human phenomena that do not belong entirely in the realm of psychology, as for instance, love, God's calling, or the prophet's discourse. They can be approached but not exhausted by psychological analysis. It is certainly for this very reason that the Ninevites' conversion in Jonah 3—4 is so briefly presented. The singer of tales wants us to understand this occurrence as a "beyondness" that is irreducible to any human explanation.

Parallel to the irrationality of the Ninevites' unexpected repentance, Jonah's anger is also to some extent illogical. God asks him: "Does anger become you?" Does it open your eyes to the meaning of what is happening? (vss. 4, 9). The first time this question is raised by God (vs. 4) it remains unanswered. This is all the more unexpected since God is conversing directly with Jonah here for the first time in the tale. Jonah should be happy, especially since God appears moved, patient, and comforting; in short, God seems to understand the prophet. But on the other hand, it is not surprising that Jonah is abashed. The irony is that, although we might expect such a dialogue to take place in the Temple in Jerusalem, Jonah has fled from YHWH's presence precisely in order that God may *not* speak to him again!

Once more, Jonah breaks the contact. He detaches himself from the commerce that moves between God and the wicked city and from the fate of Nineveh, withdrawing "out of the city," where he leaves God—if God wishes to remain. Jonah stubbornly places himself "at the east of the city," which plays on the word *qēdēm*, which means "the east," but also "the past." Jonah looks at the city from the point of view of its past history, which constitutes an ongoing judgment against it. In so doing Jonah is on solid ground. He "sits," "he builds," "he waits"; the construction of the *sukkāh* ("cabin") is, from that perspective, quite remarkable. We shall come back to this point. Let us note here the process of "distantiation" of which Erikson has so aptly spoken:

> The counterpart of intimacy is *distantiation*: the readiness to repudiate, isolate, and, if necessary, destroy those forces and people whose essence seems dangerous to one's own . . . *isolation* . . . [is] the incapacity to take chances with one's identity by sharing [in] true intimacy . . . .[19]

It has often been felt by readers of Jonah that verse 5 is out of place here.

Already in 1900, H. Winckler[20] suggested a series of transpositions in the book, including the displacement of 4:5 to follow 3:4. Winckler's thesis has been accepted by many,[21] but there have been sound objections raised to the arbitrary character of such rearrangements. Rudolph questions why verse 5 was displaced if originally it had such a fitting position after 3:4. The German critic adopts the position of the Jewish medieval commentators Redaq and Ibn Ezra, who saw in this verse a flashback, so that the verbs stand in virtual pluperfect tense. Following Lohfink, Rudolph highlights "a well-known device" of the author—portraying the reaction to a phenomenon before describing the phenomenon itself (see 1:10; 3:5 the relationship of 1:2 to 4:2; 1:5b to 1:3).[22]

Prescinding from the question of the proper placement of verse 5, we find Jonah to be in a state of expectation before a complete reversal of the situation in verse 6. He does not answer the question of God (vs. 4), but it does not mean that he has given up. Only epic characters, Homeric characters, perform in an absolute "foreground" or "present." They "wake every morning as if it were the first day of their life," says Erich Auerbach.[23] Not so with Jonah, who may sense that the last day of his life is upon him or perhaps that it marks the first day of another existence into which he will be born.

It is fitting, therefore, for Jonah to watch the course of events. Perhaps, after all, God will again change his mind and destroy Nineveh (cf. Redaq). Jonah's attitude may even be construed as defiance of God's decision to spare the city. Nineveh's wickedness may prove stronger than God's leniency. The prophet therefore builds a *sukkāh*, which is reminiscent of the Exodus from Egypt when the Hebrews dwelt in booths in the desert (Lev. 23:43). Thus, Jonah insists upon two points: he considers Nineveh to be another Egypt, which he leaves behind to its own fate, and by the same token he reminds God of his covenant with Israel, which he chose from among all nations (Exod. 19:4–5; Deut. 10:14–15).

The *sukkāh*, we soon discover, is not functional but purely symbolic.[24] The word "shadow" in Hebrew, used here in vs. 5, often carries the metaphorical meaning of protection (cf. Ps. 121:5). It is the usefulness of the *sukkāh* that is questioned in the sequel of the narrative, so it makes sense that a plant grows up in order to offer Jonah its shade. The sun is at its zenith, and the *sukkāh* (with all it represents in terms of the covenant with Israel and of remembrance of the unconditional election of Israel) is shelter no longer. Perhaps there is even something significant in the fact that the text does not say that Jonah sits *inside* the *sukkāh* but only beneath it, maybe outside under one of its walls in the shadow it provides. Later Jonah is about to faint because of the heat, but he does not shelter himself within the *sukkāh* he has built. Jonah refuses to *use* the *sukkāh*, for it was not built for a profane pur-

pose. This brings to mind the refusal of the Hittite Uriah to sleep with his
wife when he was visiting with King David (2 Sam. 11:9–11). The parallel is
all the more striking in that the word *sukkāh* is used in Uriah's story also
(vs.11).

On the psychological level, Jonah's refusal to seek refuge in the *sukkāh*
is a stark contrast to his attitude in chapters 1 and 2, which present a re-
gressive incorporation into the ship's innermost parts (1:5) and into the
fish's belly (2:1). Jonah would rather choose the state of despair and loneliness than the pseudo-comfort of a motherly womb substitute. Here again
is a definite sign of Jonah's transformation since chapter 2; here again
Israel takes her distance from the myths and rituals of the "nations." A
quotation from Eliade regarding rites of initiation indicates the profound
difference of ethos:

> In many regions, there is a hut for initiations in the bush. It is there that young
> candidates undergo a part of their ordeals and are instructed in the secret tra-
> ditions of the tribe. And the initiation-cabin symbolizes the maternal womb.[25]

Will the prophet's reminder to God concerning his covenant with his
people be heeded? Will Jonah's silent reproach have any effect on YHWH?
God's pedagogy manifests itself in an intervention that is as indirect as that
of the sea storm and the monster in chapters 1 and 2: he allows a plant to
grow up over Jonah. Jonah reacts with contentment and joy. In this way,
God reaches him better than would have been possible with words (vs. 4);
indeed, he reaches him more effectively than ever before. There is an ironic
shift of focus here, as we move from the potential destruction of "myriads"
of people to the egotistic satisfaction of one individual inconvenienced by a
hot day. But there could be another dimension to the episode. Jonah may
express deep satisfaction for being taken care of by someone who shows that
he is sensitive to Jonah's *sukkāh* ("cabin") and that he *remembers* his covenant
with him and his people.[26]

If it is so, then God's response in appointing a *qîqāyôn* tree to shed its
shadow (vs. 6)—a permanent replacement of the temporary *sukkāh* and a
God-given protection rather than a shelter made by human hands (vs. 5)—is
equivalent to God's approbation and confirmation of Jonah's expectation.
Yes, God remembers his covenant with Israel, "so Jonah was exceeding glad
about the gourd." The reprieve falls in parallel with the great fish of chapter
2: God displays mercy for Jonah's sake, so that the latter's declaration in
verse 2 would now sound quite different. Jonah is freed from his anger as his
interest shifts from the city to a tree or rather from the problem of the presence of wickedness on the earth to the discovery of God's graciousness toward Israel.[27]

The *qîqāyôn* (gourd) appears only here in the entire Bible. One thinks,
on the basis of cognate Semitic languages, of the *ricinus communis* "which

grows rapidly, has widespreading branches and large leaves, and can reach a height of forty feet, though only an annual." [28] Just as the *sukkāh* was symbolic, the mention of *qîqāyôn* or *ricinus* suggests that we are dealing with a metaphor. And just as the *sukkāh* was used in the desert for cultic purposes and represents the mobile temple in the wilderness, so *ricinus* seems to allude to its final replacement by the permanent Temple in Jerusalem. It grows up over Jonah and offers a shelter that the *sukkāh* was unable to provide.[29]

It is thus all the more paradoxical and properly intolerable when the sign of permanence, the *qîqāyôn*, symbolizing the Temple in Jerusalem, is itself smitten by a worm that has also been appointed by God! The destruction of the Temple by the enemy of Israel is presented here, as elsewhere in the prophetic books, as being stirred up by God himself, who thus becomes the real author of such destruction (see Mic. 3:12; Jer. 26:18; 7:1–15). The people lose their protecting shelter and find themselves "naked" and exposed to a scorching "wind of the east."

We encounter a quite unexpected substitution here. Instead of Nineveh being destroyed, it is the *qîqāyôn* itself, which we identify with the Temple, that is smitten and "withers." [30] The *quid pro quo* is emphasized by God himself (vss. 10–11). The vicarious function of sacrifices in the Temple is well known, but now the Temple itself is sacrificed for the sake of none other than Nineveh! The author of Jonah brings his radical interpretation of the exile in Babylon to bear upon a comprehensive view of the Temple and beyond, of Israel in the world. Once again, the *setting in life* of the book of Jonah becomes clear: In the fifth century B.C.E., when the Temple was rebuilt and the hierocratic party in Jerusalem proclaimed the advent of the theocratic restoration as announced by the prophets, the author of Jonah gave proper acknowledgment to the phenomenon. But he also recalled a decisive dimension of exile that must not be lost in the process of restoring the cult in the Temple. The exile among foreign nations represented as well Israel's reaching out toward the confines of the earth, an opportunity given to the "Ninevites" of the whole world to repent and to live. While some in the Temple milieu (represented in the Bible by the school of the Chronicler) speculated upon the impending destruction of the nations and the vindication of the sole Judaean people, others (such as Second and Third Isaiah, Second Zechariah, Joel and the anonymous authors of Ruth and Jonah) had a vision of the eschatological conversion of the non-Jews and of their coming to Jerusalem to adore Israel's God (see Isa. 55:3–5; 66; Zech. 14; etc.). In their views, the conservative party in Jerusalem was wrong since it led the people astray in the name of a reality that was only "penultimate" (the particular) and smothered that which was authentically "ultimate" (the universal). For in fact, there is no fulfillment of history in isolation from the world. If there is a lesson to be drawn from the exile in Babylon, it is that the "world

out there" must somehow be brought "in here," first into the consciousness
of Israel but ultimately into the geographical and historical, the spatial and
temporal, center of the universe.[31] It is precisely in order to avoid acknowledging this that Jonah builds a *sukkāh*, a dwelling place whose symbolism is
stressed all the more in that Jonah refuses to use it as a home, i.e., as a prag-
matic, functional object. As Eliade and others "read" the symbol of the
house, it is a private and impregnable world; but since it is in fact destructi-
ble and the indweller knows this in his heart, the house also carries with it an
expectation of destruction, *thanatos*.[32]

This inner-personal symbolism sends us back to the character Jonah and
his "fantasies." [33] We are not surprised to find him wishing again that he
were dead (vs. 8). The reason given (because the sun is too hot on his head)
would be a grotesque twist, unworthy of the genius of Jonah's author, were
it not clearly a practical joke wrought by God in order to teach a lesson to a
man who has been embittered by a much more deeply disturbing
experience.[34]

Note that Jonah leaves the protection of the city homes and, as a consequence, finds it necessary to build a substitute, a *sukkāh*. When this provi-
sional shelter becomes insufficient—while the Ninevites are comfortable
under their own roofs—Jonah understands that God has taken sides, as it
were, with the Gentiles and left his prophet to himself. So, Jonah's "pity" is
of course not for a tree "that grows up in one night and is gone in one night,"
but for himself.[35] The *ricinus*, says Cohn, is the being of Jonah. He pities
himself through a projection. But the Israelo-Dutch critic is probably wrong
when he reads the symbolism of the shriveled gourd as meaning that human
life is unexpected grace, like the growth of a plant. Just as Jonah cannot live
without the *ricinus*, so he cannot live without mercy, but he reacts to God's
dealing with the Ninevites (vss. 10–11). As Landes puts it:

> He does not object to the divine compassion and salvation directed to those
> like himself, but when it is also effective for the wicked, he cannot abide it.[36]

If at this point we adopt A. J. Greimas' observation that "the structure of
narrative consists of a breach of contract and eventual restoration of contract," [37] then the "breach of contract" is to be understood as the withering
of the *qîqāyôn* and with it the destruction of the Temple, the martyrdom of
Israel. As for the "restoration of the contract," the narrative—faithful to its
literary genre being closely related to the parable and its "subversion of the
world" [38]—brings this about in the salvation of . . . Nineveh!

As with a parable, there is present here a collision of the "structure of
hearer expectation" with the "structure of speaker expression," as Crossan
says. If we call (A) the former, and (B) the latter, we have the following
tableau:

"Structure of hearer expectation" (A):

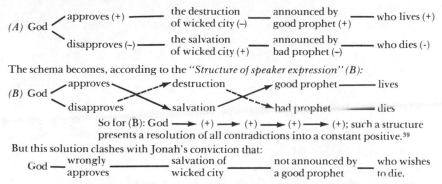

(A) God
- approves (+) —— the destruction of wicked city (–) —— announced by good prophet (+) —— who lives (+)
- disapproves (–) —— the salvation of wicked city (+) —— announced by bad prophet (–) —— who dies (-)

The schema becomes, according to the *"Structure of speaker expression" (B):*

(B) God
- approves ⟶ destruction ⟶ good prophet —— lives
- disapproves ⟶ salvation ⟶ bad prophet —— dies

So for (B): God ⟶ (+) ⟶ (+) ⟶ (+) ⟶ (+); such a structure presents a resolution of all contradictions into a constant positive.[39]

But this solution clashes with Jonah's conviction that:

God —— wrongly approves —— salvation of wicked city —— not announced by a good prophet —— who wishes to die.

Hence: God ⟶ (–) ⟶ (–) ⟶ (–) ⟶ (–); in short, the resolution of all contradictions as proposed by (B) puts each term of the structure in the negative and thus reflects negatively upon God.

The exploration of further contrasting "structures" (of expression vs. expectation) will allow us, at this point, to indicate the far-reaching and pioneering role of the book of Jonah in the development of Israel's reflections and modes of discourse. For this purpose, however, we must first go back to retrieve the motif of the "forty days" delay of the destruction of Nineveh. As we said above, "forty" is the number that accompanies a *test* in the Bible (forty days and nights of the flood; forty years in the desert; forty days of Jesus' temptations; etc.). But the outcome of the test for Israel is the antipode of its outcome for the "nations": the inheritance of *Eretz Israel* (or God's appointment to a messianic mission) on the one hand, and the utter destruction of the sinful universe on the other (cf. Exod. 24:18; 34:28; 1 Kings 19:8 vs. Gen. 7:4; Ezek. 29:11–13; and, of course, Jon. 3:4).

Now, if again we adopt Crossan's provocative schema, we will have something like the following:

(a) when the test that is symbolized by the number forty is applied to the people of God, one can expect a newness of life as its outcome;

(b) when the test is applied to the nations it provokes their doom;

(c) hence, if the syllogism is reversed as far as the nations are concerned—if they repent and are thus saved, and go into newness of life, instead of being destroyed in the process,

(d) there is at least logically the possibility that the same test applied to Israel would bring about her doom.

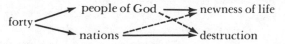

forty
- people of God ⟶ newness of life
- nations ⟶ destruction

Now such a conception of the structural reversibility of terms, introduced by a pioneer like Ezekiel (cf. 29:13f., Egypt is restored, although "diminished," i.e., unthreatening to Israel), inaugurates a logic which is found rather in the apocalyptic than the prophetic understanding of history. The prophetic view of history is teleological. It is *history* that brings about the unexpected (also in Ezekiel). The proclamation "yet forty days and X will be destroyed" means, in fact, for the prophets: as history is now oriented, or rather disoriented by human sinfulness, it is headed straight for catastrophe. Therefore, it is necessary to repent and so, reorient the course of history toward its redemption.

This is not the case in apocalyptic literature. The time for reorientation is over. It is now too late. The chips are down. After a protracted delay granted by God, history comes to its conclusion: the wicked will utterly and irremediably be destroyed by divine justice. Whereas in prophetic literature, "forty days" is the sign of the delay of grace, of the extravagance of God who still counts on the impossible possibility of humanity's turning about, in apocalyptic language on the contrary "forty days" means that by divine computation, the eschatological event will come at that time no matter what, bringing the destruction of the barbarians and the salvation of the People of God. True, the accent is on redemption, not on destruction, but it is acknowledged that the latter precedes the former.

A summary is not superfluous at this point.

1. In pre-exilic prophecy, there is introduced a logical pattern in which the "structure of hearer expectation" and the "structure of speaker expression" coincide. For instance, the forty days (years) test applied to Israel brings about repentance and restoration. Applied to a nation, the test brings about hardening of heart and condemnation.

2. In Ezekiel, the pattern is subverted so that the forty days test applied to Egypt brings about its restoration; a conception which, on the logical plane, introduces the possibility that the same test applied to Israel has not as an automatic outcome her conversion and restoration. On both ends, the possibilities remain open. A nation *may* go through the test and be restored; Israel *may* not pass the test and get "flunked" (cf. especially Ezek. 33).

3. The apocalyptic hardens the terms of the structure. "Forty days" represents the divine computation which cannot be altered (as it was before by human repentance, cf. Jer. 18:7 –10; 42:9 –10; Exod. 32:12 –14). *But* now those who are tested are (notorious) righteous and (notorious) wicked (the final judgment will only confirm their belonging to those polarized categories). The latter have replaced Israel and Egypt, although those historical realities are not foreign to the apocalyptist's argument. It is clear that the "people of the saints" of Daniel 7 (vs. 27) are recruited from among Israelites, but at least theoretically the new designation of the group by the apocalypse is more inclusive.

Structurally speaking, apocalyptic returns to a "structure of hearer expectation": the good are rewarded and the wicked are punished. This is made possible because again the message is addressed directly and exclusively to the "saints"—the apocalyptic language proves it. It makes no difference whether Antiochus IV Epiphanes hears it or not; his utter destruction is decreed by God.

4. Where is Jonah situated in this process? In the book of Jonah, something highly unusual occurs: the message is addressed not to Israel but to a foreign nation. Or rather, if we bring the classic prophecies against foreign nations to bear here, it is the first time ever in the Prime Testament that a message which is indirectly destined for Israel, is directed to Nineveh, whereas the classical prophets directly addressed oracles to Israel which were indirectly addressed to Tyre or to Edom.

In other words, if Jonah is not yet apocalyptic—the socio-religious groups contrasted are classically Israel (in the person of Jonah) and the Ninevites—the stage represented by Ezekiel's logic is however very much a *fait accompli*. The readers of Jonah are familiar with it, and the author wants them now to make a further step forward in a direction which, eventually, will lead to the apocalyptic universalistic categories of the "saints" and the "beasts."

Thus, only a *parable* was able to do, i.e., the literary genre which "subverts the world" and primarily the "structure of hearer expectation." Only a parable could push further the Ezekielian logics. Ezekiel proclaimed the open-endedness of God's scheme—hence of the historical future—*to Israel in exile*, for the comfort of those who had given up all hope to be again "God's People." The implication was the "diminution of Egypt" (and also its peace in participation with the one of Israel, like the little dogs of the Gospel eat the children's crumbs from under the table).

The storyteller in his turn makes us leave behind the Ezekielian speculation, and takes us into a heuristic (and subversive) fantasy. The roles are redistributed, all three of them: Israel or the people in exile; the "Egyptians" or the nations; Ezekiel or the prophet. Now "Israel" will be played by Nineveh, and "Ezekiel" by Jonah. There is no way to escape the conclusion that "the nations" are now played by Israel! If only for the staggering fact that in Jonah's book Israel is astonishingly and shockingly absent, it is clear that we are authorized to see in this unparalleled feature the indication that something utterly unusual is going on, and that far-reaching conclusions must be drawn. The parable has subverted Ezekiel's thinking.

We thus conclude that the book of Jonah occupies a position which mediates *logically* between prophecy and apocalyptic. That this logical mediation be also a chronological development is not thus warranted, were it not for the fact that chronologically and ideologically Jonah is situated between

Ezekiel and Daniel. The Ezekielian rigorous terms of demonstration (3:17 ff.; 33:1 ff.) are submitted to a daring twist. The oracle is proclaimed directly to Nineveh, and only indirectly to Jerusalem. Moreover, the doom is transformed, via repentance, into salvation. This implies that in the same circumstances the terms of the syllogism could be reversed as far as Israel is concerned, thus bringing her not necessarily to penance but perhaps to destruction.

The road is now open towards a reinterpretation of "Israel" and of "the nations." Prophecy is subverted by Jonah in a way which we may perhaps graphically render thus:

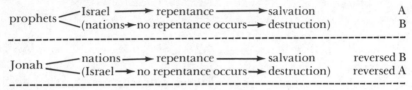

The classical categories burst open. In Jerusalem the theocratic party's ideology rests on shaky grounds. It is not enough to be Jews, to dwell in the holy city and to visit the Temple. Their splendid isolationism is sheer arrogance and dangerous delusion. They think that *"les jeux sont faits"* and the roles are forever allotted to all the actors. It is not so; among David's ancestors there may be a Ruth the Moabite, among the righteous a Job the Edomite; among the penitents the city of Nineveh—*per contra*, it may happen that Judah and Jerusalem become adversaries (Zech. 12)!

It is thus the universal history which must be considered. The stage for the *Heilsgeschichte* is not only the precinct of the Temple, it is the whole world. God's hand is visible at Nineveh or on the walls of Belshazzar's palace. "Among the inhabitants of the earth, none can stay his hand" says Nebuchadnezzar (Dan. 4:35). As for the end of time, it is still to come; it must not be confused with the Temple's restoration (whatever this latter event may mean for the former). God has not once and for all cast out the nations into outer darkness. He still appoints prophets to address the Ninevites, and visionaries to "unriddle the riddles" of history for the Babylonian kings. God still has pity on those "that cannot discern between their right hand and their left hand." All is still unaccomplished and the ending is still unfathomable. It might even take the form of all the nations coming to worship the King, the Lord of Hosts, and keep the feast of Sukkot.

It is only at face value paradoxical that apocalyptic would some time close the open-endedness maintained by Jonah (and the party of opposition in Jerusalem). For it had not been their contention that the End would never come; only that it *had* not. In order for the temporality attached to apocalyptic vision to be proposed, further steps had first to be made in terms of transforming the categories "Israel" and "Nineveh." It remains that the process was put in motion by Ezekiel and that the movement thus initiated picked up with Jonah that taut parable in the garb of a naive story.

Jonah however is not yet apocalyptic. It does not adopt the clear-cut polarized vision of the book of Daniel or 1 Enoch. The prophet is clearly ambivalent. He affected to believe that his oracle was an irrevocable description of the imminent future, which only appeased his scruples vis-à-vis his people, and made him go to Nineveh. But in the depth of his heart, he already "knew" that this was not the final word of God, even to the heathens. From this perspective, Jonah's declaration "I knew that thou art a gracious God" (4:2) is exactly what it sounds like—a censure. There is "a time to love, and a time to hate; a time for war, and a time for peace" (Qoh. 3:8). But if God himself "thinks about changing the times and the Law" (Dan. 7:25), how can life still be possible in this world? (cf. vs. 3). If the grace of God works "in time and out of time" (cf. 2 Tim. 4:2), that sounds good enough. But can it be a motive for parents' joy when the one who raped their little girl is set free by the court in the name of clemency? Is Jonah's cry so unexpected? Is not his sense of justice more understandable and sound, yea, more *just* than the court's? Is it really a tenable argument when the judge rejoins that the rapist is also a human being and that, moreover, he is such a brute that he "cannot discern between his right hand and his left hand," and that he spent all of his life with "much cattle"?

"Now O Lord take, I beseech thee, my life from me; for it is better for me to die than to live" (vss. 3, 8). This prayer of Jonah is not without parallel. Moses too said, "Blot me out of thy book which thou hast written" (Exod. 32:32). But the model of 1 Kings 19, which portrays Elijah's flight to Horeb, is even more striking. In 1 Kings 19:4 Elijah sits under a broom tree (cf. Jon. 4:6) and asks God to grant his request to die. There is, however, in both cases a reprieve: in Elijah's case, by means of an angel (vss. 5-8a), and in Jonah's by means of the *qîqāyôn* tree (vs. 6). The symbolism of "forty" appears in 1 Kings 19:8b as well as in Jonah 3.

But Jonah departs from the model at several points.

(1) Elijah initially desires death but is so much comforted and strengthened that he walks for forty days and forty nights to Horeb. As for Jonah, his desire to die is met only with a divine question that does not seem to resolve Jonah's problem any more than it answers Job's questions in the book that bears his name. Similarly, there is no direct parallel with Elijah to Jonah's *building* a booth, *sukkāh;* but Elijah is on mount Horeb in a *cave* at the place of the *Urtheophanie* while Jonah is in Nineveh and therefore needs a *sukkāh* as a substitute for the Temple (see above).

(2) There is an interesting distinction between Elijah's condemnation of

Israel, a charge that isolates him from the people, and Jonah's condemnation of *Nineveh*, although this also isolates him from the condemned; he goes out of the city and sits on the east side of the city till he might see what becomes of the city (vs. 5). As for Elijah, he journeys to the Sinai desert.

(3) The repeated question of God "does anger become you?" (vss. 4, 9) makes more sense when it is compared with the dialogue between God and Elijah. In 1 Kings 19:9, 13, God asks (also twice) the prophet: "What are you doing here, Elijah?" Elijah answers (vs. 10): "I have been very jealous for the Lord." Here also Elijah casts his shadow on the book of Jonah. As we insisted above, Jonah's attitude is also to be understood as "jealousy for the Lord." What looks at first glance like selfishness on the part of the prophet is in fact defense of God's honor. Is a God who changes his mind and "repents" still credible? Is a justice that lends itself to subjective interpretation still justice?[40]

Elijah was tired of relating to such a God. Jonah, in turn, is tired of dialoguing with someone so unpredictable. Each time that one believes that God is here, he is in fact elsewhere. Is he in the whirlwind, in the earthquake, in the sea storm, in the fish's belly, in the fire, in the breeze? Elijah and Jonah come to believe that God is not in the thundering, destructive wind, but in a "tenuous silence" (1 Kings 19:12). Both also experience the meaning of that silence to be a question: "What are you doing here, Elijah?" "Does anger become you Jonah?" The fact that the question is asked twice should be sufficient reason to reject the suggestion of some critics that verse 4 is an intrusion (because there is no answer from Jonah). The answer is delayed until the question is repeated, because until then all has not yet been said. We are just entering "the situation of being-looked-at-by-God" whose meaning, according to Paul Ricoeur, is not debasing because "the primordial sense of this look is that it establishes the *truth* of my situation, the rightness and justice of the ethical judgment on my existence. That is why that look, far from thwarting the birth of the self, stirs the self's consciousness . . . I want to know myself as I am known (Ps. 139:23 –24)."[41]

All along, nature has played a surprisingly important role in the narrative. Descriptions of places and natural phenomena abound: Joppa, Tarshish, Nineveh, the ship, the sea, the fish, the "great city," the *sukkāh*, the gourd, etc. Cohn is right when he insists upon their dynamic role in the narrative. God "appoints" storm, fish, and wind; the sea is stormy; the city is a three-day journey across, the gourd grows and dies. All are dependent upon God's word, as Jonah himself should be (2:1, 11; 3:3; 4:6, 7).[42] This, by the way, explains the use of "Elohim" on several occasions where "YHWH" might have been expected (cf. vs. 6). Rudolph, with reference to verses 7 –9, says that the shift from "YHWH" to "Elohim" underlines the unfathomable character of the God who rules nature ("deus absconditus").[43] God's sovereignty over nature is emphasized, as we said, by the divine appointment of the natural phenomena (in Jonah 4 only, vss. 6, 7, 8). It is also from this perspective that we must understand a seemingly "neutral" expression such as "when the morning rose" (vs. 7; note once more the dynamism). Ferdinand Hitzig draws a parallel at this point, again with Genesis 19 (see vss. 15, 23). Just as Lot flees at dawn before Sodom and Gomorrah are "overthrown," so Jonah expects the destruction of Nineveh at dawn. In fact, it is not Nineveh but the gourd that withers away. There is thus a distinct *historical* dimension to an expression which, at face value, is descriptive only of nature.[44]

Another example is provided by the term *ḥărîšît* (vs. 8), but this takes us onto uncertain ground. That the text should not be emended is now proven by its occurrence in Qumran (1QH 7:5), but its meaning creates a problem. The LXX and the Syriac have "burning"; the Vulgate says "hot and burning." These versions probably saw in the word the same root that is present in *ḥereš* "sun." But the Targum is interesting in that it reads "quiet" (sultry?), for *ḥrš* "to be silent." We would then, once again, have an allusion to the parallel text of 1 Kings 19:12, namely, the crucial element of "tenuous silence." In short, here again a natural phenomenon carries an *historical* (theophanic) meaning.

A third curiosity in the vocabulary of these last verses of Jonah will now take our attention. We recall that Job had been addressed by God in such a way that he was invited to share in the divine perspective (38:4 ff). In Jonah also a verb has both God and Jonah as subject. In verses 10 and 11 *ḥws* ("to have pity," "to show concern") indicates an arbitrary action. It appears here for the first time in Jonah (in parallel with Joel 2:17; Jer. 21:7; and Ps. 72:13) in connection with terms of compassion and salvation. Jonah "pitied" the gourd; YHWH "pities" Nineveh. Evidently, the meaning of the word here has to do with looking at someone or something with indulgence. As far as Nineveh is concerned, the image is clear. In the case of the gourd, however, we must understand that Jonah looks with indulgence at himself, the *ricinus* being a projection of his person (see above). But the symbolism of the *qîqāyôn* is not exhausted; it is also a metaphor for the Temple. It is thus indicated to Jonah and the ideologists in Jerusalem that it is indeed an intolerable misconception to weep over a destroyed Temple, when this blinds the mourners to the fate of the world out there writhing in the pangs or torture. "You have pity on the gourd . . . which came up in a night, and perished in a night; and should I not have pity on Nineveh the great city wherein are more than 120 thousand people who do not know their right hand from their left, and also much cattle?!" (vss. 10, 11).

As Heschel writes:

> God's answer to Jonah, stressing the supremacy of compassion, upsets the possibility of looking for a rational coherence of God's ways with the world.

> History would be more intelligible if God's word were the last word, final and
> unambiguous like a dogma or an unconditional decree. . . . Yet, beyond jus-
> tice and anger lies the mystery of compassion.[45]

From the prophet's own person or from internal, isolated concerns and
pride, the author wants to shift the attention of his contemporaries to the
world and its sufferings. When all arguments are exhausted in the theological debate, what ultimately remains is love. The mistake of Job's friends, or
of the theocratists, comtemporaries of Jonah's author, consists not of a
weakness in their theological dialectics but of a lack of love. God himself is
the first one who causes love to triumph over everything else, even his justice. This truth, which is so often and so forcefully stressed in Rabbinic Judaism, stands at the heart of the message of Jonah. "Nowhere in the Hebrew
Bible, writes S. H. Blank, do the 'person-hood' of God and his entangle-
ment in the human situation stand more clearly revealed."[46]

At the basis of love, which thus prevails over all else, lies an immense
compassion for the inadequacy of humanity. Nineveh is a city of "a dozen
myriads" of people (as Rudolph renders the text of vs. 11) "that cannot discern between their right hand and their left hand."

This latter motif has stirred much discussion. Are we to understand this
literally, as do the Bible of the French Rabbinate, the *Jerusalem Bible*, the *Interpreter's Bible*, the ATD (Weiser), the ICC (Bewer), and already Jerome,
whose commentary is: "little children and simple people whom you (Jonah)
certainly will not be able to prove to be sinners" ? [47] Or should we see in
"right" and "left" symbols of good and evil as do Parrot, Vischer, Ellul, and
the TOB? However, texts such as Deuteronomy 5:29 (32) and Joshua 1:7
do not seem to confirm the latter understanding, at least not exclusively. It is
clear that the heathens are described as boors in comparison with Israel. It is,
we think, the same conception that is expressed in Amos 3:2: "you only have
I known of all the families of the earth, therefore, I will visit upon you all
your iniquities." The nations are not guilty in the same sense as Israel can be
called guilty, for, in comparison with the latter, the former are only children
or ignoramuses. God therefore refrains from "visiting upon them all their
iniquities."

In the same vein, the connection in the text with "much cattle" prompts
Rudolph to comment "the people of Nineveh are as guiltless as the animals
that would be drawn into the catastrophe." [48] But Martin,[49] it seems to us,
has expressed the idea of this verse perfectly: "They might be adult in years,
but in character they were children—willful, passionate, perishing without
vision yet not without value . . . undisciplined and overgrown children yet
also the work of God's hands." Yes, there is inadequacy on the part of the
Ninevites but also on the part of Jonah, who felt sorry for himself (or about

an external sign of election and pride) but remained indifferent to the suffering and the "perishing without vision" of myriads of human beings, even feeling irritation at God's concern for them.[50]

> Jonah is being confronted with the inappropriate *quantity* of his anger. This leads eventually to the inappropriate quality of his anger, which is pointed out by the comparison between Jonah's pity for the plant and God's pity for Nineveh.[51]

Such is the end of the book, i.e., *open*-ended. In the words of Bickerman, ". . . we are left to believe that the Lord's rebuke convinced Jonah of his second error just as the episode of the sea monster had shown him the uselessness of his flight."[52] But one may wonder whether Bickerman's opinion is correct. It seems, on the contrary, that it is one of the important features of the book that it does *not* bring the plot to a veritable end. Is Jonah convinced? Or is he not? Perhaps the story has returned full circle to its beginning and the hero will have to go through many more expansive experiences in order to understand God's will. There will be, perhaps, another ship and another sea monster. Or perhaps there will be neither ship nor "helping animal," and the prophet, having no second chance, will sink pitifully to the bottom of the sea and into oblivion. For no form of victory is sufficient guarantee for future triumph.

It is appropriate that the author of Jonah leaves his story open-ended. Those for whom he has told his tale in the first place are themselves left with the uncomfortable necessity of creating a proper end for Jonah's story. No two ends will be alike. As Dostoyevsky wrote in the conclusion of his novel *Crime and Punishment*, ". . . .this is another story." It is a story which Dostoyevsky does not even presume to tell because it is beyond all expression and so personal to each respondent that it would be of no avail to try to generalize it.

Significantly, R. David Qimhi (Redaq) proposed in the Middle Ages that the abrupt ending of the tale is owing to the loss of a book about Jonah! Bickerman's rejoinder to this speculation is to the point: "Yet the biblical story is not about a prophet but about an unfulfilled prophecy." [53]

We should rather go beyond our uneasiness and be grateful for the missing conclusion of the book, if only because all ethical principles are overrun at this point. There is no more nobility in Jonah's being either convinced or unconvinced. God is right, and Jonah is right, although their respective stances are mutually exclusive. Who can decide between them? [54] Voicing doubt as to God's justice and equanimity may appear more "Jewish," and pleading for it more "Christian." Perhaps the book of Jonah takes us to the very heart of the Jewish-Christian problem.[55] If so, we must, like the author of the biblical book, leave the narrative without a conclusion. Jonah-Israel

does not surrender to the theological rationality of an argument that will sat-
isfy the mind in general while it is nothing other than a slap in the face of the
victim in particular. Is this to say that the particular smothers the general?
Does the tree hide the forest? On the other hand, does the admonition to
"turn and offer your other cheek" (Matt. 5:39) also mean it is not true that
"after Auschwitz the Jew has received the commandment to survive"
(Fackenheim)? Both are true. They must accompany one another until the
end of this eon. And even then, one will not prevail over the other, but they
will be reconciled like Hillel and Shammai, the rival Rabbis of the first century C.E., who when they died—according to the Talmud—looked like
twins.

Chapter VII

THE
CALL
TO
AUTHENTICITY
Listening to
the Outer Voice

[Love and conscience are the two] most striking manifestations of ... the capacity of self-transcendence. Man transcends himself either toward another human being or toward meaning. Love, I would say, is that capacity which enables him to grasp the other human being in his very uniqueness. Conscience is that capacity which empowers him to seize the meaning of a situation in its very uniqueness ....

—Viktor Frankl, *The Will to Meaning*
(New York: New American Library, 1969), pp. 18-19.

Jonah's vocation, like that of anyone else, is strictly personal. The masses of Israel are not under the commandment to move to Nineveh and to proclaim the message of God to the wicked city. But paradoxically, the particularism of the vocation does not exclude its universalism; on the contrary it grounds it. Particular in its recipient (here, Jonah), the vocation is universal in its giver, i.e., God. It participates in the absoluteness of the one who commands and thus is definitely "ethical" from a biblical point of view. In the Bible, ethics is founded on the authority of the one who issues the order. The book of Jonah does not constitute an exception to the rule. If, ultimately, Jonah goes to Nineveh despite his inner resistance to the idea of delivering a message to the archenemies of Israel, it is because of the authority of the command-giver. Jonah, without the commandment of the "outer voice" is deprived of his singularity. For no one can be said truly to exist without the commandment that is addressed to that person. What this means is that "Man is a gerundive," in the words of Van der Lieeuw. Man is not; rather, he becomes.[1] Man is his own project. Jonah's feeling of guilt stems, in fact, from his reluctance to leave the motherly womb. He suddenly realizes that we must give birth to ourselves. The first birth must be followed by a rebirth.

One could perhaps characterize the "first" birth as being-for-oneself, and the "second" birth as being-for-the-world. Those who are not "reborn" have no world; they are like stars lost in the immensity of a universe without beginning and without end. As long as Jonah does not respond to his vocation to have a world (even though it be Nineveh), he is but a ship tossed aimlessly, moving in all directions and in no direction. Only death, as the negation of all movements, can put an end to such a groundless and meaningless movement. Death then is the clearest manifestation of what has been

Jonah's condition from the beginning. Even before he started to live, at his "first" birth, such a "Jonah" was dead, i.e., soulless, "not-Jonah," just as the prophet Hosea says that Israel, in forfeiting her vocation, becomes "Not-My-People."

There is, as a matter of fact, a personal project that constitutes the very essence of the individual being. This is precisely why individuals are who they are and no one else. This uniqueness is alternatively called soul, individuality, personality, or (and this is what we are dealing with in relation to Jonah) the response to a *vocation*. Whatever name is given to this particularity, it is the very foundation of our authenticity. In other words, one is one's task; one's being lies in the decision to accept or to refuse one's vocation. All the rejoinders that attempt to explain "vocation" in terms of environment or biological contingency are choices in themselves. Speculation as to what would result from a situation in which a child is left without directive and stimulus from society and environment is an exercise in futility.

Even the genes can be understood as "invitations" to the being; they are not so much determinative of one's future as they are the parameters of an infinite range of possible options. The motherly womb is a given milieu to which also there are an infinite number of responses. Similarly, our race, skin color, sex, IQ, emotional and rational capabilities, nervous balance or imbalance, are so many "invitations" to respond. Our entire life is response.[2] All existence is interpretation; there exists both that which demands interpretation and the one who must interpret. What lies in between is the process of interpreting. "What do you see, Jeremiah?" . . . "I see a branch of an almond tree." . . . "You have seen well, for I watch over my word to perform it" (Jer. 1:12). Without Jeremiah's interpretation, the almond tree remains a message unheard and vain. Conversely, it is totally impossible to interpret a voiceless abstraction. But it is in Jeremiah's *encounter* with his milieu (here the almond tree) that something happens which is, indeed, a mutual creation.

Furthermore, an almond tree is such for anyone. No one needs to be Jeremiah in order to see it, but only Jeremiah sees it in the *way* that he sees it, so that the almond branch *becomes* different from what it is for anyone else and in fact, becomes for the first time, the almond branch that it strove to be from the beginning! As Lacordaire said: "Everyone looks at what I look at, but no one sees what I see."[3] In the words of Frankl, Jeremiah

> . . . is a particular individual with his unique personal characteristics who experiences a unique historical context in a world which has special opportunities and obligations reserved for him alone.[4]

And the Viennese psychoanalyst adds:

Thus, the ultimate meaning is no longer a matter of intellectual cognition [an almond tree] but of existential commitment. ["You have seen well, for . . ."] One might as well say that a meaning can be understood, but that the ultimate meaning must be interpreted. An interpretation, however, involves a decision.[5]

So, to say that one *is* one's choice or that there is in each of us a vocation that we have chosen from the time of our conception does not make us solipsistic beings who perform our tasks independent of environment and society. Conceived *through* and *by* communication (parental union), we are born *for* communication and are, from the outset, in constant communication with someone who is not us, although for a while we are in symbiosis with her (mother).[6] The call to communication has a character of life-giving creativity which inspired the imagination of Israel's sages. "And Adam called his wife's name Eve (*ḥawwāh*) because she was the mother of all living (*ḥay = ḥaw*)" (Gen. 3:20). This positive feature is not determined, however, for a person can at will negate that which was meant to be "good" by the creator of life. This is true physically as well as spiritually or ethically.[7]

On this ground, oriented as it was toward the historical becoming of humanity, Israel proclaimed that our common vocation as human beings, as "selves" or, if you will, as "souls" (Gen. 2:7) expresses itself specifically in a common kingship, priesthood and prophecy (Exod. 19:6 etc.). "The light enlightens everyone" (John 1:9), and everyone has a Word to say that is indispensable in the discourse of historical humanity. All are called to prophecy, but as each one is a unique person with a unique choice expressed in a unique voice each also fulfills one's vocation in a unique and irreplaceable way. This is why, when a "prophet of prophets" arises, that one is immediately understandable by all, because the prophet speaks to potential or actual prophets. In contrast, if Martians were to "speak" to us, they would probably be utterly unintelligible because we have no participation in "Martianism." As Andras Angyal has said:

A poem written in a language that no one can read does not exist as a poem. Neither do we exist in a human sense until someone decodes us. A man in the most crucial way is a symbol, a message that comes to life only by being understood, acknowledged by someone . . . .[8]

Thus, the calling is not devised by persons in order to inflate themselves with importance; rather, it is *detected*. Israel, throughout history, has said that there lies in the background of a person (be it social, racial, economical, psychological, theological, physical, or emotional) *one call* only (among millions), which is destined for that person and that person alone.[9] Israel has taken the strong position that the calling, that which actually makes someone a *person* ("but a little lower than God" himself, and "crowned with glory and honor"; see Ps. 8:6), comes from God, from the Ground of Being (Tillich). This is another although much deeper way to state that a person is a being-in-communication. Theology seeks to disclose the ultimate meaning and import in the metaphysical realm of what modern psychology rediscovers today about human beings on the phenomenological level. For the encounter with God of which Israel speaks is nothing other than the authentic encounter with "the other," which in psychological terms makes one fully human. In the words of Alfred Adler,

> . . . the individual as a complete being cannot be dragged out of his connection with life—perhaps it would be better to say, with the community.[10]

That is why the question here is *not* so much what the person expects from the community but what the community expects from the person, not so much what the person expects from life but what life expects from the person.[11]

As beings-in-communication persons must, by the necessity of their creaturely nature, choose from among many possible alternatives the one(s) which is (are) creative in the richest meaning of the word. Life itself is such a constant selection because in this way people transcend animalhood and take control of their destiny. This is also what Fromm means when he writes about one's need for transcendence (on this, see also below). Roberto Assagioli writes:

> . . . to "decide" very often means to *choose;* that is, a selection must be made from among various possibilities. But to choose implies to *prefer;* and to prefer some one thing, one action, one way, necessarily demands the discarding or eliminating of others . . . . an important criterion in choosing is to foresee in the clearest possible manner what *effects* the choice will have: not only the immediate but also the long-term ones, since the latter can turn out to be different from, and indeed opposite to, the former . . . . The act of will and intention then involves a decision to accept or not accept an impulse. Authenticity does not consist in giving in to a bad motive simply because it exists.[12]

This contrasts with what Maslow wrote in 1968: "the only way we can ever know what is right for us is that it feels better subjectively than any alternative"; and again: "what tastes good is also, in the growth sense, 'better' for us."[13] No position has been more damaging to modern society. The terms "feel" and "subjectively" as criteria for "growth" are especially deceiving. It is simply contrary to truth that one "grows" by choosing "what tastes good." In many cases the opposite is true. If the Jew Abraham Maslow were right in this, there would have been no Israel in human history. For "Israel" is precisely the name given to those who, like Abraham, prefer to leave "their own country, kindred, their own father's house" in the pursuit of an "impossible dream." Psychologically speaking, the least one can say about a patriarch Abraham who chooses to stay in Ur in Chaldea for the reason that it "feels better" is that he has missed the train of history and hence, his own "becoming." Abram, then, would never become Abraham, just as Jonah, by staying in his country because the "milk and honey" taste so good there, would never become Jonah!

During the last fifty years humanistic psychologists seem to have promoted three conflicting trends. Although they agree on basic tenets such as humanity being self-determined, free to choose, unique, etc., they still diverge in their understanding of human purpose and vocation. Some, like Kurt Goldstein, emphasize the organismic need to maintain an equilibrium (called here homeostasis or principle of equalization).[14] Others, like Maslow, go one step farther. Although they basically agree with Goldstein, they also assert that when those fundamental biological needs are fulfilled, "meta-needs" can come to the fore, but these are "less urgent or demanding, weaker." [15] Here, "self-actualization" is posited as "an end-state." "Self-actualization means working to do well the thing that one *wants* to do." [16]

The vocabulary is revealing. "Self-actualization" is an entirely different notion from "self-transcendence." So different indeed, that the question of life meaning is not dealt with, or if it is, it is treated as a luxury, as something "less urgent or demanding, weaker." People like Jung, Allport, May, Assagioli, and Frankl *(inter alia)* utterly disagree with the reduction of the human person to biological components and dictates, although they do not negate or in any way deny human "basic needs." They emphasize the constructive and necessary aspect of anxiety. "What man actually needs is not a tensionless state but rather the striving and struggling for some goal worthy of him. . . . What man needs is not homeostasis but what I call 'noö-dynamics,' . . . the spiritual dynamics in a polar field of tension where one pole is represented by a meaning to be fulfilled and the other pole by the man who must fulfill it."[17] Human self-actualization, they say (and we agree), is not "an end-state" but only a by-product in the realizing of values and in "the fulfillment of meaning potentialities which are to be found in the world rather than within himself . . . ."[18] They also assert that one must select among various immanent potentialities and aim at what is meaningful. Frankl writes:

> Man must make his choice concerning the mass of present potentials: which will be condemned to non-being and which will be actualized.[19]

One of the fundamental sources of confusion, it seems to us, lies in the abuse of the term "authenticity" to cover divergent and directly conflicting anthropological notions. There is a cause and effect relationship between one's belief system and specific actions as they are inspired or dictated by that system. We may pose the problem in the following way: Is authenticity to be equated with conformity of actions to any set of beliefs once the latter have been decided upon? There emerges one possible definition: Authenticity is an action that fits a preordained creed. If we consider the example of Abraham, the patriarch becomes authentic when and to the extent that he leaves Ur in Chaldea where he was rooted, in order to fulfill what he understands to be his vocation. In other words, the narrative presents a voice, an outer voice that utters a commandment to go, to leave a given situation in order to enter another one that will be revealed in the very process of obedience (cf. Gen. 12:1). There is for Abraham no other authenticity, because once his vocation is perceived, all other vocations become impossible.

But such a general understanding of the notion lends itself to vague relativism. *There would be as many authenticities as there are belief systems.* If one's beliefs are founded upon the ultimate value of happiness and "self-actualization," authenticity would consist precisely of realizing what "feels good" and rewarding. If, in another instance, we take a book like *Mein Kampf* as the expression of Adolf Hitler's belief system, the odious crimes of the German Führer can be said to make him authentic! Authenticity is thus a contextual notion; it does not convey in and of itself any value judgment. The fundamental question remains: Towards what is authenticity oriented? It appears that modern psychology too often uses the term authenticity with the same magical and empty content as Christian pietists use the word "faith," too seldom emphasizing that faith *per se* has no salvific virtues. Even the Nazis had a perfect faith in their evil genius! Salvation comes from God, not from sentiment.

Belief systems constitute frameworks of reference. They obviously can be as different from each other as day and night. Even when there is a commonality between them (as for example in religious belief systems), the resemblance can be so vague as to be misleading. The authentic Buddhist or the authentic animist are the antipodes of the authentic Israel. Indeed, the case could be made that any belief system is ultimately religious, so that we have not much progressed in qualifying the term authenticity as "religious," or "human." Jonah is no less human and probably no less religious when he goes to Tarshish, convinced as he is that "God" cannot command him to betray his people than when he ultimately complies with the order to go to Nineveh. As Fromm once said: "We can interpret *neurosis as a private form of religion.*" [20]

Again we must ask: to have faith *in whom?* to be authentic *to what?* Fundamentally, there are two opposing concepts of authenticity: (a) authenticity to an *inner* voice, versus (b) authenticity to an *outer* voice. The "inner voice" can be called by numerous other names—inner potentials, inner drives, personal conscience, authentic self, the self's rights and duties, etc. Individuals who listen to the inner voice fulfill their inmost potentialities according to their own convictions, norms, values, conscience, etc. There is no doubt that some among us are most demanding of ourselves and do not indulge in self-complacency. The results can be highly respectable.

But the "inner voice" is far from unequivocal. In fact, it is by its nature uncontrolled and purely subjective. Its ambiguity resides also in the fact that it is easy to confuse personally fabricated "voices" with the call that is "heard" as a message coming from without, such as the prophet who is commissioned for a task he would never have conceived for himself. Such ambiguity is always latent in even the best of situations. In the midst of the sea storm, for instance, Jonah says to the sailors. "Take me up, and cast me forth into the sea . . . for I know that for my sake this great tempest is upon you" (1:12). Jonah's self-sacrifice is a good case in point for it raises the problem of intentionality, and it allows us to stress an important aspect of our question. What prompts Jonah here? The voice of his conscience? A commandment of God? It is a moot question, for not everything that can be called an "inner voice" is indeed so. Conversely, not everything that is called an "outer voice" is indeed so. For instance, the archcriminal David Berkowitz, self-named "Son of Sam" claimed to have been "ordered" from "without" to commit his horrendous murders! When asked by the psychiatrist Dr. Abrahamson, "Who told you to kill?", Berkowitz answered simply, "Sam."

The problem would remain unsolvable were it not for the respective qualities of response yielded by obedience to a real or to a sham calling or commandment. In the case of the "Son of Sam," the obedience is a grotesque caricature. From the outset then, the question is *whose* voice is it? For here the determinative factor is the person with whom one is in communication. When one breaks the monologue with oneself and acknowledges a "Thou," one passes from what we might call a "prior-self stage" to an "authentic-self stage." The "prior-self stage" involves the innate concern for the self that is present in all human beings. Infants pull toward themselves everything they can reach. It belongs to an indispensable process of growth and maturation in all of us to discover the external world as an object that must be adapted to the self and the self to it. But ultimate maturity and personhood happens when the object is acknowledged as a subject, for then only is there dialogue and love. An individual, in the process of encountering, becomes a *person,* one who loves. In other words, the fact of recognizing the other as a person makes the lover a person. In "surrendering" to the beloved One (in Jon. 2), Jonah passes from anonymity to the stage of the authentic self. He has chosen life (cf. Deut. 30) and in fact, he lives! (Jon. 2:11).

As Buber writes:

> An individual is just a certain uniqueness of a human being. . . . He may become more and more an individual without becoming more and more human. I know many examples of man having become very, very individual, very dis-

tinct from others, very developed in their such-and-suchness without being at all what I would like to call a man. The individual is just this uniqueness; being able to be developed thus and thus. But *a person . . . is an individual living really with the world. And with the world, I don't mean in the world*—just in real contact, in real reciprocity with the world in all the points in which the world can meet man. I don't say only with man, because sometimes we meet the world in other shapes than in that of man. . . . I'm against individuals and for persons.[21]

The "prior-self stage" is thus a preliminary stage, which prepares for an eventual existential breakthrough in becoming a person. This preliminary stage is also primordial and must be overtaken and transcended but not shed like an old skin. Maturation, as we have seen above, is not metamorphosis but process. Jonah in chapter 2 or in chapter 3 is the same Jonah as in chapter 1. Similarly, the "authentic-self stage" is not built on the ruins of the "prior-self stage" although it has transcended this primary level. What actually happens is that, rather than constituting an apology for noncommitment and solipsism, the innate survival instinct becomes the ground for the act of reaching out and forgetting one's self-centeredness.

Let us pursue further this dialectic notion for it is, we believe, of fundamental import to the understanding of the Jonah story, presenting as it does a man going through *conversion* but not transmutation. The "authentic-self stage" is a complete reversal ("conversion") of the "prior-self stage" but not the abandonment of the latter as if it had no relation to the former. It is, as we said above, a process, a movement of leaving behind and of striving forward. It is an ongoing self-decentralization, a ceaseless "taking off" for which the springboard is necessarily that with which we came to life in the first place, the self. This much must be acknowledged, lest we be left with a disincarnated "agape" from which "eros" has been artificially evacuated, spirit without flesh and eventually, without reality.

But the "prior-self" is there as a means, not as a goal. It is endlessly sacrificed as a "living offering and a reasonable service" (Rom. 12:1) on the altar of the "I-Thou" relationship. One will remember at this point what Martin Buber said about the necessity to begin with oneself "but not to end with oneself . . . . True, each [soul] is to know itself, purify itself, perfect itself, but not for its own sake . . . but for the sake of the work it is destined to perform upon the world." [22] For person is person only in the process of dialoguing with the "Thou." To live means precisely to enter into the in-between-ness of the relation with the other. Ultimately, there is no other way to find life than by giving it up.[23]

Throughout the ages, the human person has desperately tried to avoid the traumatic passage from childhood to adulthood. There exist a thousand and one means to insulate oneself from the world. The deeply ingrained and universal wish to return to the golden age of the womb-stage has perennial importance. But what price does humankind pay in cultivating such an impulse? Misery, sadness, hopelessness, helplessness, isolation, absurdity, neuroses, psychoses.

Reaching authenticity is not reserved, however, for the "happy few." Everyone, at the innermost core of being, is thirsty for recognition, and that is a step in the right direction.

> Man's unacknowledged secret is his desire to be affirmed in his essence and in his existence by his fellow men. He wishes that they, in turn, would make it possible for him to affirm them, and for both affirmations to be conferred not merely within the family or perhaps at a party meeting or in a bar, but also in the course of neighborly encounters. . . by so doing, each would let the other know that he endorses his presence. It is this endorsement that constitutes the indispensable minimum of man's humanity.[24]

But, pathetically, individuals too often believe that they can "make it" on their own and find recognition within false relationships wherein others play only the role of a mirror for the self. It is a travesty of dialogue, and is in fact sheer monologue with oneself.

In its essence, monologue is static and circular. It neglects past and future and exhausts all potentialities in a phantasmic present that clouds all horizons. As is clear in our drug-culture, the "present" is reduced to an explosion, a firework that empties the self of all content and "blows your mind" in the same way that a bullet "blows your head."[25]

By contrast, dialogue is dynamic and linear. Encounter with another—so rare an occurrence as to be an extraordinary event each time[26]—is also encounter with the respective past and future of the two partners. The phantasmic is left for good, and the real is chosen for its own decisive value as an outreach toward past and future. That is why in his dialogue with Carl Rogers (April 18, 1957) Martin Buber insisted that any real relationship must begin with acceptance. He said, "Confirming means first of all, accepting the whole potentiality of the other and making even a decisive difference in his potentiality . . . . I can recognize in him . . . the person he has been . . . created to become." [27]

Here the horizons are not clouded, but on the contrary, "the other fills the horizon" (Buber); the other constitutes the "referent" of otherwise meaningless strivings and impulses. The beloved other does not "blow your mind"—although this also may happen at times on the road to communion—but restores your mind, or perhaps gives you a sound mind for the first time. "Then," says our text, "Jonah prayed to the Lord his God out of the fish's belly. . . . I will sacrifice to Thee with the voice of thanksgiving!" (2:2, 10 [English 2:1, 9]).

Thus, persons are *called* to authenticity by *somebody else* whose presence and voice are enticing and commanding. We *are* not free, said Maimonides, but we have received the commandment to be free. We can paraphrase the Jewish philosopher and say that we are not loving (by nature) but rather we have received (*qua* human beings and not just animals) the commandment to love. This is what is meant here by "the outer voice."

This phrase—the commandment to love—is problematic on two counts. First, *who* is the one who commands? Second, *why* must it be a command? With respect to the first question, the book of Jonah is written by an Israelite author who takes for granted that "the word *of the Lord* came unto Jonah" (1:1). Today, such statements are considered by many to be the products of groundless superstition. But, perhaps, this move is too precipitous. Maslow writes, ". . . the sacred is *in* the ordinary . . . it is to be found in one's daily life, in one's neighbors, friends, and family, in one's back yard . . ." [28] We are not, therefore, speaking of a meta-reality that stands over and against our down-to-earth daily existence.[29] On the contrary, on that very level—which happens to be the historical level as well—we witness (with Maslow again) a tendency within society to desacralize or devalue love, truth, respect for life and sex, in contradistinction to the reverence that previous generations gave to those things. Youth, in particular, lives in a chaotic and meaningless world. The way of "salvation," therefore, seems to lie in the resacralizing of life in all its aspects and in the reaffirming of values such as love and respect for the person.[30]

We remain on the surface of things. To express the regret that a sense of the sacredness of life has been lost with the dechristianization of the West still says nothing about "the Lord" who, for Israel, is the author of the "outer voice" and the guarantor of its trustworthiness. Were we in a mythological environment or a classically religious domain, the personality of the god in question would be definable. We would be able to resort to "biographical" stories about Zeus or Mao Tse Tung. But there is an exorbitant price to pay for such comfort: these gods belong to another realm. We watch them and their capricious, superhuman behavior, but we are not ourselves really present in the picture. Their orders have, as it were, an independent existence. They do not commit their authors and they are essentially occasional, contextual and casuistic.

Not so with the God of Israel. We cannot pursue our inquiry about who commands Jonah without considering the command itself. Here the commander and the command are essentially inseparable, the latter reflecting the personality of the former. There is no way to know who speaks other than to hear his Word. Who is "the Lord" who speaks to Jonah but the one who tells him "Arise, go to Nineveh"? Here we are entitled to take the commandment so seriously as to measure the quality of its author by that very norm. Speaker and speech build a *Gestalt*. "God is the relation with God"

(Buber). A mute Zeus would still be Zeus. "Know yourself" does not derive its ultimate meaning from the person of Socrates. But in Israel's conception, what is decisive is the "in between" space which both separates and binds the speaker and his word, as well as the addresser and the addressee. What is all-important is the phenomenon of *speaking and the dynamism of speaking to* someone who is also a subject, i.e., a *responsible* being capable of the best and the worst, of creating life with the creator, and of destroying the world in an anti-God suicidal move (cf. Freud's "Thanatos").

But a person's choice is not uniformed. Heschel said, "Man is not alone." The *voice from without* tells him, "choose life in order to live," in the same manner that parents lovingly teach their children a way of life guided by values. That is why the very nature of God's Word is a commandment, and the genuine form of the commandment in Israel is apodictic (unconditional).[31] Far from being conceived as curtailing a congenital, organic, and natural freedom, the commandment creates for the first time the conditions of the possibility of freedom. This is why the very first word addressed by the creator to Adam is an order (Gen. 1:28).

From the same perspective, the "Ten Commandments" have shown their mettle. Some will perhaps be content to speak about them in terms of profound wisdom, of genial knowledge, of human spirituality, etc. Those compliments remain unsatisfactory, however, because they can so easily sound like mere lipservice paid to a cultural achievement that is as obsolete as it is admirable. We must rather ask *what* makes the Ten Words life-giving, *what* makes the commandment to Jonah a possibility for his rebirth.

At the basis of the outer voice and its commandment, there is love. Human beings are under command because they are loved, and the order they receive makes them love in turn. The commandment pulls people up from animality to humanity. Buber writes, "Whoever goes forth to his You (the other) with his whole being and carries to it all the being of the world, finds him whom one cannot seek."[32]

All this has been an attempt to show how indispensable it is to detect not so much one's needs, desires, and aspirations, but the demands of life itself. Moreover, without diminishing the usefulness of philosophical or theological systems, for setting useful parameters to human choices, such systems are ultimately adequate only for the general and the customary. They are incapable of bringing any valid response to Job. They apply automatic criteria of judgment to the murderous acts of Moses, Yael, Ehud, or Judith, hailed by Israel's tradition as saviors appointed by God himself. Such systems are "bourgeois," and are paralyzed by anything that is out of the ordinary. They are adapted to everyone, and so, to no one. They know nothing of eccentricity, of extravagance, of holy disobedience. They frown at Bonhoeffer's dream of killing Hitler. They know nothing of us.

That is why one must go beyond both psychology and theology (e.g., the theology of Job's friends). What goes beyond any ethical norm is what is called here "the outer voice." By nature it cannot be systematized. In order for persons to proclaim their obedience to the voice from without, to God's voice, they must admittedly place their existence beyond the controllable. But it is nonetheless the ultimate criterion. In the penultimate realm, we may heed the useful directions indicated by respectable masters such as Freud, Jung, Assagioli, Fromm, and many others. But they go only so far, not beyond. The claim to be guided as Jonah is guided to Nineveh by the "outer voice" must in the last resort be judged by God himself.

Chapter VIII

THE JONAH COMPLEX REVISITED

Each step forward is a step into the unfamiliar and possibly dangerous. It also means giving up something familiar and good and satisfying. . . . It also often means giving up a simpler and easier and less effortful life, in exchange for a more demanding, more responsible, more difficult life.

—Abraham Maslow, *Toward a Psychology of Being* (Princeton, NJ: D. Van Nostrand, 1968), p. 204.

The temptation to run away from responsibility, pain and loneliness has been widely acknowledged in psychotherapeutic literature.[1] Jung, in fact, calls this pathological wish to regress to a womb-like state the "Jonah-and-the-Whale complex."[2] The social sciences, as well as philosophy, psychology, and theology have clearly demonstrated that more often than not, we fear change and growth because it means leaving behind old patterns, attitudes, and behaviors for new ones. This is similar to what Angyal said of the nature of neurosis, that its main features are twofold: evasion of growth (fear of change) and ambivalence toward commitment to any particular value or person.[3] Adler makes the same observation and describes neurosis as essentially a hesitation or a "yes-but" attitude toward any type of commitment.[4] He notices how tempting it is for people to do what they please ("private sense") instead of behaving in a manner that would benefit not only the subject but others as well ("common sense"). "Evasion of responsibility," he once wrote, "is bound up with the lack of interest in other people."[5] Cowardice (lack of courage to live in an altruistic cooperation with others) is what restrains men and women from investing themselves in the project of helping humankind move toward a better, healthier way of living in peace and harmony.

The avoidance of new knowledge of oneself (growth) and of social responsibility has been shown to have its roots in one's fear of *doing*. Maslow, for example, convincingly highlights this point by giving the following account:

> It was certainly safer for the Germans living near Dachau not to know what was going on, to be blind and pseudo-stupid. For if they knew, they would either have had to do something about it or else feel guilty about being cowards.

> More than any other kind of knowledge we fear knowledge of ourselves, knowledge that might transform our self-esteem and our self-image. . . . the more impersonal the knowledge . . . the less resistance there will be.[6]

Frank Manual, a colleague and friend of Maslow, was the first to label this resistance to growth and authenticity the "Jonah syndrome."[7] It is to Maslow himself, however, that we owe credit for elaborating upon this existential phenomenon in his attempt to integrate it within the framework of a theory of healthy growth and motivation. He first called this defense mechanism "fear of standing alone," "fear of one's greatness," "evasion of one's destiny," or "fear of knowledge" until he adopted Manual's term.

What precisely is the Jonah syndrome? Maslow writes:

> It is a falling short of what one could have been, and even one could say, of what one *should* have been.
>
> . . .We all have unused potentialities or not fully developed ones. . . . We enjoy and even thrill to the godlike possibilities we see in ourselves in such peak moments. And yet we simultaneously shiver with weakness, awe and fear before these very same possibilities.
>
> I have found it easy enough to demonstrate this [the Jonah syndrome] to my students simply by asking . . . "Who aspires to be a saint, like Schweitzer, perhaps? Who among you will be a great leader?" Generally everybody starts giggling, blushing, and squirming until I ask, "If not you, then who else?"[8]

It is interesting to note that both Maslow and Manual have wavered in their use of the expression "Jonah syndrome" or "Jonah complex" without ever defining either term. In fact, neither scholar had studied the biblical book of Jonah prior to introducing his concept. For example, Maslow's paper "Neurosis as a Failure of Personal Growth," which first introduced the "Jonah syndrome," was published in 1967, but when it appeared in *The Farther Reaches of Human Nature* (1971) the "Jonah syndrome" became the "Jonah complex" without an explanation of the switch of terms.[9]

What is a complex? Jung, who was the first to introduce that term, described it as a cluster of ideas, impulses, and memories, often repressed, which strongly conflicts with other aspects of one's personality. Complexes are outside the control of (immediate) consciousness or "conscious intentions."[10] They indicate that there are unresolved conflicts within one's psyche, arising from the clash "between the requirement of adaptation and the individual's constitutional inability to meet the challenge."[11] They are, on the positive side, potential openings for "new possibilities of achievements."[12] Thus, complexes do not necessarily imply abnormality and can be used to describe "associations of desires, impulses, and sentiments which occur in normal persons."[13]

"Jonah complex" is to be preferred to "Jonah syndrome" because the lat-

ter would indicate sheer accidentality and circumstantiality. The Jonah narrative then, would be relevant only for some very specific, even unusual,
occasions. A "Jonah syndrome," as the term is used in psychiatry and psychology, would represent a rare phenomenon (like Freud's success neurosis
erupting only in a few nonrepresentative individuals).

The Jonah complex is not so much a fear of one's own immanent potentialities as it is a fear of actualizing one's vocation, i.e., to serve God. One of
the fundamental differences between Maslow's concept and ours (the Jonah
complex revisited) lies in the *context* against which evasion from growth is
interpreted. It can of course be viewed from a solipsistic point of reference
which interprets "happiness," "success," "meaning," etc. solely in terms of
the individual's private standards (or we could say in terms of a Voice from
Within). This is Maslow's viewpoint. But another standpoint is possible according to which the ambivalence toward one's greatness is seen as the endeavor to reject the sublime (the Outer Voice, God) and this also is very
much a human immanent potentiality!—so much so that the Jonah complex
means that one rejects the sublime and the sacred in life. It means that *for all
and always, there is a congenital fear of one's humanness and of one's vocation to
act "with a view to the welfare of humanity as a whole," past, present and future.*[14] The problem therefore is not whether some have a vocation like
Jonah, while some do not; all men and women face the necessity of fulfilling
their humanness.[15] The resolution of evasion of growth and pathological
conformity, then, lies in an ongoing *process* of choosing to go *beyond* ourselves, beyond our potentialities precisely, and to be "attuned" to transcendence. Then really we discover the norm for assessing the meaning and
purpose of our lives. By this we mean an existential awareness that accentuates Awe, Wonder, and Sacredness as the primary foci for one's perceptions
and beliefs, while not negating the wisdom of the biological. The latter,
however, is not left to its dictates; it is under the control of superior imperatives which at times may demand the subjugation of our natural desires and
aspirations. This context of listening to the Outer Voice shifts one's fascina-
tion with oneself to a level of full humanness and respect for life. "The highest knowledge," Albert Schweitzer once said, "is to know that we are
surrounded by mystery."[16]

Why do most people opt to listen to the Voice from Within and live in a
state often referred to as one of a "spiritual lobotomy"?[17] Here Haronian's
thinking becomes particularly helpful. In one of his papers he defines the
sublime as the realm in which men and women discover their feelings of
brotherhood and sisterhood and their wish to get involved, with the direct
intent of contributing to others' welfare.[18] The "Jonah complex" *is repression
of the Sublime.* It is also *Fear of Death* or, rather terror before death. Let us
start with this latter aspect. Death appears as the "ultimate enemy." It is hu-

manity's curse *par excellence*; it has a character of aggression that, common as it is, is however the irruption of the unexpected. Death is not only our finality; it is also the absolute negation of all meaning, the anti-life, and anti-being. Everyone "dies by chance" (Sartre). It is always, and even in the best of cases, an accident—an accident which befalls kings as well as slaves. It is *derekh eretz,* the way of the earth (of all people), says Joshua 23:14, the terrible leveler which joins in the same embrace the righteous and the wicked, the murderer and the innocent. To fear such a gruesome monster is only natural. The feeling is not simple but extremely complex. Fear of Death is also "life fear," the fear of loneliness and individuality.[19] It brings one to look for refuge in pathological conformity and prompts Jonah to get lost in the anonymity of the crowd en route to Tarshish. Thus, by "disappearing" in the mass, the hope is to escape loneliness and the awareness of death. People are willing to sacrifice everything, including their own potentialities and humanness, to avoid being singled out by the "eyes" of death. Death, as well as life, is in need of interpretation so that we neither understand it nor accept it as blind fate.

Like life itself, death is not deterministic, nor is it a geometrical point at the end of a line. It is a reality we carry with us all our lives. I live with my death and my death is always present to me—so present that it is not a foreign body over which I have no control: stone in my kidney, bullet in my leg; for I am pregnant with my worst enemy, my death *is* me. In other words, I shape my death as I shape my life. In consequence, even death can be made positive! The enemy can be made a friend. Death is dialectical. It is not always where one expects it. *Tanhumah b. Berakhot* 28b says:

> the righteous even after their death may be called living, whereas the wicked, both in life and in death may be called dead.

In the process of its transcendance, death has changed its nature. As Reuven P. Bulka writes, "death makes life meaningful" for, "man would not be faced with an imperative to act and accomplish if his life were endless. That his existence may be terminated suddenly is a reality which forced, or should force, man to utilize his allotted moments as meaningfully as possible."[20]

To live with the awareness that we are mortals transforms our perception of the world. Everything is interpreted under a new light, within a new context. Ultimately, in the affirmation of the self lies the acceptance, even the appreciation of death. Race, money, power, social status, education, ultimately mean very little. They do not redeem our lives. We still will die. As Becker puts it, using Montaigne's insight: ". . . on the highest throne in the world man sits on his arse."[21]

Empathy is asked of us because we all die. One aspect of the "Jonah complex" is the refusal to accept that death binds us all into a human family.

Death, our finitude, when brought to the level of conscience, provides a vantage point *sub specie aeternitatis*. It puts things in perspective. It especially gives the philosopher or the prophet a sense of compassion for the people "humiliated and offended" (Dostoyevsky) by a life which is "a dying" from its start. Existence becomes a race against the meaninglessness of its disappearance at the end. Existence and its finitude cannot be stretched one inch beyond its "horizontal" span, but it can, indeed it must be *fulfilled* vertically so to speak. We live fully to the extent to which we devote our lives to a vocation that is beyond our self-centered interests and which accentuates the respect, protection and enhancement of all that lives. One must start with oneself, but not end with oneself, in the context of respect and reverence for all that lives. "Sin," Tillich once said, "is the turning towards ourselves, and making ourselves the center of our world." [22] Life is a *loan* which must be returned through death. Its ultimate meaning therefore lies in the response to this reality.

We can now turn to the Jonah complex as "Repression of the Sublime" which we equated with the resistance to the pressing invitation or commandment of the Outer Voice. Theoretically such reflection is puzzling. Those whose backs are trained to carry the "yoke of Torah" consider it perfectly evident that one should "choose life in order to live." But one reason for the suppression of the Outer Voice is well put by two modern thinkers:

> ... the more one is conscious of one's positive impulses, of one's urges toward the sublime, the more shame one feels for one's failure to give expression to these impulses. There ensues a painful burning of the conscience, a sense of guilt at not being what one could be, of not doing what one could do. This is not superego guilt but rather the cry of the Self for its actualization. [23]

> We fear the sublime because it is unknown and because if we admit the reality of higher values, we are committed to act in a more noble way. [24]

Contrary to overoptimistic conceptions it is to be emphasized that one rather listens to one's desires and libido, thus denying the uniqueness and dedication to a cause that would transcend one's animality and raise one to the level of humanness. By choosing a solipsistic context, one lives in a world where myth supersedes history, and rites are substitutes for existential involvement. One is truly a "homo religiosus" as one lives in magics and superstitions.

For to be "religious" does not mean that one has transcended one's superstitious and solipsistic beliefs. Even neurosis, as we saw with Fromm earlier, is a private form of religion. Religiosity applies to all who behave according to their convictions, be they selfish, altruistic or neurotic. Therefore, it is our belief that regardless of what meaning in life one selects, one is *always* religious. What matters is not so much whether one is or is *not* religious as it is *how* one interprets one's religiosity.[25] Even atheism is a "post-religious faith, a faith for a post-religious age," according to Paul Ricoeur.[26] True, the adjective "religious" is somewhat vague. Its "best" aspect is highlighted by Eliade when he speaks of a religious person (homo religiosus) as one who believes in the sacred as life's absolute reality,

> which transcends this world but manifests itself in this world, thereby sanctifying it and making it real. He [homo religiosus] further believes that life has a sacred origin and that human existence realizes all of its potentialities in proportion as it is religious—that is, participates in reality.[27]

But this phenomenological approach is an eye-opener that needs to be followed by the commitment of this one to this God. The criterion of Paul Ricoeur is sharp and illuminating:

> This is the first stage, the first level of thought that starts from symbols. But one cannot rest here; for the question of *truth* has not yet been posed. If a phenomenologist should give the name truth to internal coherence, to the systematization of the world of symbols, it is a truth without belief, truth at a distance, a reduced truth. From such truth this question has been eliminated: *Do I myself believe that? What do I personally make of these symbolic meanings?* Now this question cannot be raised as long as one remains at the level of comparativism, passing from one symbol to another without taking a stand. This stage can only be a stage, the stage of an understanding that is horizontal and panoramic, curious but not concerned. We now have to enter into a relationship with symbols that is emotionally intense and at the same time critical. To do so I must leave the comparativist point of view aside; I must follow the exegete and become implicated in the life of one symbol, one myth.[28]

What the book of Jonah is teaching us is that we are called to give unique responses to life's unique demands. In consequence, there is only one answer per situation, the *right* one[29] or the "Yes-Choice." This response can be defined as a decision made in total honesty, integrity, and freedom. We agree with Maslow that "Conscious awareness, insight, and 'working through' à la Freud is . . . the best path I know to the acceptance of our highest powers. . . ."[30] To this we add that the Yes-Choice always has as its context the commitment to enhance the human condition through our best talents and potentialities. Such "Ethical Choice," as May labels it,[31] is always made through listening to the Voice from Without.

Pleasure or displeasure are not adequate arguments for or against the advisability of any decision or action. The former is not within our grasp but exists only as a side-effect of performing a meaningful task. To this also the book of Jonah testifies. At no point does the principle of happiness nor even of "being O.K." (as for the Ninevites, they are certainly not O.K.!) come in consideration. Neither is Jonah to be content, nor are the inhabitants of Nineveh to "feel good" about themselves. Quite the contrary, Jonah must go whither he does not want to go, and he must accept the reality of Nineveh's pardon while he would rather see the city razed to the ground. Similarly, the Ninevites must not silence their guilt feelings and "auto suggestion" themselves that everything is for the best in the best possible world. They have to repent and to be forgiven.

All narcissism has subsided. The inner voice of a deceiving conscience (cf. Freud's exercise of suspicion) has been superseded by another voice, which is not deceitful because it does not flatter but does *order* and thus does respect our human responsibility. Jonah and the Ninevites hear the "Voice from Without." The latter repent and are forgiven; the former—so we are left to believe—renounces his religious or theological constructions and allows God to be God.

Conclusion

At the end of this study of the prophet Jonah and the book that bears his name, it may be useful to look back at the ground that has been covered and to embrace in one glance the whole countryside. The book of Jonah is a folk tale and must be read as such. Oral versions of the narrative may have existed and may have been used by the biblical author for his own purpose. Composed in the fifth century B.C.E., its story was particularly fit as a polemical response to the isolationism of a powerful religious party among the returnees from Babylon in Jerusalem. Consequently, what had perhaps been an entertaining story seasoned all along with humor and irony became a parable, i.e., a "world subverting" tale meant to provide a merciless mirror for an awry and somewhat monstrous attitude in life that deliberately ignored the fate of non-Jews.

To reach his goal, the author does not render facile his task. He has a profound understanding of the rationales behind his opponents' refusal to "go to Nineveh." It is the grandeur of Jonah that the "others" are not naive "savages" ready for the proclamation of the Gospel but are symbolized by the Ninevites, i.e., by the archenemies and torturers of Israel. In other words, the "prophet" Jonah has all the reasons not to bother with a nest of vipers at whose bites his people suffered so much. Until the end of the story, the reader is left with the most uneasy feeling that perhaps Jonah has been right from the first, and God's obstinacy in sending his Jew to Nineveh has been from the first wrong. There is a time when the greatest justice and the profoundest mercy in principle become outrageous injustice.

Such is the framework for a reflection which the author pursues without complacency. Is there any reason why God would call an unimportant man such as Jonah? Do we know in advance the parameters within which God's call is contained? Is there any law regulating the alternation of judgment and pardon in God? Is the divine promise to Jeremiah and Ezekiel to break the determinism of the condemnation of generations valid for others besides Israel? Are non-Jews also capable of repentance? Are foreigners susceptible to the action and the word of the Living God? Would such an opening of pagan hearts to Israel's God have an adverse bearing on the contrasting procrastination of Israel? Under what conditions can a prophetic oracle remain unfulfilled and still be authentically commissioned by God? This last ques-

tion was especially relevant in the post-exilic community of Jerusalem, ago-
nizing about the nonfulfillment of solemn promises by prophets concerning
the advent of eschatological conditions with the restoration. Imagining as
the author does that the nonaccomplishment of a prophecy happens in the
case of a promise of destruction to a pagan nation (instead of a promise of
eschatological blossoming to the holy people) only seemingly reverses the
terms. Nineveh is the antipode of Jerusalem; her impending destruction is
the very opposite of the expected glory of Zion. Could it be that her repentance bringing divine forgiveness is also a foil for the arrogance of some in
Jerusalem bringing the divine punishment of the nonfulfillment of the
prophecies? In the former case the lack of accomplishment spells out salvation, and it is initiated by the repentance of the Ninevites; in the latter case it
spells out doom, and it is wrought by the callous solipsism of a complacent
establishment. Perhaps one would wish for the reversal of the situation, i.e.,
for the glorification of Zion and the "overthrow" of Nineveh, but the book
of Jonah indicates that this cannot be accomplished by a simple algebraic op-
eration (cf. Jon. 4:10–11). For if the revocation of God's decision regarding
Nineveh resulted from the repentance of the whole population, it is implied
the realization of prophetic promises regarding Zion will require a profound
transformation of the situation in Jerusalem.

* * * * * * * *

Clearly, this theological kerygma could have been presented in another
form by the author of Jonah. However, he chose to be a "singer of tales,"
and this should be taken with the utmost seriousness. If the "content" is decisive for the "form," as a river opens up its own bed, the "form," reflects
upon the "content" and is instrumental in restricting or enlarging its sway.
No literary genre is more encompassing than the narrative. Even when it
conveys a very focused message—as is the case with Jonah—narrative makes
the message immediately universal because it is presented as a human experience indefinitely repeatable under some circumstances. In other words,
the story renders paradigmatic a situation or an event that otherwise could
appear as isolated in time and limited in scope.
    The story of Jonah is not only a religious manifesto but also a psychologi-
cal tableau of the human condition. Jonah is not just a Jew of Palestine called
out of his anonymity by a commissioning voice from without. He is a human
being, every person. The theological beam focuses on a specific known
prophet (2 Kings 14:25) with a specific and unique task: to preach the destruction of Nineveh. The psychological pencil of rays reveals human characteristics and contributes to what Ricoeur calls the process of suspicion
about ourselves. Jonah as every human being exemplifies our call to our

task. He is also a paradigm of our resistance to election by God, for nothing is more repulsive to us than to be designated (elected, chosen) by the Outer Voice for a self-transcending task, when we would rather follow our inner voice and our biological dictates ("what feels good") for our self-satisfaction and our self-aggrandizement.

This universal resistance to a vocation which breaks our solipsism and thus provides with a sense of responsibility the authentic liberty, we call "the Jonah complex." This is of course an anthropological pronouncement. What it implies is that always and everywhere the human being is "distinguished" by the Outer Voice for a task of communication. The very meaning of life is the love of others for their own sake, in their own right, even if they are "Ninevites." That is why such a love transcends eros and is anti-heroic (which is narcissistic), anti-deterministic (and therefore "bears all things, believes all things, hopes all things, endures all things"), anti-"functional" (it does not expect recompense).

But the "Jonah" in us wishes rather to regress to the motherly womb (Jung speaks of "Jonah-and-the-whale-complex"), i.e., to a stage *before* an existential decision must be made. "Jonah" wants to "kill time," not to "redeem time," he wants to reduce the human being to scientific formulas (love as biological function, e.g.), to legalistic imperatives (satisfaction of biological needs, e.g.), to deterministic rules (genes, heredity). He still prefers the uncertainty of a perilous escape to "Tarshish" to the *mysterium tremendum* of God's revelation and of human performativeness. Rather to die than to become. Rather the hate of Ninevites than the love of God; the former is comprehensible and all too fathomable, the latter is the unknown and hence a threat to our security.

The author of Jonah had the amazing boldness to show the "anti-Jonah" in the persons of the wicked Ninevites. To the Jonah who hungered for certainty they opposed the ultimate uncertainty of "perhaps." They thus opened an immense possibility, namely, that God might choose extravagance over determinism, that a human person might be a gerundive rather than an animate puppet manipulated by genetic and other laws.

The author of Jonah was an Israelite. He chose to give to his story a double ending: the wager of the Ninevites was vindicated; God, according to Israel, gives victory to those who risk everything. And as for Jonah himself, he is pondering still whether or not it is advantageous to side with the Ninevite extravagance.

Chicago, Yom Kippur 1980,
when Jonah is read in all Synagogues.

Abbreviations

Aen.	*Aeneid*
Altoriental. Forsch.	*Altorientalische Forschung*
ANET	*Ancient Near Eastern Texts Relating to the Old Testament*, ed. J.B. Pritchard.
Ant.	Josephus, *Jewish Antiquities*
ATD	Das Alte Testament Deutsch
b.	babli (of Babylon)
Bibl. Sacra	*Bibliotheca Sacra*
BJ	*Bible de Jérusalem*
BK	Biblischer Kommentar
BQ	Baba Qamma
BZ	*Biblische Zeitschrift*
CAT	Commentaire de l'Ancien Testament
CBQ	*Catholic Biblical Quarterly*
DB	*Dictionnaire de la Bible*
DBS	*Dictionnaire de la Bible, Supplément*
E	Elohist
EB	Etudes bibliques
Enc. Bibl.	*Encyclopedia Biblica*, ed. T.K. Cheyne and J.S. Black (London: Adam and Charles Black, 1899)
EThR	*Etudes théologiques et religieuses*
FRLANT	Forschungen zur Religion und Literatur des Alten und Neuen Testaments
HAT	Handbuch zum Alten Testament
HUCA	*Hebrew Union College Annual*
IB	*Interpreter's Bible*
ICC	International Critical Commentary
IDB	*Interpreter's Dictionary of the Bible*
IDB Supp.	*Interpreter's Dictionary of the Bible, Supplementary Volume* (Nashville: Abingdon, 1976)
Interp.	*Interpretation*
j.	*jerushalmi* (of Jerusalem)
J	Jahwist
JBL	*Journal of Biblical Literature*

JE	*Jewish Encyclopedia*
J. of Ps. and Theol.	*Journal of Psychology and Theology*
JQR	*Jewish Quarterly Review*
KAT	Kommentar zum Alten Testament, ed. E. Sellin
LXX	Septuagint
MT	Masoretic Text
NT	New Testament
OT	Old Testament
PG	J. Migne, Patrologia graeca
PL	J. Migne, Patrologia latina
Q	Qumran
1QH	Hodayot from Qumran Cave 1
RB	*Revue biblique*
RGG	*Die Religion in Geschichte und Gegenwart*
RHPR	*Revue d'histoire et de philosophie religieuse*
SBT	Studies in Biblical Theology
Scott. J. of Theol.	*Scottish Journal of Theology*
Str.-Bill.	H. Strack and P. Billerbeck, *Kommentar zum Neuen Testament*
Tg.	Targum
ThDNT	*Theological Dictionary of the New Testament,* ed. G. Kittel; trans. G.W. Bromiley (Grand Rapids: Eerdmans)
Theol. St. u. Krit.	*Theologische Studien und Kritiken*
ThR	*Theologische Rundschau*
ThZ	*Theologische Zeitschrift*
TOB	Traduction Oecuménique de la Bible
VT	Vetus Testamentum
VT Sup	Supplements to *Vetus Testamentum*
ZAW	Zeitschrift für die Alttestamentliche Wissenschaft.

Notes

Chapter I

1 Elias Bickerman, *Four Strange Books of the Bible* (*Jonah/Daniel/Koheleth/Esther*) (New York: Schocken Books, 1967), p. 3.

2 Bickerman, *Four Strange Books*, pp. 3-4.

3 James D. Smart, *The Interpreter's Bible* (Nashville: Abingdon, 1956), vol. 6, pp. 871 ff.

4 Gerhard von Rad, *Der Prophet Jona* (Nürnberg: Laetare, 1950), p. 11. See also Leslie C. Allen, *The Books of Joel, Obadiah, Jonah, and Micah*, The New International Commentary on the OT (Grand Rapids: Eerdmans, 1976), p. 229: "What religious monster is this?"

5 Bickerman, *Four Strange Books*, p. 15, quoting Jerome; *Comm. on Jonah*, 1:3.

6 See, e.g., Louis Ginzberg, *The Legends of the Jews* (Philadelphia: Jewish Publication Society, 1955), vol. 6, pp. 348-352.

7 Quoted by Joachim Jeremias, *ThDNT*, vol. 3, p. 408, n. 17 (under *Iōnas*).

8 Hans Schmidt, *Jona, eine Untersuchung zur vergleichenden Religionsgeschichte*, FRLANT 9 (Göttingen: Vandenhoeck & Ruprecht, 1907).

9 Cf. "Ten just people are enough to save Sodom" (Gen. 18:22-23). See also Jeremiah 5:1, but compare 31:29.

10 Adolphe Lods, *Histoire de la littérature Hébraïque et Juive* (Paris: Payot, 1950), ad loc.

11 See Peter R. Ackroyd, *Israel Under Babylon and Persia* (Oxford: Oxford University Press, 1970), p. 338.

12 Representative of those who accept the allegorical hypothesis are Kleinert, Bloch, Cheyne, König, Smith, and Ackroyd.

13 See most recently Peter R. Ackroyd, *Exile and Restoration*, (Philadelphia: Westminster, 1968), pp. 244-245. (The book of Jonah fulfills the same role as Isaiah 65:1 in that God is found by those who were not looking for him.)

14 We shall note here as a curiosity Jacques Ellul's connection with the *yônāh* which brought back to Noah the sign of the end of God's wrath in Genesis 8:11 (see "Le livre de Jonas," *Foi et Vie* 50 [1952]: 84). Let us recall also the identification made by the NT with the Holy Spirit (see Matt. 3:16). A notable Rabbinic interpretation sees the dove as representing Israel unjustly persecuted, in *Baba Qamma* 93a (on the basis of Ps. 74:19, where the word is not *yônāh* but *tôr*).

15 George A. F. Knight, *Ruth and Jonah*, Torch Bible Commentaries (London: SCM, 1950). See also F. Weinreb, *Das Buch Jonah, der Sinn des Buches Jona nach der ältesten Jüdischen Überl* (Zurich: Origo Vlg, 1970), p. 118. Weinreb also, like Ellul, draws a parallel with Noah's dove (see note 14 above; Weinreb, *Das Buch Jonah*, pp. 126, 132).

16 "Die Komposition des Buches Jona," *ZAW* 7 (1887): 222-284. Boehme grounds his argument concerning the model of the Pentateuch on the most unreliable basis—the variation of divine names in the book. As a matter of fact, God is some-

times called YHWH (hence source "J" for Boehme), sometimes Elohim (hence his source "E"), or even as, for example, in Genesis 2, YHWH-Elohim (1:9; 2:2; 4:6; hence Boehme's JE redaction).

17 "Die Komposition des Buches Jona," *ZAW* 25 (1905): 285-310.

18 Allen, *Joel, Obadiah, Jonah, and Micah*, pp. 197, 200.

19 In Jonah 1:4, therefore, one might have expected the use of Elohim rather than YHWH, but it is made clear by the author that the storm on the sea concerns Jonah exclusively. It is a *historical* gesture in the disguise of a natural phenomenon.

20 On the preceding development, see Gabriël H. Cohn, *Das Buch Jona im Lichte der biblischen Erzählkunst* (Assen: Van Gorcum, 1969); see also below note 33.

21 Cohn, *Das Buch Jona*, p. 37.

22 André Parrot, *Nineveh and the Old Testament*, trans. B.E. Hooke (New York: Philosophical Library, 1955).

23 With the exception of Genesis 24:3, 7 (J).

24 See George M. Landes, "The Kerygma of the Book of Jonah," *Interp*. 21 (1967): 3-31, and before him A. Loretz "Herkunft und Sinn der Jona-Erzählung" *BZ* 5 (1961): esp. 19-24.

25 See *Genesis Rabbah* 98 (p. 62a).

26 André Feuillet, "Les Sources du livre de Jonas," *RB* 54 (1947): 176.

27 Albert Lord, *The Singer of Tales* (Cambridge, Mass.: Harvard University Press, 1973), p. 207.

28 John D. Crossan, *The Dark Interval* (Niles, IL: Argus Communications, 1975).

29 The use of irony by the author of Jonah has been stressed by various commentators (see Chapter II). Along the same line, Allen (*Joel, Obadiah, Jonah, and Micah*) sees also parodies of 1 Kings 19:4 in Jonah 4:4, 8; of Jeremiah 18:7, 8, 11; in Jonah 3:9, 10; of *Joel* especially (2:13-14) in Jonah 3:9; 4:2. (On the use of Joel in Jonah, see Hans Walter Wolff, *Studien zum Jonabuch*, Biblische Studien 47 [Neukirchener Verlag: Neukirchen-Vluyn, 1947 (Köln, 1965)]).

30 See Paul Hanson, *The Dawn of Apocalyptic* (Philadelphia: Fortress Press, 1975).

31 Hanson, *The Dawn of Apocalyptic*, p. 68.

32 See André Lacocque, "Date et milieu du livre de Ruth," *RHPR* 3 –4 (1979): 583-593. Note at this point the ongoing reappraisal of Deuteronomic laws. See Isaiah 56:3 –8 on the presence of eunuchs and strangers in the community of YHWH: see also Ruth contrasting Deuteronomy 23:4 (cf. Zech. 14 broadening the Levitical laws of purity).

33 Y. Kaufmann's reaction to modern misconceptions about Jonah is refreshing. He sees in the book the moral opposition of justice and mercy, not of Israel and the Gentiles (*The Religion of Israel* [Chicago: University of Chicago Press, 1960], p. 283). Cohn also is on the right track when he sees the contrast between the way of humanity and the way of God. Only God's word shows the right direction and is the essence of life (*Das Buch Jona*). For the author of Jonah, the ideologists' stance is "the way of humanity."

34 Allen, *Joel, Obadiah, Jonah, and Micah*, p. 191.

35 Wilhelm Rudolph (*Joel-Amos-Obadja-Jona*, KAT 13/2 [Gütersloh: Mohn, 1971]) has correctly seen that the adversaries of the author are the disciples of Ezra-Nehemiah. The author of Jonah is deeply upset by pagan dominion over Israel as a thorn in the flesh that cannot be ignored, since it is an obstacle to the coming of the *eschaton* (p. 369). (This opinion is expressly rejected by Gerhard von Rad [*Old Testament Theology* (New York: Harper & Row, 1965), vol. 2, p. 291], A. Loretz

["Herkunft und Sinn der Jona-Erzählung," p. 28], Otto Eissfeldt [*Old Testament: An Introduction* (New York: Harper & Row, 1965), p. 405], P. Trible ["Studies in the Book of Jonah" (Ph.D. Dissertation, Columbia University, 1963), pp. 262-263].) But the author describes the adversaries with tact, like Cervantes, who ridicules the sham chivalry of his time in the person of Don Quixote. In both cases, the treatment of the subject is not devoid of a profound respect.

36 See the commentary on Jonah 1 below. As Brevard Childs writes, ". . . the canonical setting of the story in the period of Jeroboam II (2 Kings 14), rather than placing it in the post exilic period, ensures seeing the issue raised by the book as constitutive to the theological relation between Israel and the nations" (*Introduction to the Old Testament as Scripture* [Philadelphia: Fortress, 1979], pp. 425-26).

37 See Paul Ricoeur, *The Conflict of Interpretations*, ed. D. Ihde, (Evanston, IL: Northwestern University Press, 1974), pp. 349-350: ". . . .a *textual* exegesis is abstract and remains meaningless for us so long as the 'figuratives' it comments on are not inserted into the affective and representative dynamism. . . . The symbol is a phantasm disavowed and overcome but not at all abolished."

38 Pindarus exhorts man to become all he can be.

Chapter II

1 See, for example "Paul Ricoeur on Biblical Hermeneutics," *Semeia* 4, ed. John D. Crossan (Missoula, MT: Scholars Press, 1975); or *Interpretation Theory: Discourse and the Surplus of Meaning* (Ft. Worth: Texas University Press, 1976).

2 Crossan, *The Dark Interval*, p. 66. He also writes: ". . . the most magnificent parable in the Hebrew Bible is the book of Jonah which is the precursor for the parables of Jesus and the distant ancestor of the contemporary parabolic genre" ("Parable, Allegory, and Paradox," in *Semiology and Parables*, ed. D. Patte [Pittsburgh: Pickwick Press, 1976], p. 251).

3 Robert Scholes and Robert Kellogg, *The Nature of Narrative* (London: Oxford University Press, 1966).

4 Roland Barthes ("An Introduction to the Structural Analysis of Narrative," tr. by Lionel Dinsit, in *New Literary History* 6 [Winter 1975]: 237-72) reviews three possibilities in respect to the narrator's role in the classic literary approach: (a) the narrator is the actual author and the narrative is his mirror; (b) the narrator is an all-knowing consciousness, a "god" in control of the world within the actors and without; (c) the narrator limits his presentation to the viewpoints of the characters. (For Barthes all of these are inadequate, as, for him, author and characters are grammatical entities, not real people.) Jonah's author would be a mixture of (b) and (c). He is Jonah and outside Jonah. Jonah represents both his people—with whom he can identify—and a caricature of his people, namely, the hierocratic party in Jerusalem, from whom he keeps his distance (see above, Chapter I).

5 Scholes and Kellogg, *The Nature of Narratives*, p. 229.

6 Crossan, "Parable, Allegory, and Paradox," p. 251.

7 Paul Ricoeur spoke, as we saw above, of "disorientation" and "reorientation" by the narrative. It is striking that Jonah chooses to go toward the totally foreign and properly "disoriented" world of Tarshish in the West.

8 See John A. Miles, Jr., "Laughing at the Bible: Jonah as Parody," *JQR* 65 (January 1975): 168-181.

9 See D. O. Via, *The Parables* (Philadelphia: Fortress, 1967), p. 105. Ricoeur uses rather the term "extravagance."

10 As far as Jonah is concerned, its understanding depends directly upon its historical setting in the fifth century situation in Jerusalem; "... the relation is an event, and hence narration is the proper form to describe it. The decisive word-form in the language of the Bible is not the substantive, as in Greek, but the verb, the word of action" (G. Ernest Wright, *God Who Acts*, Studies in Biblical Theology 8 [London: SCM Press, 1952], p. 90). Thus it is clear that especially in Israel the relation between "story" and "history" is very close. According to Scholes and Kellogg (*The Nature of Narrative*, p. 151), "science seems to have demonstrated that Aristotle's distinction between history and fiction was one of degree, not of kind." Any report of event is representational fiction.

11 Quoted by Helen M. Crawford, *A Reluctant Missionary* (Chicago: U.P.C. Board of Education, 1965), p. 34.

12 Herman Melville, *Moby Dick or the Whale* (New York: Holt, Rinehart and Winston, 1957), pp. 40-41.

13 Even though the fish in Jonah 2 is commonly known as a whale, the biblical text does not specify its genus. It is described only as a "great fish," meaning Leviathan or a mythological animal of chaos. As George Orwell aptly says, "The Whale's belly is simply a womb big enough for an adult" (*Inside the Whale* [London: Victor Gollancz, 1940], p. 177).

14 B. Zeigarnik, "Über das Behalten von erledigten Handlungen," *Psychologie Forschung* 9 (1927): 1-85.

15 R. M. Goldenson, *The Encyclopedia of Human Behavior*, 2 vols. (New York: Doubleday, 1970), p. 1382, summarizing Zeigarnik.

16 Bruno Bettelheim, *The Uses of Enchantment* (New York: Alfred A. Knopf, 1976).

17 Hyman Fingert, "The Psychoanalytic Study of the Minor Prophet Jonah," *The Psychoanalytic Review* 41 (1954): 55-65.

18 Fingert, "Psychoanalytic Study," p. 58.

19 Fingert, "Psychoanalytic Study," p. 61.

20 Fingert, "Psychoanalytic Study," p. 62.

21 The nature and function of the Bible, from a psychoanalytical viewpoint, is essentially the expression of Oedipal struggles, according to D. F. Zeligs ("A Psychoanalytic Note on the Function of the Bible," *American Imago* 14 [Spring 1957]: 57-58).

22 Joseph More (Muggia), "The Prophet Jonah: The Story of an Intrapsychic Process," *American Imago* 27 (1970): 3-11.

23 More (Muggia), "Prophet Jonah," p. 6.

24 More (Muggia), "Prophet Jonah," p. 7.

25 More (Muggia), "Prophet Jonah," p. 7.

26 More (Muggia), "Prophet Jonah," pp. 7-8.

27 Carl G. Jung, *Two Essays on Analytical Psychology* (Princeton, NJ: Princeton University Press, 1953), p. 97.

28 Jung, *Two Essays*, p. 97; see also *Symbols of Transformation* (New York: Pantheon, 1956), p. 348; *Critique of Psychoanalysis* (Princeton, NJ: Princeton University Press, 1975), p. 128; and *The Psychology of Transference* (New York: Bollingen Foundation, 1966), p. 137.

29 But Jonah, as we saw, is not a Greek hero but an antihero. He does not hurt or kill the fish; his concern is not with the latter but with his divine calling.

30 Jung, *Symbols of Transformation*, pp. 109-110, 156, 419.

31 Jung, *Symbols of Transformation*, p. 331.

32 Rollo May, *Man's Search for Himself* (New York: W. W. Norton, 1953), p. 121; see also *Love and Will* (New York: Dell, 1969), p. 166.
33 See Jung, *Symbols of Transformation*, p. 348.
34 Erich Fromm, *The Forgotten Language* (New York: Grove Press, 1937), p. 22.
35 Erich Fromm with R. I. Evans, *Dialogue with Erich Fromm* (New York: Harper & Row, 1966), p. 119.
36 Erich Fromm, *Man for Himself* (Greenwich, CT: Fawcett, 1947), p. 105.
37 See Jeremiah 20:7.
38 Viktor Frankl, *Psychotherapy and Existentialism* (New York: Simon and Schuster, 1967), p. 12; cf. pp. 30, 68.
39 Viktor Frankl, *The Doctor and the Soul* (New York: Alfred A. Knopf, 1955), p. x.

Chapter III

1 Frankl, *Psychotherapy and Existentialism*, p. 9.
2 Abraham Maslow, *Toward a Psychology of Being* (New York: D. van Nostrand, 1968), p. 61.
3 Abraham Maslow, "Neurosis as a Failure of Personal Growth," *Humanitas* 3 (1967): 165-166.
4 For *j. Sukka* 5, 55a, 54 Jonah's (call) occurred on the second day of Sukkoth when his heart was merrying (cf. Str.-Bill. Vol. I, p. 643).
5 Maslow, *Toward a Psychology of Being*, p. 195.
6 Martin Buber, *Knowledge of Man* (New York: Harper Colophon Books, 1965), p. 47.
7 In the first two one has recourse to games, then to clichés. The fourth and last stage is the fear of death (Frederick Perls, *Gestalt Therapy Verbatim* [Lafayette, CA: Real People Press, 1969], pp. 55-56).
8 See e.g., Rollo May, *Man's Search for Himself* (New York: W. W. Norton, 1953), p. 24; and Viktor Frankl, *Man's Search for Meaning* (Boston: Beacon Press, 1962), p. 103.
9 Carl G. Jung, *Modern Man in Search of a Soul* (New York: Harcourt, Brace, and World, 1933), p. 65.
10 Suffice it here to refer to Zepheniah 2:13 or to the book of Nahum. Nineveh was the capital of Assyria when Sennacherib conquered the kingdom of Juda (702 B.C.E.). The city was destroyed in 612 by the Medes. It is curious that, according to a popular etymology, Nin-naveh would mean the "place of the fish." The cuneiform pictogram for the city shows "Nina, a sign of representing an enclosure with a fish inside" (*IDB*, vol. 3, p. 552). Moreover, in Hellenistic times, a parallel was drawn with the Greek god Ninos, who was a god-fish.
11 R. E. Clements, "The Purpose of the Book of Jonah," Congress Volume, Edinburgh, 1974, VTSup 28 (Leiden: Brill, 1975), p. 18. This leads Clements to so minimize the element of Nineveh that it all but disappears from the picture (p. 21, ". . . it makes no difference to the point that is being made" [sic!]). For a similar point of view, see Trible, "Studies in the Book of Jonah."
12 On the generic sense of "Nineveh," cf. the Demotic papyrus "The Lamb" (Peḥib) ca. seventh-eighth centuries C.E. but representing a tradition going back probably to the Ptolemies. It announces the conquest of Egypt by "Nineveh"!
13 Cf. 1 Corinthians 12:4, 7; see also below Chapter VII. As Frankl puts it, "No man, and no destiny can be compared with any other man or any other destiny. No situation repeats itself, and each situation calls for a different response"

(*Man's Search for Meaning*, p. 77); ". . . each human being is not comparable with any other in his innermost being. To compare yourself with anyone else is to do an injustice either to yourself or to the other person" (*The Doctor and the Soul* [New York: Alfred A. Knopf, 1955], p. 173).

14 See James M. Redfield, *Nature and Culture in the Iliad, The Tragedy of Hector* (Chicago: University of Chicago Press, 1975).

15 When we compare, for instance, the deluge story as told in Babylon and in the Bible, it appears clearly that in Israel the flood does not interrupt history; here rather, *mythos* is complemented by *ethos*. Noah is a righteous man. Similarly, the vocation of Jonah is to be righteous.

16 ". . . I don't think one can be a hero in any really elevating sense without some transcendental referent, like being a hero for God, or for the creative powers of the universe. The most exalted type of heroism involves feelings that one has lived to some purpose that transcends one" (Ernest Becker, "The Heroics of Everyday Life," in *Voices and Visions*, ed. Sam Keen [New York: Harper & Row, 1974], p. 183).

17 See Rollo May, *Existential Psychology* (New York: Random House, 1960), p. 81: "Anxiety is the state of the human being in the struggle against that which would destroy his being. . . . One wing of this struggle will always be against something outside the self. But even more portentous and significant for psychotherapy is the inner battle, . . . namely, the conflict within the person as he confronts the choice of whether and how far he will stand against his own being, his own potentialities."

18 In the words of Ernest Becker, "Neurosis is another word for describing a complicated technique for avoiding misery, but reality is the misery. That is why from earliest times sages have insisted that to see reality one must die and be reborn" (*The Denial of Death* [New York: Free Press, 1973], p. 57).

19 Cf. M. Solovine, *Démocrite. Doctrines philosophiques et réflexions morales* (trad. et notes précéd. d'une intro), (Paris: Alcan, 1928).

20 Carl G. Jung, *Symbols of Transformation*, p. 110.

21 One will notice the *centrifugal* character of the book of Jonah. The myth of the Center is broken (see *Myths and Symbols: Studies in Honor of Mircea Eliade*, ed. Joseph M. Kitagawa and Charles H. Long [Chicago: University of Chicago Press, 1969]).

22 "The Kerygma of the Book of Jonah," p. 19. The same opinion is present in the Targum, Ibn Ezra, and Redaq on this verse.

23 Rudolph, *Joel-Amos-Obadja-Jona*, p. 337. "See ye not then, shipmates, that Jonah sought to flee world-wide from God?" (Melville, *Moby Dick*, p. 41).

24 Rudolph, *Joel-Amos-Obadja-Jona*, ad loc. 4:2; contra Ellul, Vischer, Keller, *et al.*

25 Str.-Bill., vol. I, p. 643.

26 Landes, "The Kerygma of the Book of Jonah," p. 4.

27 So N. Lohfink, "Und Jona ging zur Stadt hinaus (Jon. 4, 5)," *BZ* 5 (1961): 200; Trible, "Studies in the Book of Jonah" p. 206; Allen, *The Books of Joel, Obadiah, Jonah, and Micah*, p. 204.

28 " 'Al Sepher Yonah,' " *Mahanayim* 47 (1961): 45-48, quoted by Cohn, *Das Buch Jona*, p. 67, n.2.

29 Hans Walter Wolff speaks of "weisheitlische Lehrerzählung" and of "Weisheitdichtung" (*RGG* 3, vol. III, cols. 853-56).

30 See Isaiah 51:9 –10; Psalms 74:13 –15, 89:10 –11; Job 26:12.

31 Cohn, *Das Buch Jona*, p. 78, n. 1.

32 Cohn, *Das Buch Jona*, p. 88, n. 3.

33 Harry S. Sullivan, *The Psychiatric Interview* (New York: W. W. Norton, 1954), p. 218. Alfred Adler, in the same vein, speaks of "exclusion tendencies"(*The Individual Psychology of Alfred Adler*,ed. Hans and Rowena Ansbacher [New York:Harper and Row, 1956], pp. 277-78).

34 See André Lacocque, "A Return to a God of Nature?" in *Sources of Vitality in American Church Life*, ed. R. L. Moore (Chicago: Exploration Press, 1978), pp. 108-119.

35 Fromm, *The Forgotten Language* , p. 22.

36 The Hebrew word for fish that is used in Jonah 2:2 is a feminine form.

37 See above, Chapter I.

38 R. B. Y. Scott, "The Sign of Jonah," *Interp.* 19 (1965): 16-25.

39 W. Vischer,"Jonas," *EThR* 24 (1949): 117.

40 *Pirqe de Rabbi Eliezer*, trans. with notes by Gerald Friedlander (New York: Hermon Press, 1965), chap. X, "The Story of Jonah."

41 See below our reflections on verse 7 and anti-Semitism.

42 Fromm, *The Forgotten Language*, p. 21. See also More (Muggia), "Prophet Jonah," p. 3.

43 Allen,*Joel, Obadiah, Jonah, and Micah*, p. 207.

44 This has been noticed also by Cohn, *Das Buch Jona*, p. 57.

45 This progression corresponds to the "stair style" of which Cohn speaks. So, for example, as Jonah increases the gap with God, the sailors come even closer to him:

    vs. 5 "they feared the divine"

    vs. 10 "these men feared of a great fear"

    vs. 16 "these men feared of a great fear YHWH."

We see the same thing re the story:

    vs. 4 "and there was a great storm on the sea"

    vs. 11 "for the sea continued to rage"

    vs. 13 "for the sea continued to rage against them" (Cohn, *Das Buch Jona*, p. 53).

46 Clearly, this confirms the direct relationship that exists between perception and need as D. Snygg and A. W. Combs have amply demonstrated in their work: "What is perceived will always be a function of the individual's need and the antecedent field which he possesses at the moment" (*Individual Behavior*, 2d ed. [New York: Harper and Row, 1959], p. 35).

47 See Melville, *Moby Dick*, p. 45. On God creator of sea and dry land, see Psalm 95:5.

48 May, *Man's Search for Himself*, p. 88.

49 May writes: ". . . [modern man] has significance only if he gives up his own significance. . . . [he] maintains a protective coloring so that he won't be singled out from the others and shot at. To this extent you are said to be significant, but it is a significance that is bought precisely at the price of giving up one's significance" ("Modern Man's Image of Himself," *The Chicago Theological Seminary Register*, 52 [October 1962]: 2).

50 Roberto Assagioli, *Psychosynthesis* (New York: Viking Press, 1971); Alfred Adler, *Social Interest: A Challenge to Mankind* (New York: G. P. Putnam's Sons, 1964), p. 39.

51 Becker, *The Denial of Death*, p. 82.

52 In the words of Paul Tillich, "Anxiety strives to become fear. . . . It is impossible

for a finite being to stand naked anxiety for more than a flash of time. People who have experienced these moments . . . have told of the unimaginable horror of it [naked anxiety]. This horror is ordinarily avoided by the transformation of anxiety into fear of something, no matter what" (*The Courage to Be* [New Haven: Yale University Press, 1952], p. 39). And as May writes, "In fear we know what threatens us. . . . In anxiety, however we are threatened without knowing what steps to take to meet the danger. Anxiety is the feeling of being 'caught,' 'overwhelmed' and instead of becoming sharper, our perceptions generally become blurred or vague" (*Man's Search for Himself,* p. 39).

53 Maslow, *Toward a Psychology of Being,* pp. 60-67.

54 May, *Man's Search for Himself,* pp. 247, 250.

55 Becker, *The Denial of Death,* p. 73. Following Sullivan, one could say that the real characteristics of Jonah as perceived by the sailors are distorted for their convenience, a process called "parataxic distortion."

56 More (Muggia), "The Prophet Jonah," p. 8.

57 Friedlander, *Pirqe de Rabbi Eliezer* , p. 67, n. 10.

58 Jerome, Letter LX (Jerome's approach is of course Christocentric). See *Select Letters of St. Jerome,* with an English translation by F. A. Wright, The Loeb Classical Library (Cambridge, Mass.: Harvard University Press, 1933), pp. 267-269.

59 For Haller and Trible, verse 12 is the final attempt to evade his mission. For Smart, Brockington, Keller, Ellul, on the contrary, it is a gallant bid for vicarious sacrifice.

60 Erik Erikson, *Identity, Youth, and Crisis* (New York: W. W. Norton, 1968), p. 140.

Chapter IV

1 Allen Wheelis, "How People Change," *Commentary* 47 (May 1969): 65.

2 Wheelis, "How People Change," p. 65.

3 Smart, "Jonah," *IB,* vol. 6, p. 874. So C. H. H. Wright, "The Book of Jonah Considered from an Allegorical Point of View," *Biblical Essays* (1886): 34-98, quoted by Trible, "Studies in the Book of Jonah," p. 155, n. 3.

4 As once said by Vischer, "One should notice this true to life contradiction: the very one who fled away from the Lord, is now in anguish for fear of being 'cast out from His presence.' " ("Jonas," *EThR* 24 [1949]: 118). And St. Jerome writes: "Jonah, that headstrong prophet, once fled from me, yet in the depths of the sea he was still mine" (Letter XXIX, 3 in *The Principal Works of St. Jerome,* tr. Fremantle, Lewis and Martley, Nicene and Post Nicene Fathers, Series 2 [Grand Rapids: Eerdmans, n. d.], p. 51).

5 Rollo May, *The Courage to Create* (New York: W. W. Norton, 1975), p. 59.

6 "When this breakthrough of a creative insight into consciousness occurs, we have the subjective conviction that the form should be this way and no other way. It is characteristic of the creative experience that it strikes us as true. . . . And we think, nothing else could have been true in that situation, and we wonder why we were so stupid as not to have seen it earlier" (May, *The Courage to Create,* p. 68).

7 "But observe his prayer, and learn a weighty lesson. For sinful as he is, Jonah does not weep and wail for direct deliverance. He feels that his dreadful punishment is just. . . And here, shipmates, is true and faithful repentance . . ." (Melville, *Moby Dick,* p. 46).

8 From "prior-self" to "authentic self"; see our discussion of these categories below in Chapter VII on the Outer Voice.
9 Trible, "Studies in the Book of Jonah," p. 80; cf. Wolff, *Studien zum Jonabuch.*
10 Theodore H. Robinson and F. Horst, *Die Zwölf Kleinen Propheten,* HAT 1/14 (Tübingen: Mohr-Siebeck, 1964), p. 117.
11 Wilhelm M. L. Dewette appears to have been the first to contend for the inauthenticity of the psalm here, in *Lehrbuch der historisch-kritischen Einleitung in kanonischen und apokryphen Bücher des A.T.* (Berlin: G. Reiner, 1817), p. 298 (see Landes, "The Kerygma of the Book of Jonah," 3-31).
12 See Y. Kaufmann, *Toldot ha-emunah ha-yisraelit* (Tel Aviv. Bialik Institute, 1963), vol. 4. (it has been inserted by the author himself from an extant Psalm collection); so also Allen (*The Books of Joel, Obadiah, Jonah, and Micah,* p. 183): "The motifs and metaphors of this Psalm are stereotyped vehicles of devotion used by spiritual folk in many a situation of distress." See also A. R. Johnson, "Jonah 2:3 –10: A Study in Cultic Fantasy," in *Studies in Old Testament Prophecy,* ed. H. H. Rowley and Theodore H. Robinson (New York: Scribner's, 1950), pp. 87-100; Eissfeldt, *The Old Testament: An Introduction;* pp. 121-124; and especially Landes, "The Kerygma of the Book of Jonah," pp. 3-31.
13 Paul Tillich, *The Eternal Now* (New York: Charles Scribner's Sons, 1963), p. 128. For Heidegger, the way to freedom is the conversion to Being. The inauthentic existence is a negative sign of its reference to Being; its sense can always be reversed.
14 Max Scheler; "Repentance and Rebirth," in *On the Eternal in Man* (New York: Anchor Books, 1972), pp. 41-42. See also note 7 above.
15 Mircea Eliade, *Myths, Dreams and Mysteries,* (New York: Harper and Row, 1960), pp. 225, 237.
16 Of course, we do not mean to say that numbers overcome solitude. Each of the millions in the Nazi camps was desperately alone.
17 "This prayer of Jonah's appears to be a symbolic representation of the childhood fantasy of being in the mother's womb. . . . Here we find symbolically represented a fantasy of a person being in the womb, the amniotic fluids and the placenta membranes about him. Even the sex of the engulfing being is clearly represented in the phrase; 'the earth with her bars closed upon me forever' " (Fingert, "Psychoanalytic Study of the Minor Prophet Jonah," p. 59).
18 Eliade, *Myths, Dreams and Mysteries,* p. 223. In the Greek parallels of the Jonah story, the fish is a dolphin. Carl G. Jung and K. Kerenyi see in it a delph-uterus, an etymology which we have been unable to verify (see *Einführung in das Wesen der Mythologie* [Zurich: Rascher, 1951], pp. 73 ff.). We refer the reader to the myth of Herakles who is swallowed by a sea monster before he is saved. Arion (ca. 625 B.C.E.) is said to have been carried on a dolphin's back to land after a shipwreck. Significantly, Abarbanel defends the historicity of the miracle through analogy with the living embryo living for nine months in the mother's womb.
19 *The History of Religions,* ed. Eliade and Kitagawa (Chicago: University of Chicago Press, 1959), chap. 5; see also Mircea Eliade, *Myths, Dreams and Mysteries,* p. 223 and *The Sacred and the Profane* (New York: Harper and Row, 1961), pp. 130-131.
20 G. Campbell Morgan, *The Minor Prophets* (London: Pickering, 1960), p. 69.
21 Friedlander, *Pirqe de Rabbi Eliezer,* p. 69.
22 Friedlander, *Pirqe de Rabbi Eliezer,* p. 73, n. 1.
23 J. Steinmann, *Le livre de la consolation d'Israël et les prophètes du retour de l'exil* (Paris: Cerf, 1960), p. 290 (our English translation).

24 G. B. Stanton, "The Prophet Jonah and His Message," *Bibl. Sacra* 108 (1951):371.
25 Landes, "The Kerygma of the Book of Jonah," pp. 12-13. So also Rudolph, *Joel-Amos-Obadja-Jona,* ad loc. 2:1 P. Reymond, *L'eau, sa vie et sa signification dans l'Ancien Testament,* VTSup 6 (Leiden: Brill, 1958), p. 198; *et al.* For the opposite view, see Cheyne, van Hoonacker, Bewer, Feuillet, Weiser, Trible, etc.
26 Despite the affirmation of Trible ("Studies in the Book of Jonah," pp. 139, 141) that the fish is "an instrument of salvation," not at all a "chaos-dragon monster," one must realize that in Judaism and in Christianity, as soon as there is descent into water, the symbol is uniformly a catabasis into the shapeless death realm where the dragon dwells. Even the baptism of Jesus in the little threatening Jordan was so interpreted by a unanimous Christian tradition (see H. Riesenfeld, "La signification sacramentelle du baptême johannique," *Dieu Vivant* 13 [1949]: 29-37; cf. *Odes of Solomon* 24:1-3 and the study by R. Harris, *The Odes and Psalms of Solomon* [Cambridge: Cambridge University Press, 1909], p. 123). It is possible to go even farther. The descent of Jesus into the river has been seen as a messianic process of purification of the waters. *So also was the catabasis of Jonah* viewed by the Rabbis, who see in Jonah the Messiah ben Joseph (see Ignatius of Antioch, *Letter to the Ephesians* XVIII, 2; in Jewish tradition, see *Exodus Rabbah* 18, 97 –98; for Jonah as a type of Christ, see Matt. 12:39; Luke 11:29).
27 Rollo May, "Modern Man's Image of Himself," *The Chicago Theological Seminary Register* 52 (October 1962): 14. Cf. Tillich, "Remembrance of the past preserves the identity of a human being with himself" (*The Eternal Now,* p. 29) and H. Feifel, "The past is an image that changes with our image of ourselves" ("Death-relevant variable in psychology," in *Existential Psychology,* ed. Rollo May [New York: Random House, 1960], p. 59).
28 For Fromm, e.g., the fish symbolizes "the state of isolation and imprisonment which his lack of love and solidarity has brought upon him" (*Man for Himself,* p. 105; cf. *Dialogue with Erich Fromm* [New York: Harper & Row, 1966], p. 119).
29 The great sixteenth-century Rabbi, the Maharal of Prague, has eloquently shown that, in the number three, the focus is on the middle term; the middle term simultaneously separates and binds, distances and approximates, differentiates and homogenizes, rends by hatred and mends by love. "Three" is the in-between, the "no man's land" which is open to any and every possibility both the most rewarding and the most painful. André Neher refers to Hosea 6:2 which shows, he says, that the number of three days is symbolic of the maintenance of the "life of time." "Whether time is crossed by illness and death, within three days it shall not be exhausted: wait for healing or resurrection at the end in certainty. Beyond, there is the hazard of a fatal accident" (*L'exil de la parole* [Paris: Seuil, 1970], pp. 28-29 (our English translation).
30 It is interesting to note with Landes ("Jonah," *IDB Supp.,* p. 490; "The Kerygma of the Book of Jonah," pp. 11-12; or again in *JBL* 86 [1967]: 446-450), that three days are necessary for covering the distance from here to the nether world, according to the Sumerian myth of the Descent of Inanna to the Netherworld (*ANET,* p. 55, cf. Part II, li. 169-173). The theme has been reversed here; it takes three days to bring back Jonah to the world of living. On the basis of Hosea 6:2 and Genesis 42:18, the Rabbis concluded that God does not leave his righteous ones in need more than three days (*Genesis Rabbah,* 56; 57; *Yalqut* to Josh. 2:16). As Job 40 seems to identify the Behemoth with the common hippopotamus, and Job 41 Leviathan with the crocodile, Jonah may here allude to the latter

as a "big fish." Verse 4 here uses a term like "billows," which is elsewhere in the Bible a synonym of "abyss" (cf. Exod. 15:5; Neh. 9:11; Mic. 7:19 from where God saves his elect, Ps. 68:23; 69:3, 16, etc.). In the Gilgamesh Epic, Siduri, the goddess of life, has her throne in the sea *(ANET,* p. 90).

31 Cf. Frankl: "What man actually needs is not a tensionless state but rather the striving and struggling for some goal worthy of him" *(Man's Search for Meaning,* p. 107) or again ". . . meaning must not coincide with being, meaning must be ahead of being" *(Psychotherapy and Existentialism,* p. 12).

32 Address delivered at Temple Emanuel, Chicago, 1971.

33 "Thank you for what my eyes have seen, and for the deeper insight I was granted when I became blind" (Reconstruction by memory of Old Lodge Skins' parting words in Arthur Penn's film "Little Big Man.")

34 Mere contemplation implies that the visionary remains somewhat uninvolved. He stands, as it were, on an aesthetic level. What ravishes him is an *object,* always unreachable, as in a dream.

35 In our days, the rebirth of the state of Israel, on the heels of Auschwitz, is a historical phenomenon entirely congruent with the past of that literally "extra-ordinary" people.

36 See André Neher, *Amos, contribution à l'étude du prophétisme* (Paris: J. Vrin, 1950), (particularly his development on Amos's visions, chaps. 7 ff.).

37 Erich Fromm, *The Art of Loving* (New York: Harper and Row, 1956), p. 39.

38 "Thus whenever the psychiatrist's attempt to discover what the patient is talking about leads the patient to be somewhat more clear on what he is thinking about or attempting to communicate or conceal . . ."(Sullivan, *The Psychiatric Interview,* pp. 23-24).

39 Martin Buber, *The Way of Man* (New York: Citadel Press, 1967), p. 34.

40 Cf. Jerome: "You will note that where you would think should be the end of Jonah, there was his safety" (quoted by Bickerman, *Four Strange Books of the Bible* p. 12).

41 Frankl, *The Doctor and the Soul,* p. 122.

42 Frankl, *Psychotherapy and Existentialism,* p. 50.

43 Becker, *The Denial of Death,* p. 58.

Chapter V

1 Already in 1799, J. C. Nachtigal made a distinction between Jonah 2:3—4:11, on the one hand, and 1:1—2:2 on the other. The former passage was written during the Exile against Jewish particularism, the latter in the time of Ezra-Nehemiah. More recently this thesis has been adopted by A. Thoma ("Die Entstehung des Büchleins Jona," *Theol. St. u. Krit.* [1911]: 47 ff.; cf. Nachtigal in *Eichhorns allgemeine Bibliothek der bibl. Literatur* [Lips: Weidmannschen Buchhandlung, 1799], IX, pp. 221 ff.).

2 Cf. Bettelheim, ". . . the dominant feeling a myth conveys is: this is absolutely unique; it could not have happened to any other person, or in any other setting; such events are grandiose, all-inspiring and could not possibly happen to an ordinary mortal like you or me" *(The Uses of Enchantment,* p. 37).

3 "A second time" is, however, also understood in Jewish tradition as being restrictive, namely, there is no third time, which sanctions Jonah's looking "for the glory of the son (Israel), but not of the father (God)" *(Mekilta on Exodus* 2a on 12:1).

4 R. D. Laing writes: "To be eaten does not necessarily mean to lose one's identity.

Jonah was very much himself even within the belly of the whale" (*The Divided Self* [Baltimore: Penguin Books, 1965], p. 49).

5 Rudoph, *Joel-Amos-Obadja-Jona*, pp. 357-358.

6 "The Ninevites might be the source of dramatic suspense in easily imaginable variations of the plot. But the biblical book is about Jonah" (Bickerman, *Four Strange Books*, p. 9).

7 See "extravagance" in *The Oxford Universal Dictionary*, 1955. Also see the final chapter of André Lacocque, *Where Was God at Auschwitz?* forthcoming.

8 Melville, *Moby Dick*, p. 47.

9 E.g., the four cardinal points, the four seasons. Nineveh is to be destroyed in forty days, a multiple of four after the model of the flood, of the time spent by the Israelites in the desert, of Elijah's trip to Horeb (cf. Jesus' trial in the desert, etc.). On the size of Nineveh, see Diodorus Siculus II:3. Its actual circumference was seven and one half miles, an extraordinary size for the time.

10 Psalm 11:5 uses the word *ḥāmās* in connection with Sodom and Gomorrah.

11 Redaq in the Middle Ages had already called attention to the necessary connection with the fate of Sodom and Gomorrah. Long before him, Cyril of Alexandria had made the same point (see Bickerman, *Four Strange Books*, p. 13).

12 As one can see, the Bible is not "behavioristic." Lot and Jonah were involved in similar situations but they had conflicting purposes, attitudes, and results.

13 YHWH is the proper name of the God in covenant with Israel, whereas Elohim is a common noun and can be translated "God," "the divine," "the divinity," etc. On the decisive importance of the use of YHWH and Elohim for the understanding of biblical texts, see Lacocque, "Job or the Impotence of Religion," to be published in *Semeia* in 1981.

14 *'Abot de Rabbi Nathan* 1:8.

15 Again here, behaviorism seems to miss the real existential issue. With the book of Jonah we are far from a statement like the one that follows, by H. J. Eysench, "there is no neurosis underlying the symptom but merely the symptom itself. Get rid of the symptom, and you have eliminated the neurosis" (*Behavior Therapy and the Neuroses* [Oxford: Pergamon Press, 1960], p. 9). It is to be noted that Wolpe's systematic desensitization therapy is based on this credo.

16 Or, as the book of Jonah entertains the fiction of an eighth century B.C.E. prophet speaking to Nineveh, that wicked city is destined some day to assault Jerusalem and its Temple. Thus, if Jonah's preaching is the occasion of repentance and salvation for Nineveh, the prophet is instrumental in keeping in existence the future destroyer of Zion and the House of God! That he could be conscious of this is not inconceivable for Jewish tradition. The Rabbis say: There is no "before" and no "after" in the Bible.

17 Wolf Mankowitz, "It Should Happen to a Dog," *Religious Drama, III*, selected and introduced by Marvin Halverson (Meridian, NY: Living Age Books, 1959), p. 131.

18 Cf. Servius ad Vergil *Aen.* 4.696: "Sunt fata quae dicuntur denuntiativa, sunt alia fata quae condicionalia vocantur. Denuntiativa sunt quae omnimodo eventura decernunt . . . non potest aliter evenire." (The revelation of destiny can be unconditional—*denuntiativa*; it then occurs in any case, nothing else can happen.) (Quoted by Elias Bickerman, "Les deux erreurs du Prophète Jonas," *RHPR* 45 [1965]: 252, n. 75).

19 R. Ami wept when he came upon the [following] verse: "let him put his mouth in

the dust, perhaps there may be hope" (Lam. 3:29). He said: "All this for a Perhaps!?" (*Hagiga* 4b; cf. Zeph. 2:3; Joel 2:14).

20 Neher, *L'exil de la parole*, pp. 258-259 (our English translation).

21 According to the so-called "short text"; cf. Josephus, *Antiquities* 9.10.2 § 214.

22 According to the Rabbis (*Sanhedrin* 89b), "Jonah did not know whether Nineveh would be 'overthrown' towards good (convert), or if it would be overthrown by evil." In a somewhat similar vein, St. Augustine says that from a material point of view, it is true Jonah appears to be a liar, but from a spiritual viewpoint it is true that sinful Nineveh was "overthrown" (Quoted by Bickerman, "Les deux erreurs," p. 255). *Yalqut* to Jonah 3:3 (§ 550) says that because the Ninevites did penance, God restrained his wrath for forty years in accord with the forty days of the oracle.

23 "In Israel, whoever does not believe in the miracle is not a realist" (J. Ben Gurion).

24 Neher, *L'exil de la parole*, pp. 254-255 (our English translation).

25 We must, however, credit Bickerman for pointing out the difference between Jewish "repentance" and Greek *metanoia*. Whereas the former is contrition of heart, the latter implies a mere intellectual value judgment (cr. A. D. Nock, *Conversion* [Oxford: Clarendon, 1933], p. 181) and is oriented toward future behavior rather than the moral condemnation of the past. Similarly note the contrast between the Hebrew concept of revolt against God and the Greek *hamartia*; cf. Bickerman, "It's not sin, it's a mistake" ("Les deux erreurs," p. 257, n. 90 [our English translation].

26 Philo, *De Jona* (quoted by Bickerman, *Four Strange Books*, p. 47).

27 Calvin, for example, emphasizes here the wisdom of God, which reaches beyond human understanding (*Opera* LXVIII [1890], p. 264).

28 Carl Rogers, *On Becoming a Person* (Boston: Houghton Mifflin, 1961); cf. Jahoda, Maslow, Royce, etc.

29 The title is startling and may be a token of the age in which Jonah was written. But Landes warns that this should not be pressed, for the formula "X king of Y" is a Hebrew form of identification (1 Kings 21:1; 2 Kings 1:3). The same phenomenon is present in Neo-Assyrian inscriptions (Landes, "Jonah," *IDB Supp.*, p. 490).

30 Theodor H. Gaster, *Myth, Legend, and Custom in the O.T.* (New York: Harper and Row, 1975), vol. 2, p. 655.

31 *Four Strange Books*, p. 40. St. Jerome also opposes Jonah to Jeremiah, or at least sees a response to Jonah's question in Jeremiah 18:7 (see Jerome, *Dogmatic and Polemical Works*, trans. by J. N. Hritzu, The Fathers of the Church, vol. 53 [Washington: Catholic University, 1965], pp. 356-357).

32 André Feuillet, *Etudes d'Exégèse et de Théologie Biblique, Ancien Testament* (Paris: Gabalda, 1975), p. 422 (our English translation).

33 Vischer, "Jonas," p. 119.

34 Feuillet, *Etudes d' Exégèse*, p. 422 (our English translation).

35 See *Sanhedrin* 59a; *BQ* 38a; *'Aboda Zara* 3a; *Sifra Shemoth* 13 (ed. Weiss, 86b).

36 Bickerman's remarks upon the nature of God or his "attributes" are somewhat misleading. God is all that Jonah 4:2 says he is, within the framework of his covenant with Israel. That he appears to act with other nations as he does with Israel is as shocking to Israel as it is to a wife who witnesses her husband's infidelity!

37 Feuillet, *Etudes d'Exégèse*, p. 427 (our English translation).

38 The Tetragrammaton is judiciously used here as the tale makes sure that we un-

derstand the sailors' move to be one of conversion, and not a religiously vague act. We shall therefore take exception here to Ibn Ezra's remark (on 1:1) that the text does not say anything about the destruction by the heathens of their altars and idols. For Bickerman as well, there is no mention of the conversion of pagans in Jewish literature before 2 Maccabees. "The Ninevites (and the sailors on the ship) simply acknowledge the power of the Lord" ("Les deux erreurs," p. 250, n. 67 [our English translation]).

39 See Lacocque, *But as for Me* (Atlanta: John Knox Press, 1979).

40 E. M. Cioran, *La tentation d'exister* (Paris: Gallimard, 1956), p. 82 (our English translation).

Chapter VI

1 There is an interesting parallel here with the ending of the book of Job when God asks Job "Where were you?"

2 Allen, *The Books of Joel, Obadiah, Jonah, and Micah,* p. 227. Allen makes the constant mistake, however, of depicting the audience of the tale as antipathetic to Jonah. On the contrary, those for whom the narrative was conceived in the first place, namely, the ideologists of Jerusalem, must have been perfectly attuned to Jonah's reaction. The *grandeur* of Jonah lies in the fact that such a stance, although rejected by the author, is not subjected to wholesale ridicule. To be sure, irony and satire are present here, but only in light strokes and with discretion.

3 *Mekilta,* tractate *Pisha* I, 80–82 (edited by Lauterbach).

4 Cohn, *Das Buch Jona,* ad loc. 4:1.

5 Cohn, *Das Buch Jona,* p. 100 ("Es ist der Eifer für Gott, welcher Jona sich *gegen* Gott wenden lässt").

6 Quoted by Rudolph (*Joel-Amos-Obadja-Jona,* ad loc. 4:1; "desperat de salute Israelis. . . . Non contristatur, ut quidam putant, quod gentium multitudo salvetur, sed quod pereat Israel"). Rudolph quotes also Andrea di S. Vittore (d. 1175): "penitencia gencium ruina Judaeorum."

Let us add that the Gospel shares the same perspective. Matthew 12:41 says: "at Judgment when this generation is on trial, the men of Nineveh will appear against it and ensure its condemnation for they repented at the preaching of Jonah; and what is here is greater than Jonah." There is an interesting parallel to this in the Midrash on Lamentations (*Midrash Ekah Rabbati* on Zepheniah 3:1, alluded to by Bickerman, *Four Strange Books,* p. 17: the repentance of the Ninevites in contrast to the hardening of Israel's heart led to the latter's exile).

7 J. T. Hower, "The Misunderstanding and Mishandling of Anger," *J. of Ps. and Theol.* 2 (1974): 270.

8 "Some Thoughts on a Biblical View of Anger," *J. of Ps. and Theol.* 2 (Summer 1974): 212; see also Karen Horney, *The Neurotic Personality of Our Time* (New York: W. W. Norton, 1964), p. 66: "The main reasons why awareness of hostility may be unbearable are that one may love or need a person at the same time that one is hostile toward him."

9 See R. B. Y. Scott, "The Sign of Jonah," *Interp.* 19 (1965): 25: "In the name of divine justice [those who had suffered so much at the hands of enemies] were all too sure of their *right* to be angry."

10 Crossan, *The Dark Interval,* p. 76.

11 Cohn, following Wolff (*Studien zum Jonabuch,* p. 118), calls attention to the prophet's use (nine times) of the first person singular in verses 2–3.

12 In an Armenian text translated by Bickermann *Four Strange Books,* p. 34.
13 Sullivan, *The Psychiatric Interview,* p. 135.
14 "Die Gedanken sind frei."
15 Bickermann, *Four Strange Books,* p. 44.
16 Hence the surprising insistence of God that Jonah and no one else must go to Nineveh in Jonah 1–2.
17 Carl Rogers, "The Necessary and Sufficient Conditions of Therapeutic Personality Change," *Journal of Consulting Psychology* 21 (1957): 95–103; or *Client-Centered Therapy* (Boston: Houghton Mifflin, 1951).
18 The Israelite documents present numerous examples of brutal orders that were followed, most paradoxically, by compliance. We alluded above to the vocation narratives concerning Abraham, Moses, Jeremiah, Ezekiel, etc. The same is true in the New Testament, where the call to discipleship by Jesus is also strikingly abrupt, extravagant—and efficacious! See, e.g., Matthew 9:9, which is echoed by Paul in Acts 9:4. No psychological explanation is sufficient to justify their moves. Psychological reasons are enlightening, but they always fall short of explaining the veritable drive that brings Matthew or Paul to their transformation ("conversion").
19 Erikson, *Identity, Youth and Crisis,* pp. 136–137.
20 H. Winckler, "Zum Buche Jona," *Altoriental. Forsch.* 2 (1900): 260–65. Trible ("Studies in the Book of Jonah," p. 198 in particular) says that the structure dictates that 4:5 be displaced after 3:4. Her argument, however, is misleading; on the contary 4:5 may perfectly stay where it is as it falls in parallel with 2:11b (use of nature: fish in parallel with tree; departure from the fish to resume mission and departure from Nineveh to witness the results of mission). See Alexander Rofé, "Classes in the Prophetical Stories: Didactic, Legends and Parables," *Studies in Prophecy,* VTSup 26 (Leiden: Brill, 1974), p. 157, n. 71.
21 See Sellin, KAT; Weiser, ATD; Robinson, HAT; von Rad *Theologie* II, p. 299, n. 16; Trible, "Studies in the Book of Jonah," etc.
22 See Rudolph, *Joel-Amos-Obadja-Jona,* p. 362; Lohfink, "Und Jona ging zur Stadt hinaus (Jon. 4,5)," 185–203; Allen, *Joel, Obadiah, Jonah, and Micah,* p. 231; Wolff, *Studien zum Jonabuch,* pp. 44–48, Cohn, *Das Buch Jona,* p. 57.
23 Erich Auerbach, *Mimesis: The Representation of Reality in Western Literature* (Princeton, NJ: Princeton University Press, 1953), p. 12.
24 Even Rudolph, who denies all allegorical interpretations of the book of Jonah, acknowledges that the *sukkāh* refers to the "Laubhütten" festival. On this very basis, he adds, it may be said that its roof was not sufficient for an effective protection against the sun (*Joel-Amos-Obadja-Jona,* p. 365).
25 Eliade, *Myths, Dreams and Mysteries,* p. 198.
26 On the meaning of remembrance in the book of Jonah, see above, Chapter IV.
27 "God is good, compassionate, and kind, and hesitant to punish. In origin this formula belongs firmly to an Israelite setting of application." Allen, *The Books of Joel, Obadiah, Jonah, and Micah,* p. 193).
28 E. Kraeling, *Commentary on the Prophets* (Camden, NJ: Nelson, 1966), vol. 2, p. 202–203.
29 That the *sukkāh* represents the Temple is clear in a text such as Psalm 27:5 where it stands in parallel with "house," "palace," and "tent" (twice). In Jonah 4 the motif is set in balance with Jonah 1:3, e.g., "the Lord's Presence."

At this point, let us mention the very interesting reading of C. H. H. Wright ("The Book of Jonah considered from an Allegorical Point of View," *Biblical Es-*

says: or Exegetical Studies on the Books of Job and Jonah [Edinburgh: T. and T. Clark, 1886], pp. 55 ff.) who sees in this chapter of Jonah a symbol of the activity of Israel during the restoration. So the oracle of Nineveh's doom corresponds to the often predicted downfall of the nations (especially the Persian empire); the booth represents the "poor shelter in their desolated country;" Jonah's displeasure reflects the frustration at the nonfulfillment of exilic prophecies; the plant is Zerubbabel (cf. Ezra 1:8; 1 Chron. 3:19)—like the *qîqāyôn*, Zerubbabel disappeared "overnight" from the scene. With regard to the identification of Zerubbabel with the *qîqāyôn* of Jonah, one will remember the use of the term *ṣemaḥ* in Zechariah with its messianic overtones to designate the royal figure.

30 On the motif of destruction in this chapter, see Trible, "Studies in the Book of Jonah," pp. 195–196. The theme, she says, "is central in the legend."

31 On Zechariah 14, see e.g., André Lacocque, "II Zacharie," CAT XIb (Neuchâtel: Delachaux et Niestlé, 1981).

32 Eliade, *Myths, Dreams and Mysteries,* p. 198.

33 Again here, the "Freudian" psychologists seem to extrapolate abusively; they speak about the hut as "nocturnal erection and detumescence" and as a "breast-penis composite." See More (Muggia), "The Prophet Jonah," p. 10.

34 George M. Landes ("Jonah: A Mašal?" in *Israelite Wisdom: Theological and Literary Essays in Honor of Samuel Terrien,* ed. J. G. Gamie [Missoula, MT: Scholars Press, 1978], pp. 137–158) stresses the contrast: the Ninevites respond to God with faith and repentance and they live; Jonah responds with anger and complaint, and he desires to die. The ensuing episodes, says Landes, are to move the prophet to do what both the Ninevites and God have done: change one's mind (p. 147).

35 See Scott, "The Sign of Jonah," p. 24: "Jonah did not 'pity' the plant, as the English versions put it. He 'was sorry' about it because he pitied himself."

36 Landes, "The Kerygma of the Book of Jonah," p. 29.

37 Following Robert Detweiler, *Story, Sign and Self* (Philadelphia: Fortress, 1978), p. 121 (on Greimas's *Sémantique structurale* [Paris: Larousse, 1966]).

38 Crossan, *The Dark Interval.*

39 J. Steinmann exclaims, "Blessed be the Author who, at a time when Ezra was creating racism, responded in behalf of God with that explosion of laughter, the only effective rejoinder capable of saving the message of the prophets" *Le livre de la consolation d'Israël* [Paris: Cerf, 1960], p. 290; our English translation).

40 "One of the things people need most is a feeling of living in a world they understand" (Mildred Neuman and Bernard Berkowitz, *How to Be Your Own Best Friend* [New York: Ballantine Books, 1971], p. 46). When such an understanding collapses, as in the case of Elijah or Jonah, there results despair or depression. L. Bellak writes, ". . . depression is the equivalent of intra-aggression" (in *Specialized Techniques in Psychotherapy,* ed. E. Bychowski and J. Louise Despert [New York: Grove Press, 1952], p. 328).

41 Paul Ricoeur, *Finitude et culpabilité. II. La Symbolique du mal* (Paris: Aubier Montaigne, 1960), pp. 85–86 (our English translation).

42 See Cohn, *Das Buch Jona,* p. 59. Note also the extensive use by God of natural phenomena in his communication with Elijah in 1 Kings 19:11–12.

43 The Syriac has the combination "YHWH-Elohim" throughout the book of Jonah, a sign of its embarrassment before the variations in the MT. Such puzzlement is, however, unnecessary, and one need not agree with the statement of Otto Eissfeldt, followed by P. Trible, according to which a satisfactory explana-

tion of the problem has yet to be found (Eissfeldt, *The Old Testament: An Intro-duction,* p. 496; Trible, "Studies in the Book of Jonah," p. 85).

44 Genesis 19 is not the only place besides Jonah 4:7 where the expression '*alôt haš-šahar* occurs. However, each time these words are used they indicate that a dra-matic event is about to happen: Genesis 32:25, 27 (Jabbok); Joshua 6:15 (Jericho); Judges 19:25 (collective rape); 1 Samuel 9:26 (Saul's anointing); Nehe-miah 4:15 (rebuilding in arms of Jerusalem). See Hitzig, *Die Zwölf Kleinen Propheten,* ad loc.

45 Abraham Heschel, *The Prophets* (New York: Harper Torchbooks, 1962), vol. 2, p. 67.

46 S.H. Blank, "Doest Thou Well to Be Angry? A Study in Self-Pity," *HUCA* 26 (1955): 41. The Rabbis said, "As Jonah did not pity the Ninevites nor call them to repentance, he found himself in need. He had to beg God to rule His world with the measure of compassion, cf. Daniel 9:9, (so as to be himself at the benefit of that disposition)" (*Yalqut* on Jonah 4:8).

In turn, Fromm writes, "God's answer to Jonah is to be understood symbolical-ly. God explains to Jonah that the essence of love is to 'labor' for something and 'to make something grow,' that love and labor are inseparable. One loves that for which one labors, and one labors for that which one loves" (*The Art of Loving* p. 23).

47 *Dogmatic and Polemical Works,* trans. J. N. Hritzu; The Fathers of the Church 53 (Washington, DC: Catholic University of America Press, 1965), pp. 356–57; see also p. 374.

48 Rudolph, *Joel-Amos-Obadja-Jona,* p. 368.

49 A. D. Martin, *The Prophet Jonah: The Book and the Sign* (London/NY: Longmans, Green and Co., 1926), p. 87.

50 The motif of "120,000" is found again in Judith 2:5, 15 (cf. Rev. 7:4 where 144,000=12,000 × 12).

51 More (Muggia), "The Prophet Jonah," p. 5.

52 Bickerman, *Four Strange Books,* p. 14.

53 Bickerman, *Four Strange Books,* p. 38.

54 As Rudolph, in a very Ricoeurian vein, so aptly writes regarding the lack of an ending here: "Das gibt zu denken" (*Joel-Amos-Obadja-Jona,* p. 368).

55 If it seems to some that the problem of the relationship between Judaism and Christianity is artificial here, suffice it to recall that from the time of the Fathers of the Church until our own day, the book of Jonah has been used argumenta-tively to prove the "superiority" of Christianity. Bickerman recalls the pamphlet of a Protestant minister, published in a time ominously close to the irruption of German Nazism in 1920: *Biblisher Antisemitismus. Der Juden Weltgeschichtlicher Charakter, Schuld und Ende in des Propheten Jona Judenspiegel* (Biblical Anti-Semi-tism. The universal character, sin, and end, of the Jews in the mirror of Jewish soul provided by the prophet Jonah).

Chapter VII

1 Karl Jaspers said, "What man is, he ultimately becomes through the cause which he has made his own" (quoted by Frankl, *Psychotherapy and Existentialism,* p. 9).

2 When Noam Chomsky, e.g., reflecting upon the acquisition of language by the child, suspects that "from the start, . . . we are dealing with a species-specific ca-pacity with a largely innate component," the question of nature of such compo-

nent arises. In fact, what is innate is not Platonic Ideas but the *energy*. What is universal is the *will*, i.e., the capacity to fulfill one's vocation, or to respond to the Message as it has been perceived by the person "Recent Contributions to the Theory of Innate Ideas" in *Boston Studies in the Philosophy of Science*, vol. 3, ed. R. Cohen and M. Wartofsky [Dordrecht: Reidel, 1968], p. 123).

3 "Tout le monde regarde ce que je regarde, mais personne ne voit ce que je vois."

4 Frankl, *Psychotherapy and Existentialism*, p. 44.

5 Frankl, *Psychotherapy and Existentialism*, p. 34

6 "Community, of course, is implicit in the creature of flesh and blood by reason of his very origin in the mother's womb . . ." (Scheler, *On the Eternal in Man*, p. 374).

7 In a time when some potential mothers try to convince themselves and others that the embryo in their uterus is "their own body," it is perhaps not useless to recall that even the embryo is no "soulless" clay. Let us state unequivocally that an interruption of pregnancy is the interruption of a communication that has begun and has given to an "other" (the infant) the opportunity of *choice*, of being self, of *being*. Our ontological root is encounter. Our ontological need is encounter.

8 Andras Angyal, *Neurosis and Treatment: A Holistic Theory* (New York: John Wiley and Sons, 1965), p. 18.

9 Frankl writes: "No man and no destiny can be compared with any other man or any other destiny . . . no situation repeats itself, and each situation calls for a different response" *(Man's Search for Meaning* p. 77); "To compare yourself with anyone else is to do an injustice either to yourself or to the other person" *(The Doctor and the Soul*, p. 173).

10 Adler, *Social Interest*, p. 39.

11 Cf. Frankl, *The Doctor and the Soul*, p. 80; *The Unconscious God* (New York: Simon and Schuster, 1975), pp. 23 –24.

12 Roberto Assagioli, *The Act of Will* (Baltimore: Penguin Books, 1973), pp. 166 –167, 167 –168, 143.

13 Maslow, *Toward a Psychology of Being*, pp. 45, 48.

14 K. Goldstein, *The Organism* (New York: American Book Co., 1939); "Effect of Brain Damage on Personality," in *Theories of Psychopathology and Personality*, ed. T. Millon (Philadelphia: W. B. Saunders Co., 1973).

15 Abraham Maslow, *The Farther Reaches of Human Nature* (Baltimore: Penguin Books, 1971), p. 312. Further, "man's higher nature rests upon man's lower nature needing it as a foundation and collapsing without this foundation. . . . Man's higher nature is inconceivable without a satisfied lower nature as a base" *(Toward a Psychology of Being*, p. 173). Maslow defines self-actualization as "the full use and exploitation of talents, capacities, potentialities . . ." *(Motivation and Personality* [New York: Harper and Row, 1970], p. 150).

16 Maslow, *The Farther Reaches*, p. 46

17 Frankl, *Man's Search for Meaning*, p. 107.

18 Frankl, *Psychotherapy and Existentialism*, p. 68.

19 Frankl, *Psychotherapy and Existentialism*, p. 46; see also Assagioli, *The Act of Will*, pp. 143, 167-168.

20 Fromm, *Psychoanalysis and Religion* (New Haven: Yale University Press, 1950), p. 27.

21 Buber, *Knowledge of Man*, p. 184 (italics added).

22 Buber, *The Way of Man*, pp. 31 –32, 34.

23 Similarly, Israel gives up nature and historicizes it; she gives up matter and spiritualizes it. Nature on the one hand and matter on the other hand are the terrain of history and of spirit. As there is no tree without humus, there is nothing spiritual without the material. But the humus exists for the tree, not the tree for the humus. And what is true for a tree is a thousand times truer for a person. Now the ultimate scandal for Israel's tradition is that the human being, instead of becoming spirit, returns to humus!

24 Martin Buber, *The Way of Response,* ed. N. N. Glatzer (New York: Schocken Books, 1966), p. 207.

25 The "Original guilt" Buber said, "consists in remaining with oneself," *(The Knowledge of Man,* p. 49).

26 "He only earns his freedom and existence who daily conquers them anew," said Goethe (quoted by May, "Existential Psychology and Human Freedom," *The Chicago Theology Seminary Register* 52 [October 1962]: 19).

27 Buber, *The Knowledge of Man,* p. 182.

28 Maslow, *The Farther Reaches,* p. 333.

29 This dualistic conception has proven to be lethal for Christianity and has been propounded by the Christian "Establishment" ever since the Church Fathers. It is responsible for the most detrimental misunderstanding of the Gospel in the modern world.

30 See, e.g., Maslow, *The Farther Reaches,* p. 48. The Brandeis scholar thus confirms what Jung said in 1933: " . . . we psychotherapists must occupy ourselves with problems which, strictly speaking, belong to the theologian," p. 241, see the whole page.

31 Cf. Albrecht Alt, *Die Ursprünge des israelitischen Rechts* (Leipzig: S. Hirzel, 1934).

32 Martin Buber, *I and Thou* (New York: Charles Scribner's Sons, 1970), p. 127.

Chapter VIII

1 E.g., S. H. Cohen, "A Growth Theory to Neurotic Resistance to Therapy," *Journal of Humanistic Psychology* 1 (Spring 1961): 48–63; Frankl, *The Doctor and the Soul,* p. 67; and May, *Man's Search for Himself,* p. 250.

2 Jung, *Symbols of Transformation,* p. 419. See also Assagioli, *The Act of Will,* pp. 112–113. The courage to be alone has been widely acknowledged in the psychotherapeutic literature as being an important aspect of mental health. May (*Man's Search for Himself,* p. 121), for instance, speaks of the need for "cutting the psychological umbilical cord," while Jung (*Symbols of Transformation,* p. 348) refers to the "battle for deliverance from the maternal grip." What both authors imply is that to reach maturity one must be able to get rid of morbid dependency ties which bind the person to significant others (e.g., parents).

3 Angyal, *Neurosis and Treatment: A Holistic Theory,* e.g., p. 127; "Evasion of Growth," *American Journal of Psychiatry,* 110 (1953–1954): 358–362, e.g., p. 358 ff.

4 ". . . [neurotics] resort to detours, truces, retreats, tricks and stratagems as soon as the question of socially necessary decisions comes up" (Adler, *Individual Psychology of Alfred Adler,* p. 236). Throughout his writings Adler stressed that the neurotics, psychotics, criminals and all those having deep inner turmoils are those who refuse to help others and to commit themselves socially (see e.g., *The Individual Psychology of Alfred Adler,* pp. 149, 253; see also his *Social Interest,* passim).

5 Adler, *Social Interest* p. 160.

6 These two quotes are respectively from Maslow's *Toward a Psychology of Being*, p. 66; and *The Psychology of Science* (Chicago: Henry Regnery Co., 1966), p. 16. Among Maslow's best contributions on the fear of knowledge is his paper "The Need to Know and the Fear of Knowing" (*Toward a Psychology of Being*, pp. 60–71).

7 As early as 1915, Freud had noticed that during the treatment of psycho-neuroses, an unusual phenomenon would arise in some of his patients: success in their work brought them acute anxieties. He explained this by postulating that for some, success meant the symbolical murder of the parent of the same sex. Such fantasy, in turn, would create intense anxiety and guilt feelings, precipitating a state of melancholy which, in some cases, could last for years. Freud described these persons as "those wrecked by success" ("Some Character-types Met with in Psychoanalytic Work," [1915] *Collected Papers* [New York: Basic Books, 1959], pp. 318-344; see esp. pp. 341, 323).

8 Maslow, "Neurosis as a Failure of Personal Growth," *Humanitas* 3 (1967): 161, 163. It is well known how negative towards religiosity was Freud. For him it is a question of neurosis as a result of a traumatizing primal event: the massacre of the father in order to steal from him his wives. Religiosity is repressed guilt which lurks under a sublimated form. (*Civilization and Its Discontent* [New York: W. W. Norton, 1930], pp. 31–32). Perhaps, but as Auerbach writes: "if Don Quijote had not gone mad, he would not have left his house. And then Sancho too would have stayed home, and he could never have drawn from his innate being the things which—as we find in delighted amazement—were potentially contained in it. The multifarious play of action and reaction between the two and their joint play in the world would not have taken place" (*Mimesis*, p. 350).

9 E.g., compare pages 34 and 293 of *The Farther Reaches of Human Nature*. See also *The Healthy Personality* in collaboration with H.-M. Chiang (New York: Van Nostrand Reinhold Co., 1969), and compare pages 39 and 46.

10 Jung, *Modern Man in Search of a Soul*, pp. 78 ff. See also J. Jacobi, *The Psychology of C. G. Jung* (New Haven: Yale University Press, 1962), p. 36.

11 Jung, *Modern Man*, p. 80.

12 Jung, *Modern Man*, pp. 79–80. Such viewpoint is also shared by existential psychotherapists; Rollo May, *Power and Innocence* (New York: W. W. Norton, 1977), p. 223.

13 J. P. Chaplain, *Dictionary of Psychology* (New York: Dell Publ. Co., 1968), p. 97.

14 Adler, *Social Interest*, p. 160. Though it has not been emphasized yet, there are of course other Old Testament prophets whose names could be used to label the complex to which we refer here. Besides Jeremiah and Moses fearing God's commands, the reader will also remember similar reactions in Isaiah and Ezekiel among other prophets.

15 In the words of Carl Jung, "vocation, or the feeling of vocation, is not perchance the prerogative of great personalities, but also belongs to the small ones" (quoted by Assagioli, *The Act of Will*, p. 115).

16 *The Wit and Wisdom of Albert Schweitzer*, ed. C. R. Joy (Boston: Beacon Press, 1949), p. 66.

17 This expression is Assagioli's (see "The Synthetic Vision: A Conversation with Roberto Assagioli," in *Voices and Visions*, ed. S. Keen [New York: Harper and Row, 1974], p. 214).

18 Frank Haronian, "Repression of the Sublime" in *The Proper Study of Man* (N.Y.: Macmillan, 1971), pp. 239–246.

19 Otto Rank, *Will Therapy and Truth and Reality* (N.Y.: Alfred A. Knopf, [1936] 1964).

20 Reuven P. Bulka, "Death in Life — Talmudic and Logotherapic Affirmations," *Humanitas*, 10:1 (Feb. 1974): 33–43.

21 Becker, *The Denial of Death*, p. 31.

22 Tillich, *The Eternal Now*, p. 56.

23 Haronian, "Repression of the Sublime," p. 135.

24 Assagioli in "The Synthetic Vision," p. 214.

25 See also Jung, *Modern Man*, p. 67.

26 Paul Ricoeur *The Conflict of Interpretations*, ed. D. Ihde (Evanston, IL: Northwestern University Press, 1974), p. 441.

27 Mircea Eliade, *The Sacred and the Profane* (New York: Harper & Row, 1961), p. 202.

28 Paul Ricoeur, *The Symbolism of Evil* (New York: Harper & Row, 1967), pp. 247–298.

29 Frankl is particularly helpful on this point. See *The Doctor and the Soul*, p. 63; and *The Will to Meaning* (New York: New American Library, 1969), p. 61, where he elaborates on such belief.

30 Maslow, *The Farther Reaches*, p. 36.

31 "To the best of my lights at the moment this is what I choose to do, even though I may know more and choose differently tomorrow" (May, *Man's Search for Himself*, p. 219).

Bibliography

Ackroyd, Peter R. *Exile and Restoration*. Philadelphia: Westminster, 1968.
_____. *Israel Under Babylon and Persia*. Oxford: Oxford University Press, 1970.
Adler, Alfred. *The Science of Living*. Garden City, NY: Garden City Publishing Co., 1929.
_____. *Social Interest: A Challenge to Mankind*. New York: G. P. Putnam's Sons, 1964.
_____. *Superiority and Social Interest*. Edited by H. and R. Ansbacher. Evanston, IL: Northwestern University Press, 1964.
_____. *Problems of Neurosis*. New York: Harper & Row, 1964.
_____. *Individual Psychology of Alfred Adler*. Totowa, NJ: Littlefield, Adams & Co., 1969.
_____. *The Education of Children*. Chicago: Henry Regnery Co., 1970.
Allen, Leslie C. *The Books of Joel, Obadiah, Jonah, and Micah*. The New International Commentary on the Old Testament. Grand Rapids: Eerdmans, 1976.
Allport, Gordon W. *Becoming*. New Haven: Yale University Press, 1955.
Angyal, Andras. "Evasion of Growth." *American Journal of Psychiatry* 110 (1953-1954): 358-362.
_____. *Neurosis and Treatment: A Holistic Theory*. New York: John Wiley & Sons, 1965.
Ansbacher, Hans, and Ansbacher, Rowena, eds. *The Individual Psychology of Alfred Adler*. New York: Harper & Row, Colophon Books, 1956.
Assagioli, Roberto. *Psychosynthesis*. New York: Viking Press, 1971.
_____. *The Act of Will*. Baltimore: Penguin Books, 1973.
_____. "The Synthetic Vision: Conversation with Roberto Assagioli." In *Voices and Visions*. Edited by S. Keen. New York: Harper & Row, 1974.
Auerbach, Erich. *Mimesis: The Representation of Reality in Western Literature*. Translated by W. R. Trask. Princeton, NJ: Princeton University Press, 1953.

Becker, Ernest. *The Denial of Death*. New York: The Free Press, 1973.
_____. "The Heroics of Everyday Life." In *Voices and Visions*. Edited by S. Keen. New York: Harper & Row, 1974.
Bellak, Leopold. "The Emergency Psychotherapy of Depression." In *Specialized Techniques in Psychotherapy*. Edited by E. Bychowski and J. L. Despert. New York: Grove Press, 1952.
Bettelheim, Bruno. *The Informed Heart*. New York: The Free Press, 1960.
_____. *The Uses of Enchantment*. New York: Alfred A. Knopf, 1976.
Bewer, Julius A. *The Book of the Twelve Prophets*. International Critical Commentary. Edinburgh: T. and T. Clark, 1949.
Bickerman, Elias. *Four Strange Books of the Bible: Jonah, Daniel, Koheleth, Esther*. New York: Schocken Books, 1967.
_____. "Les deux erreurs du Prophète Jonas" *RHPR* 45 (1965): 232-64.

Blank, Sheldon H. "Doest Thou Well to Be Angry? A study in Self-Pity." *HUCA* 26 (1955): 29-41.

Boehme, W. "Die Komposition des Buches Jona," *ZAW* 7 (1887): 224-84.

Bonhoeffer, Dietrich. *Letters and Papers from Prison*. Edited by E. Bethge. Translated by R. H. Fuller. New York: Macmillan, 1972 (enlarged edition).

Brande, M. *Scriptural Psychiatry*. New York: Froben Press, 1946.

Brockington, Leonard H. "Jonah." In *Peake's Commentary on the Bible*. Edited by M. Black and H. H. Rowley. London: Nelson, 1962. Pp. 627-629.

Buber, Martin. *The Prophetic Faith*. New York: Harper & Brothers, 1960.

_____. *Knowledge of Man*. New York: Harper & Row, 1965.

_____. *The Way of Response*. New York: Schocken Books, 1966.

_____. *The Way of Man*. New York: Citadel Press, 1967.

_____. *I and Thou*. New York: Charles Scribner's Sons, 1970.

Bulka, Reuven P. "Death in Life—Talmudic and Logotherapeutic Affirmations," *Humanitas,* 10:1 (Feb. 1974): 33-34.

Calvin,n John. *Opera Selecta*. Edited by P. Barth and G. Niesel. Vols. I-VI. Munich: Kaiser, 1926-1936.

Chaplin, James P. *Dictionary of Psychology*. New York: Dell Publishing Co., 1968.

Cheyne, Thomas K. "Jonah, A Study in Jewish Folklore and Religion." *ThR* 57 (1877): 211-19.

_____. "Jonah." *Enc. Bibl. II*. London: Adam and Charles Black, 1901. cols. 2565-71.

Childs, Brevard S. *Introduction to the Old Testament as Scripture*. Philadelphia: Fortress Press, 1979.

_____. "Jonah: A Study in Old Testament Hermeneutics." *Scott. J. of Theol.* 11 (1958): 53-61.

Chomsky, Noam. "Recent Contributions to the Theory of Innate Ideas." In *Boston Studies in the Philosophy of Science*. Edited by R. Cohen and M. Wartofsky. Vol. 3. Dordrecht: Reidel, 1968.

Cioran, E. M. *La tentation d'exister*. Paris: Gallimard, 1956.

Clements, R. E. "The Purpose of the Book of Jonah." *Congress Volume. Edinburgh, 1974*. VTSup 28. Leiden: Brill, 1975. Pp. 16-28.

Cohen, S. H. "A Growth Theory of Neurotic Resistance to Therapy." *Journal of Humanistic Psychology* 1 (Spring 1961): 48-63.

Cohn, Gabriël H. *Das Buch Jona im Lichte der biblischen Erzählkunst*. Assen: Van Gorcum, 1969.

Collodi, E. *Pinocchio, the Story of a Puppet*. Translated by M. A. Murray. New York: E. P. Dutton & Co., 1956.

Combs, Arthur and Snygg, Donald. *Individual Behavior: A Perceptual Approach to Behavior*. New York: Harper & Brothers, 1959.

Crawford, Helen M. *A Reluctant Missionary*. Chicago: Board of Christian Education, United Presbyterian Church, 1965.

Crossan, John D. *The Dark Interval*. Niles, IL: Argus Communications, 1975.

_____. "Parable, Allegory, and Paradox." In *Semiology and Parables*. Edited by D. Patte. Pittsburgh: Pickwick Press, 1976.

Detweiler, Robert. *Story, Sign and Self*. Philadelphia: Fortress, 1978.

DeWette, W. M. L. *Lehrbuch der historish-kritischen Einleitung in kanonischen und apokryphen Bücher des A. T.* Berlin: G. Reiner, 1817.

Dostoyevsky, Fyodor. *Crime and Punishment.* New York: E. P. Dutton, 1933.

Eissfeldt, Otto. "Amos und Jona in Volkstümlicher Überlieferung." *F. S. Ernst Barnikol,* Berlin 1964, 9-13 = *Kl. Schr.* IV, 1968, 137-142.
_____. *The Old Testament: An Introduction.* Translated by P. R. Ackroyd. New York: Harper and Row, 1965.
Eliade, Mircea. *Birth and Rebirth.* New York: Harper & Brothers, 1958.
_____. *Myths, Dreams and Mysteries.* New York: Harper & Row, 1960.
_____. *The Sacred and the Profano.* New York: Harper & Row, 1961.
Ellul, Jacques. "Le Livre de Jonas," *Foi et Vie* 50 (1952): 81-184. In English, *The Judgment of Jonah.* Translated by G. W. Bromiley. Grand Rapids: Eerdmans, 1971.
Erikson, Erik H. *Young Man Luther: A Study on Psychoanalysis and History.* New York: W. W. Norton, 1961.
_____. *Insight and Responsibility.* New York: W. W. Norton, 1964.
_____. *Identity, Youth and Crisis.* New York: W. W. Norton, 1968.
_____. *Life History and the Historical Moment.* New York: W.W. Norton, 1975.
_____, with R. I. Evans. *Dialogue with Erik Erickson.* New York: E. P. Dutton, 1969.
Eysenck, H. J. *Behavior Therapy and the Neuroses.* New York: Pergammon Press, 1960.

Feuillet, Andrè. "Les sources du livre de Jonas." *RB* 54 (1947): 161-186.
_____. "Les sens du livre de Jonas." *RB* 54 (1947): 340-61.
_____. "Le livre de Jonas." In *BJ.*
_____. "Le livre de Jonas." *DBS* IV: cols. 1104-31.
_____. *Etudes d'Exégèse et de Théologie Biblique. Ancien Testament.* Paris: Gabalda, 1975.
Fingert, H. H. "Psychoanalytic Study of the Minor Prophet, Jonah." *The Psychoanalytic Review* 41 (1954): 55-65.
Fohrer, Georg. See E. Sellin.
Frankl, Viktor E. *The Doctor and the Soul.* New York: Alfred A. Knopf, 1955.
_____. *Man's Search for Meaning.* Boston: Beacon Press, 1962.
_____. *Psychotherapy and Existentialism.* New York: Washington Square Press, 1967.
_____. *The Will to Meaning.* New York: New American Library, 1969.
_____. "Meaninglessness: A Challenge to Psychologists." In *Theories of Psychopathology and Personality.* Edited by T. Millon. Philadelphia: W. B. Saunders Company, 1973.
_____. *The Unconscious God.* New York: Simon and Schuster, 1975.
Freud, Sigmund. "Some Character-types Met with in Psychoanalytic Work" (1915). In *A General Selection from the Works of Sigmund Freud.* Edited by J. Rickman and C. Brenner. New York: Liveright Publishing Co., 1957. Also in *Collected Papers.* Chap. XVIII. New York: Basic Books, 1959.
_____. *Civilization and Its Discontents* (1930). New York: W. W. Norton, 1961.
_____. *The Psychopathy of Everyday Life.* New York: W. W. Norton, 1965.
Friedlander, Gerald, ed. *Pirke de Rabbi Eliezer.* New York: Hermon Press, 1965.
Fromm, Erich. *Escape from Freedom.* New York: Holt, Rinehart & Winston, 1941.
_____. *Man for Himself.* Greenwich, CT: Fawcett, 1947.
_____. *Psychoanalysis and Religion.* New Haven: Yale University Press, 1950.
_____. *The Forgotten Language.* New York: Grove Press, 1951.

_____ . *The Art of Loving*. New York: Harper & Row, 1956.
_____ . with R. I. Evans. *Dialogue with Erich Fromm*. New York: Harper & Row, 1966.

Gaster, Thedor H. *Festivals of the Jewish Year*. New York: William Sloane, 1953.
_____ . *Myth, Legend, and Custom in the O.T.* Vols. I-II. New York: Harper & Row, 1975.
Goldenson, Robert M. *The Encyclopedia of Human Behavior*. Garden City, NY: Doubleday, 1970.

Haller, E. "Die Erzählung von dem Propheten Jona." *Theologische Existenz Heute* n. s. 65 (1950): 5-54.
Hanson, Paul. *The Dawn of Apocalyptic*. Philadelphia: Fortress, 1975.
Haronian, Frank. "Repression of the Sublime." In *The Proper Study of Man*. Edited by F. Fadiman. New York: Macmillan, 1971.
_____ . "The Repression of the Sublime." *Synthesis*, 1 (1977): 125-136.
Harris, J. R. *The Odes and Psalms of Solomon*. Cambridge: Cambridge University Press, 1909.
Heschel, Abraham. *Man Is Not Alone*. New York: Farrar, Straus & Giroux, 1951.
_____ . *The Prophets*. Vols. I & II. New York: Harper Torchbooks, 1962.
_____ . *The Wisdom of Heschel*. New York: Farrar, Straus & Giroux, 1970.
Hitzig, F. *Die Zwölf Kleinen Propheten*. Leipzig: S. Hirzel, 1863.
Hoonacker, A. van. *Les 12 petits prophètes*. EB. Paris: Gabalda, 1908.
Horner, M. "The Motive to Avoid Success and Changing Aspirations in College Women." In *Readings on the Psychology of Women*. Edited by J. Bardwick. New York: Harper & Row, 1972.
Horney, Karen. *The Neurotic Personality of Our Time*. New York: W. W. Norton, 1964.
Hower, J. T. "The Misunderstanding and Mishandling of Anger." *J. of Ps. and Theol.* 2 (1974): 269-275.

Jacobi, Jolande. *The Psychology of C. G. Jung*. New Haven: Yale University Press, 1962.
Jahoda, Marie. *Current Concepts of Positive Mental Health*. New York: Basic Books, 1958.
Jeremias, Joachim. "Ionas." *ThDNT*, Vol. 3, pp. 406-410.
Jerome, St. *Selected Letters of St. Jerome*. Translated by F. A. Wright. The Loeb Classical Library. London: Heinemann, 1933.
_____ . *Dogmatic and Polemical Works*. Translated by J. N. Hritzu. The Fathers of the Church, 53. Washington, DC: The Catholic University of America Press, 1965.
Johnson, Aubrey R. "Jonah 2:3-10: A Study in Cultic Fantasy." In *Studies in O.T. Prophecy*. Edited by H. H. Rowley and T. H. Robinson. New York: Charles Scribner's Sons, 1950.
Jourard, Sidney M. *The Transparent Self* (1964). New York: D. Van Nostrand, 1971.
Joy, Charles R., ed. *Albert Schweitzer: An Anthology*. New York: Harper & Row, 1947.
_____ . *The Wit and Wisdom of Albert Schweitzer*. Boston: Beacon Press, 1949.
Jung, Carl G. *Modern Man in Search of a Soul*. New York: Harcourt, Brace & World, 1933.
_____ . *Psychological Types*. London: Harcourt, Brace & Co., 1938.

_____. *Two Essays on Analytical Psychology*. Princeton, NJ: Princeton University Press, 1953.
_____. *Symbols of Transformation*. New York: Pantheon Books, 1956.
_____. *The Undiscovered Self*. New York: New American Library, 1958.
_____. *Alchemical Studies*. Princeton, NJ: Princeton University Press, 1967.

Kaufmann, Yehezkel. *The Religion of Israel*. Translated and abridged by M. Greenberg. Chicago: University of Chicago Press, 1960.
_____. *Toldot ha-emunah ha-yisraelit*. Vol. 4. Tel Aviv: Bialik Institute, 1963.
Keller, C. A. "Jonah, le portrait d'un prophète." *ThZ*, 21 (1965): 329-40.
_____. *Joel, Abdias, Jonas*. CAT 11a. Neuchâtel: Delachaux et Niestlé, 1965.
Knight, George A. F. *Ruth and Jonah*. Torch Bible Commentaries. London: SCM Press, 1950.
König, E. "Jonah." *DB*. New York: Charles Scribner's Sons, 1911. 744-53.
Kotchen, T. A. "Existential Mental Health: An Empirical Approach." *Journal of Individual Psychology* 16 (1960): 174.

Lacocque, André. "Date et milieu du livre de Ruth." *RHPR* 59:3-4 (1979), *Mélanges, Edmond Jacob*, 583-593.
_____. *Where Was God at Auschwitz?* Forthcoming.
_____. *But As for Me*. Atlanta: John Knox Press, 1979.
_____. "A Return to a God of Nature." In *Sources of Vitality in American Church Life*. Edited by Robert L. Moore. Chicago: Exploration Press, 1978.
Laing, R. D. *The Divided Self*. Baltimore: Penguin Books, 1965.
Landes, George M. "The Kerygma of the Book of Jonah." *Interp*. 21 (1967): 3-31.
_____. "Jonah, Book of." *IDB Supp*. Nashville: Abingdon, 1976. Pp. 488-91.
_____. "Jonah: A Mašal?" *Israelite Wisdom: Theological and Literary Essays in Honor of Samuel Terrien*. Edited by J. G. Gamie. Missoula, MT: Scholars Press, 1975. Pp. 137-158.
Lods, Adolphe. *Histoire de la littérature hébraïque et juive*. Paris: Payot, 1950.
_____. *The Prophets and the Rise of Judaism*. Translated by S. H. Hooke. London: Routledge & Kegan, 1950.
Lohfink, N. "Und Jona ging zur Stadt hinaus (Jon. 4,5)." *BZ* N.F. vol. 5, 2 (1961): 185-203.
Lord, Albert. *The Singer of Tales*. Cambridge, MA: Harvard University Press, 1973.
Loretz, O. "Herkunft und Sinn der Jona Erzählung." *BZ* n.s. 5 (1961): 18-29.
_____. *Gotteswort und menschlische Erfahrung. Eine Auslegung der Bücher Jona, Rut, Hohes Lied und Qohelet*. Freiburg: Herder, 1963.

Mankowitz, Wolf. "It Should Happen to a Dog." *Religious Drama III*. Selected and Introduced by M. Halverson. Meridian, NY: Living Age Books, 1959.
Martin, A.D. *The Prophet Jonah, the Book and the Sign*. London/NY: Longmans, Green and Co. 1926.
Maslow, Abraham H. *The Psychology of Science*. Chicago: Henry Regnery Co., 1966.
_____. "Neurosis as a Failure of Personal Growth." *Humanitas* 3 (1967): 153-169.
_____. *Toward a Psychology of Being*. Princeton, NJ: D. Van Nostrand (1962), 1968.
_____. *Motivation and Personality*. New York: Harper & Row, 1970.
_____. *The Farther Reaches of Human Nature*. New York: Penguin Books, 1971.
_____ and Chiang, H. M. *The Healthy Personality*. New York: Van Nostrand Reinhold Co., 1969.

May, Rollo. *Man's Search for Himself.* New York: W. W. Norton, 1953.

———. *Existential Psychology.* New York: Random House, 1960.

———. "Modern Man's Image of Himself." *The Chicago Theological Seminary Register* 52 (October 1962): 1-11.

———. "Existential Psychology and Human Freedom." *The Chicago Theological Seminary Register* 52 (October 1962): 11-19.

———. *Existential Psychotherapy.* Toronto: Bryant Press, 1967.

———. *Love and Will.* New York: Dell, 1969.

———. *The Courage to Create.* New York: W. W. Norton, 1975.

———. *Power and Innocence.* New York: W. W. Norton, 1977.

Melville, Herman. *Moby Dick or the Whale.* New York: Holt, Rinehart & Winston, 1957.

Miles, John A. "Laughing at the Bible: Jonah as Parody." *JQR,* 65 (January 1975): 168-181.

More (Muggia), Joseph. "The Prophet Jonah: The Story of an Intrapsychic Process." *American Imago* 27 (1970): 3-11.

Morgan, G. Campbell. *The Minor Prophets.* London: Pickering, 1960.

Neher, André. *L'Essence du Prophétisme.* Paris: Seuil, 1955.

———. *L'exil de la parole.* Paris: Seuil, 1970.

———. *Amos, contribution à l'étude du prophétisme.* Paris: G. Vrin, 1950.

Orwell, George. *Inside the Whale and Other Essays.* London: Victor Gollancz, 1940.

Otto, Rudolf. *The Idea of the Holy* (1929). Oxford: Oxford University Press, 1958.

Parrot, André *Ninive et l'Ancien Testament.* Neuchâtel: Delachaux et Niestlé, 1953.

Pederson, J. E. "Some Thoughts on a Biblical View of Anger." *J. of Ps. and Theol.* 9 (1974): 210-215.

Perls, Frederick. *Gestalt Therapy Verbatim.* Lafayette, CA: Real People Press, 1969.

Rad, Gerhard von. *Der Prophet Jona.* Nürnberg: Laetare, 1950.

Rank, Otto. *Will Therapy and Truth and Reality.* New York: Alfred A. Knopf, 1964.

Redfield, James M. *Nature and Culture in the Iliad: The Tragedy of Hector.* Chicago: University of Chicago Press, 1975.

Reymond, P. *L'eau, sa vie et sa signification dans l'Ancien Testament.* VTSup 6. Leiden: Brill, 1958.

Ricoeur, Paul. *The Conflict of Interpretations.* Edited by D. Ihde. Evanston: Northwestern University Press, 1974.

———. *Finitude et culpabilité II. La Symbolique du mal.* Paris: Aubier Montaigne, 1960.

Robinson, Theodore H. *Prophecy and the Prophets in Ancient Israel.* London: G. Duckworth, 1953.

———. and Horst, F. *Die Zwölf Kleinen Propheten.* HAT 1/14. Tübingen: Mohr-Siebeck, 1964.

Rofé, A. "Classes in the prophetical stories: Didactic legenda and parable." *Studies on Prophecy.* VTSup 26. Leiden: Brill, 1974. Pp. 143-164.

Rogers, Carl R. *Client-Centered Therapy.* Boston: Houghton Mifflin, 1951.

———. "The Necessary and Sufficient Conditions of Therapeutic Personality Change." *Journal of Consulting Psychology* 21 (1957): 95-103.

———. *On Becoming a Person.* Boston: Houghton Mifflin, 1961.

Rowley, Harold H. *The Missionary Message of the Old Testament.* London: Carey Press, 1945.
Royce, James E. *Personality and Mental Health.* Milwaukee: Bruce, 1955.
Rudolph, Wilhelm. *Joel-Amos-Obadja-Jona.* KAT 13/2. Gütersloh: Mohn, 1971.

Scheler, Max. *On the Eternal Man.* New York: Anchor Books, 1972.
Schmidt, Hans. "Die Komposition des Buches Jona." *ZAW* 25 (1905): 285-310.
Scholes, Robert and Kellogg, Robert. *The Nature of Narrative.* London: Oxford University Press, 1966.
Schweitzer, Albert. *Out of My Life and Thought.* New York: Henry Holt and Co., 1933.
_____ . "The Ethics of Reverence for Life." *Christendom* 1 (Winter 1936): 225-239.
_____ . *The Schweitzer Album.* New York: Harper & Row, 1965.
_____ . *Reverence for Life.* New York: Harper & Row, 1969.
_____ . *Civilization and Ethics* (1923). London: Adam & Charles Black, 1946.
Scott, R.B.Y. "The Sign of Jonah." *Interp.* 19 (1965): 16-25.
_____ . *The Relevance of the Prophets.* New York: Macmillan, 1969.
Sellin, E. *Das Zwölfprophetenbuch.* KAT 12. Leipzig: A. Deichert, 1922.
Sellin, E. and Fohrer, G. *Introduction to the Old Testament.* Translated by D. E. Green. Nashville: Abingdon, 1968.
Smart, James D. "Jonah." *Interpreter's Bible.* Vol. 6. New York: Abingdon-Cokesbury, 1956.
Smith, George A. *The Book of the Twelve Prophets.* Vol. 2. Garden City, NY: Doubleday-Doran & Co., 1929.
Stanton, G. G. "The Prophet Jonah and His Message." *Bibl. Sacra* 108 (1951): 237-249, 363-376.
Steinmann, J. *Le livre de la consolation d'Israël et les prophètes du retour de l'exil.* Paris: Cerf, 1960.
Strack, Hermann L. and Billerbeck, Paul. *Kommentar zum Neuen Testament aus Talmud und Midrasch.* Vol. I. Munich: Beck, 1926.
Sullivan, Harry S. *The Psychiatric Interview.* New York: W. W. Norton, 1954.
Swift, Jonathan. *Gulliver's Travels.* New York: The Modern Library, 1931.

Tec, L. *The Fear of Success.* New York: Reader's Digest Press, 1976.
Thoma, A. "Entstehung des Büchleins Jona." *Theol. St. u. Krit.* (1911): 479-502.
Tillich, Paul. *The Courage to Be.* New Haven: Yale University Press, 1952.
_____ . *The Eternal Now.* New York: Charles Scribner's Sons, 1963.
_____ . *Morality and Beyond.* New York: Harper & Row, 1963.
_____ . *Religious Perspective.* New York: Harper & Row, 1963.
Tresmer, D. *The Fear of Success.* New York: Plenum Press, 1977.
Trible, P. "Studies in the Book of Jonah." Ph.D. Dissertation. Columbia University, 1963.

Vischer, W. "Jonas." *EThR* 24 (1949): 116-119.

Weinreb, F. *Das Buch Jonah, der Sinn des Buches Jona nach der ältesten jüdischen Überl.* Zürich: Origo. Vlg., 1970.
Weiser, A. *Das Buch der Zwölf Kleinen Propheten.* Vol. 1. ATD 24. Göttingen: Vandenhoeck & Ruprecht, 1959.

Weiss, M. "Einiges über die Bauformen des Erzählens in der Bibel." *VT* 13 (1963): 456-475.

———. "Weiteres über die Bauformen des Erzählens." *Biblica* 46 (1965): 181-206.

Wheelis, Allen. "How People Change." *Commentary* 47 (May 1969): 56-66.

Winckler, H. "Zum Buche Jona." *Altoriental. Forsch.* Leipzig: E. Pfeiffer. 1900.

Wolff, H. W. "Jonabuch." *RGG*. Tübingen: Mohr-Siebeck, 1959. Vol. 3. Cols. 854-855.

———. *Studien zum Jonabuch*. Biblische Studien 47. Neukirchener Verlag: Neukirchen-Vluyn, 1947 (Köln, 1965).

Wolpe, Joseph. *Psychotherapy by Reciprocal Inhibition*. Stanford, CA: Stanford University Press, 1958.

Wright, Charles H. H. "The Book of Jonah Considered from an Allegorical Point of View." *Biblical Essays: or Exegetical Studies on the Books of Job and Jonah*. Edinburgh: T. and T. Clark, 1886.

Wright, G. Ernest. *God Who Acts: Biblical Theology as Recital*. Studies in Biblical Theology, First Series 8. London: SCM Press, 1952.

Zeigarnik, B. "Über das Behalten von Erledigten Handlungen." *Psychologie Forschung* 9 (1927): 1-85.

Zeligs, Dorothy F. "A Psychoanalytic Note on the Function of the Bible." *American Imago* 14 (Spring 1957): 57-60.

Author Index

Topical Index